BASIC
CONCEPTS OF
CRIMINAL
LAW

BASIC CONCEPTS
OF
CRIMINAL LAW

George P. Fletcher

New York   Oxford
OXFORD UNIVERSITY PRESS
1998

Oxford University Press

Oxford   New York
Athens   Auckland   Bangkok   Bogota   Bombay
Buenos Aires   Calcutta   Cape Town   Dar es Salaam
Delhi   Florence   Hong Kong   Istanbul   Karachi
Kuala Lumpur   Madras   Madrid   Melbourne
Mexico City   Nairobi   Paris   Singapore
Taipei   Tokyo   Toronto   Warsaw

and associated companies in
Berlin   Ibadan

Published by Oxford University Press, Inc.,
198 Madison Avenue, New York, New York 10016

Oxford is a registered trademark of Oxford University Press

Library of Congress Cataloging-in-Publication Data
Fletcher, George P.
Basic concepts of criminal law / George P. Fletcher
        p.   cm.
Includes bibliographical references and index.
ISBN 0-19-512170-8; 0-19-512171-6 (pbk.)
1. Criminal law.   I. Title.
K5015.4.F58   1998
345—DC21   97-33550

3 5 7 9 8 6 4 2

Printed in the United States of America
on acid-free paper

For Deborah and Rebecca
Each Internationalist in her Own Way.

Acknowledgments

This book began not as a scholarly enterprise but as a service to the text-hungry law faculties of Russia and other post-Communist countries in Asia and Eastern Europe. I wanted to write a book that would introduce Russian law students to Western ways of thinking about criminal law. Indeed, I conceived of doing a series of books for Russian law students on basic concepts of law, with an emphasis on jurisprudential and comparative issues. The Constitutional and Legislative Policy Institute in Budapest, then headed by Stephen Holmes, thought that this was a good idea, and we entered into a contract to supply the first two books in the series, one on criminal law and one on property. Ugo Mattei, then of the Hastings and Trento, Italy, law faculties, agreed to write the book on property.

Once I decided to organize the book around the twelve dichotomies that lie at the foundation of criminal justice everywhere, I realized that the approach had merit as well for American and Western European students of law. The result is a series of books based, more or less, on the modular text that lies before you. In each foreign edition, a local commentator takes charge of the translation and adds material on the way the twelve universal distinctions discussed in this book find expression in the local positive law.

This approach, which stresses the common philosophical dimensions of criminal law, will soon be known around the world. The Spanish edition, prepared by Francisco Muñoz Conde of Sevilla, Spain, appeared in late 1997 under the title *Conceptos Basicos de Derecho Penal*. The publisher is Tirant Lo Blanch in Valencia. The Russian edition, with extensive commentary by Anatolij Naumov from Moscow, is almost ready for publication. It will be distributed, with a subsidy from George Soros, to all the law faculties in Russia. The Italian edition, under the tutelage of Michele Papa of Modena, Italy, is in preparation. Other editions are under negotiation. The full collection of books based on this modular text will provide an excellent library of comparative criminal law.

The process of working with collaborators in various countries has greatly enriched my thinking about criminal law. Emboldened by the experimental nature of this project, I have ventured some new ideas and arguments that have advanced my understanding of the basic structure of criminal law. The ideas presented here go far beyond an introductory text. I hope that the presentation is sufficiently straightforward to be easily grasped by beginners as well as scholars of criminal law who are used to more conventional modes of analysis.

Many friends, collaborators, assistants, and students have helped me keep the text direct and simple. I am indebted to Bruce Ackerman, Russell Christopher, Anthony Dillof, Albin Eser, Manfred Gabriel, Kent Greenawalt, and James Jacobs for thoughtful comments along the way. I hope that this new way of thinking about criminal law will stimulate a new generation of students and scholars to explore the foundations of criminal justice.

Contents

BASIC CONCEPTS OF CRIMINAL LAW

Introduction

Criminal law has become codified law. Everyplace you go in the Western world, you will find a criminal code that lays out the definitions of offenses in the code's "special part" and prescribes general principles of responsibility in the code's "general part." Germans are proud of their code enacted in 1975. Americans cherish their Model Penal Code, which has provided the model for the recent reform of criminal codes in at least thirty-five states. The French show off a new 1994 code, as do the Spanish in their 1995 innovation. One of the first items of business in the post-Communist countries of Eastern Europe is to adopt new criminal codes to reflect their new emphasis on human rights and the just treatment of criminal suspects.

One consequence of codification is that every country goes its own way. Every country has adopted its own conception of punishable behavior, its own definitions of offenses, its own principles for determining questions of self-defense, necessity, insanity, negligence, and complicity. Criminal law has become state law, parochial law. If there was ever much unity among the countries that succeeded to the domain of Roman law, there is none now. If there was ever a common vocabulary and set of principles used by common law jurists, that commonality has long since disintegrated. In the United States today, it is almost impossible to find two states that have the same law of homicide. Every state that has followed the Model Penal Code has amended and adapted the model code to meet its own local preferences. The republics of the former Soviet Union once had criminal codes that were, as the expressions of a single centralized policy, by and large the same. Now as each independent state in the region drafts its own code, we await a cacophony of policies and principles. Soon we will have as many bodies of criminal law as there are distinct flags flying over sovereign states.

Yet as the world has in fact become more localized in criminal justice, the contrary aspiration has become stronger. The talk today in the European Union is of the "Europeanization" of criminal law. How will this form of legal unification be possible in the light of intense national and cultural differences?

The thesis of this book is that there is already much greater unity among diverse systems of criminal justice than we commonly realize. In order to perceive this underlying unity, we must take a step back from the details and the linguistic variations of the criminal codes. The unity that emerges is not on the surface of statutory rules and case law decisions but in the debates that recur in fact in every legal culture. My claim is that a set of twelve distinctions shapes and guides the controversies that inevitably break out in every system of criminal justice. Whether you start from the Model Penal Code or the German Criminal Code, you will inevitably confront disputes about these questions:

1. What is a rule of *substantive* (or material) criminal law? What is a rule of *procedural* criminal law? How do we tell the difference?

2. How do we mark the boundaries of *criminal punishment* as opposed to other coercive sanctions, such as deportation, that are burdensome but non-criminal?

3. What is the difference between treating the suspect as a *subject* and an *object*, both in terms of the criminal act and the unfolding of the criminal trial?

4. What is the difference between *causing* harm and harm simply occurring as a *natural event*?

5. What is the difference between determining whether a crime, or *wrongdoing*, has occurred, and *attributing* that wrongdoing to a particular offender, that is, holding that person responsible for the crime?

6. What is the distinction between *offenses* and *defenses*?

7. How should we distinguish between *intentional* and *negligent* crimes?

8. Why should there be defenses both of *self-defense* and *necessity*, and what is the distinction between them?

9. Why are some mistakes *relevant* to criminal liability and other mistakes *irrelevant?*

10. How should we distinguish between *completed offenses* and *attempts* and other inchoate offenses?

11. What is the difference between someone who is a *perpetrator* of an offense and someone who is a mere *accessory* to the offense?

12. In the end, how do we distinguish between *legality* and *justice* in the criminal process?

Some of these distinctions may be difficult to understand. At this stage, it is not important to grasp the full significance of all of them. They illustrate the underlying thesis of this book that a basic set of distinctions generates the "deep structure" of all systems of criminal law. This is, as it were, the universal grammar of criminal law. As Noam Chomsky developed a universal grammar underlying all the particular languages of the world, here, in these twelve distinctions lies the grammar of criminal law.

Understanding the deep, universal structure of criminal law provides an antidote for the positivist bias of recent decades. It is true that every country has a criminal code, but these codes should be understood as local answers to the universal questions that constitute the foundation of criminal law. Different countries may pose different resolutions to the same twelve underlying distinctions, but these resolutions on the surface of the law should not obscure the unity that underlies apparently diverse legal cultures. If the basic questions remain constant, then legal cultures have more in common than they might otherwise think.

There are many reasons why students of criminal law should welcome this approach. Mastering these twelve distinctions will not only enable the student to understand the grammar of the legal culture but also will facilitate appreciation of the unity of the world's legal systems. Some students might object. I imagine various types of students and their complaints:

Ms. Patriot: This student is simply interested in her own legal culture. She does not want to learn the underlying grammar of legal cultures around the world. To her, I say:

> Good, perhaps you should be interested just in your own culture. But this method of learning distinctions will enable you to appreciate your local legislation as something more than just the arbitrary rulings of the legislature. In the local rules that you learn, you will find a lasting message, a solution to a basic problem that runs to the foundation of the legal system. You have reason to be proud of your local law, for it represents an answer—and perhaps the correct answer—to questions that criminal lawyers and judges pose all over the world.

Mr. Efficient: This student is concerned only about learning the local law as quickly and efficiently as possible. All that counts is committing the rules and precedents to memory so that he can spout them back on examinations. To him, I say:

> Good, I agree that this is an important value. Learn the law efficiently. This method will help you do it. If you master the basic skeleton of twelve distinctions and understand what they are about, the data of your legal culture will provide the flesh for your local body of law. It is easier to learn twelve distinctions and their implications than to memorize, say, 200 distinct rules.

Ms. Professional: This hip student wants only to know how to prepare and to try cases. She wants to get into court as soon as possible. What is the use of all this theory? Teach me how to win cases, she insists. To her, I respond:

> Good, prepare to win cases. But you cannot prosecute or defend unless you understand what is at stake when you argue basic questions of law. Anyone can look up the rules in a handbook. What you need to excel in court is an understanding of the deeper dynamic of the law, the hidden structure that influences and shapes the thinking of judges. If you delve into the deep distinctions that shape the contours of the law, you will have an edge on the pedestrian lawyers who tread on the surface of the law.

Mr. Sport: This guy is only interested in who wins and who loses. Why should we care about the ideas of the law, when these ideas might not impact on juries or judges who decide whether the defendant is guilty? To him, I reply:

> Good, winning is what it is all about. But it is important to know what the prosecution and the defense are actually winning and losing. There is more at stake in the contests of the law than just the fate of a single individual. When O.J. Simpson is found not guilty, the repercussions are felt across the country. The consequences hit those concerned about race, battered women, controlling the police, and the reliability of the jury system. In all important cases, there is more at stake than one person's winning or losing. Tennis may be only about the player who wins; the law is also about the ideas that prevail.

Maybe these replies will win over the skeptics. Maybe not. The better way to prove the merit of this approach to criminal law is to immerse oneself in it. It should become obvious as we proceed that mastering the deep structure of the law enables one to understand the significance of local details and variations.

1

Substance versus Procedure

When you look at the law from a distance, you see a maze of rules. This is the maze that ensnared the accused Joseph K. in Kafka's *The Trial* when he tried to determine whether he was guilty of a crime. If you look at the maze more carefully, you find that the rules break down into two general categories, rules of substance and rules of procedure. The substantive rules define the crimes that are punished in the particular state or country. If Joseph K. was guilty of a crime, that crime would have been defined in the substantive rules of the local criminal law. If those rules are secret or too complicated or too vague to understand, then the legal system inhumanely drives people to anxiety about whether they are guilty of a transgression against the rules.

Being guilty is one thing; being prosecuted and punished another. Whether one is ever held liable for a particular offense depends on the rules of procedure. These rules determine how the state enforces the criminal law by proving the occurrence of crime and convicting and punishing those responsible for the crime.

In general terms, we can say that the substantive rules establish "guilt in principle." The procedural rules determine whether individuals are "guilty in fact." Whether guilt in principle becomes guilt in fact depends on several factors—on the evidence available, on the rules for introducing and evaluating this evidence, and on the personalities and talents of those charged with making the decision of guilt. The

7

agony of Joseph K. derives not only from the inscrutable rules of substance but from the torture of undefined procedures.

The rules of legal procedure allocate functions among the lawyers, the judge, and the jury or the lay people who assist the judge in finding the facts of the cases. They also determine the scope of admissible evidence, prescribe provisions for appeal, and establish criteria for reversing judgments and starting all over again. These rules determine the way the game is played. And the game is always played the same way, whether in the particular case the rules lead to what appears to be a just result or not.

In real games and sports, curiously, we rarely find procedures for litigating disputes. The substantive rules of card games, chess, baseball, hockey, and other games determine when one side scores a point, loses a piece, or commits a foul. If there is a dispute about the facts to which the rules apply (did the ball hit on this or that side of the line?), the rules for settling disputes are typically no more complicated than "the umpire decides" or "each side calls its own fouls." In most areas outside of the law, we make do with informal processes that depend on the good faith of all concerned.

Games assume the good faith of all participants. But the law assumes rather that litigants are motivated by self-interest. To secure their ends, they might well act in bad faith. For this reason, the procedures for settling disputes are as important as the rules that determine, in principle, who should win and who should lose.

We may understand the general points behind the distinction between substance and procedure, but do we understand how the distinction works in practice? Let us consider the problem more deeply.

Our reflections on establishing guilt under the law are summarized in the following syllogism:

Major: Whoever intentionally kills another person is
                guilty of murder.

Minor: On January 1, 1996, John Jones intentionally
                killed Bruce Barnes.

Conclusion: John Jones is guilty of murder.

This is the "syllogism of legal guilt." The major premise is defined by the rules of substantive law. The minor premise is a matter of fact, and the facts are established by following the procedures laid down in procedural rules, namely, the rules for conducting a fair trial.

Note there is also a process or a procedure for determining the major premises. The rules of substantive law are not self-evident. The trial judge determines what these rules are by researching the law in the books or by asking for briefs from the lawyers on questions of law. Surprisingly, there are no fixed rules for fathoming the rules of substantive law. The process is informal, and much depends on how particular judges like to work.

In a system based on jury trial, as in the United States, the judge expresses the major premises of the law in his instructions to the jury. The jury determines the factual issues in the minor premises, and then, when the system works properly, the jury applies the law to the facts, the major premise to the minor. Jury instructions also contain procedural rules, such as one requiring the jury to be convinced beyond a reasonable doubt that a fact relevant to the minor premise is true. If the jury has doubts that it identifies as reasonable, then it may not regard the fact as proven.

Most constitutions of the world are more concerned about procedural rights than about rights to a substantive law of a certain sort. The Fifth and Sixth Amendments to the U.S. Constitution list an array of rights (e.g., right to counsel, jury trial) that are designed primarily not to promote the efficiency of the trial but to protect the interests of the accused.

With regard to substantive law, the most common constitutional provision today bespeaks the liberal principle that states must advise their citizens in advance of the substantive rules of conduct which might trigger criminal liability. The U.S. Constitution expressly prohibits ex post facto laws [no legislation after the fact].[1] The same rule is made explicit in the 1949 German Basic Law and in virtually all modern constitutions.[2] This excludes a certain set of possible major premises, namely, those rules that are legislated as statutory law after the facts in the minor premise have occurred. It follows that the date of the law's enactment is critical to whether the major premise is constitutionally acceptable. A more complete version of the major premise in the example would read, therefore:

> As of January 1, 1996 (the date mentioned in the minor premise), it was the law of this state (or country) that:
> Whoever intentionally kills another person is guilty of murder.

Adding one complication invites another. Now that we have tied down the law to a particular date and place, we must add the qualification the crime occurred in the place (or under other circumstances) that give the court "competence" over the alleged crime. Adding the requirement of judicial competence changes both the major and minor premises of the syllogism of legal guilt. The full statement becomes:

Major: As of January 1, 1996, it was the law of this state (or country) that: Whoever intentionally kills another person within the competence of the court is guilty of murder.

Minor: On January 1, 1996, John Jones intentionally killed Bruce Barnes within the competence of the court.

Conclusion: John Jones is guilty of murder.

1.1 The Philosophical Problem: Substance versus Procedure

It seems as though we have a good idea of the difference between substantive rules and procedural rules. In many borderline cases, however, this distinction is hardly obvious. Take, for example, the statute of limitations, which prescribes the time limit within which the state may prosecute a particular crime. This looks like a procedural rule, but it could be interpreted as substantive by redrafting the major premise. Suppose that the limitation period for murder is twenty years. Then the major premise of our example might read:

> As of January 1, 1996 (the date mentioned in the minor premise), it was the law of this jurisdiction that:
> Whoever intentionally killed another person on or after January 1, 1976 is guilty of murder.

Note that this formulation shifts the tense of the major premise from the present to the past. The prohibition is transformed from one against murder in the abstract to one that exposes the offender to liability for a period of twenty years. It is as though the major premise read: if you kill someone, you are guilty of murder for twenty years and no longer. But what is wrong with this formulation? The question, I suppose, is whether we desire to have the norms of the criminal law express general moral principles or whether they should define the conditions under which the state may deprive an individual of his or her liberty. If you take the view that the criminal law should state moral rules, the prohibition should be against murder in general; if the purpose is to define the conditions of liability, the latter approach is preferable.

It turns out, then, that in borderline cases the distinction between substance and procedure raises philosophical issues. We cannot clarify the distinction without a theory both about the nature of substantive law and the particular issue we are trying to classify, in this case, the statute of limitations.

Assessing the nature of the statute of limitations became a burning political issue in Germany after World War II. The question was how long the West German government would be able to prosecute concentration camp murders under their homicide statute, which carried a prescriptive period, a statute of limitations, of twenty years. The initial German position was that the twenty-year period began running in May 1945 when the Third Reich collapsed and prosecution became politically feasible. When the statutory period was about to run out in May 1965, the Bundestag [Parliament] of the Federal Republic extended the period for ten years. Before the prescriptive limit took hold in 1975, the legislature abolished it altogether. When alleged war criminals were prosecuted after 1965 or after 1975, could they legitimately claim that they were being subject to an ex post facto law, namely, a rule on prosecuting homicide that was enacted after they committed their offenses?

There is something unsettling about prosecuting concentration camp killers on the basis of the German homicide statutes in force at the time. There is no doubt that if they killed innocent inmates, they violated the statute. They could claim an exception, perhaps on the basis of administrative regulations or military orders. Contemporary German courts reject defenses of this sort on the ground that the implicit instructions to kill were themselves secret and therefore unlawful.[3] What remains is the statute prohibiting homicide. There is no difference, in the view of German courts, between killing someone in a 1943 Berlin robbery or killing someone in a 1943 Auschwitz gas chamber.

The legislature's extending the statute of limitations differs arguably from the courts' disregarding unjust orders to kill. By extending the prescriptive period, the legislature changes the time period in which the alleged criminal is subject to liability. That requires us to answer the question whether the twenty-year prescriptive period enters in the definition of the crime that the guards committed. There are two interpretations, one substantive, one procedural:

The substantive interpretation:	If you intentionally kill an innocent person, you are guilty of murder for twenty years. [After the twenty year period has run, you are no longer guilty.]
The procedural interpretation:	If you intentionally kill an innocent person, you are guilty of murder. You are subject to prosecution for a period of twenty years. [After the twenty-year period has run, you are still guilty but you cannot be prosecuted.]

Note that in the substantive interpretation, the time period enters into the definition of guilt; in the procedural case, the time period applies merely to rules for prosecuting the offense. Is it coherent and plausible to interpret the concept of guilt to include a time period? The conventional answer requires us to decide whether the statute of limitations is substantive or procedural. How do we decide that question?

The general prohibition against retroactive criminal legislation (ex post facto laws) provides some guidance to answering the question.[4] The principle behind this prohibition is that individuals have a right to know what the "law" is at the time that they supposedly violate it. The principle is expressed as well in the Latin maxim: *nullum crimen, nulla poena sine lege* [There is no crime, no punishment, without prior legislative warning]. While the 1787 U.S. Constitution contains a prohibition against ex post facto legislation, the 1949 German Constitution enacts the broader prohibition against punishing in the absence of prior legislative warning.[5] The basic principle is this:

> Individuals have a right to know what the "law" is at the time that they are said to violate it.

But how much of the "law" is included in this principle? Do individuals have the right to know all aspects of the procedural as well as the substantive law? Does the individual have the right to know precisely what evidence might be introduced against him at trial? If, for example, O.J. Simpson is guilty of murdering his former wife and Ron Goldman, did he have the right to know at the time he committed the offense that the prosecution would use evidence of prior spousal abuse against him? Suppose the law at the time of the killings was that evidence of the defendant's spousal abuse was not admissible. Suppose further that after the murder, the legislature intervened and changed the law to make the evidence of spousal abuse admissible. Would this have been unfair to Simpson as a criminal defendant?

Whether the evidence of spousal abuse is admissible or not has little to do with the definition of murder. Simpson had a right to know how murder was defined in California at the time he allegedly acted, but it would seem odd to say that he also had a right to know what evidence the prosecution might use to try to convict him. After all, if he was guilty, he was guilty of murder—not murder as it could be proved by admitting evidence of prior spousal abuse.

Some courts would solve this problem simply by saying that the evidence of prior spousal abuse is an "evidentiary" or "procedural" matter and therefore there would be nothing wrong with changing the rule after the date of the suspected murder. In other words, the classification as procedure would settle the issue.

But the classification is not always so easily made. On borderline issues, such as the statute of limitations, we have to reach back to the principle that motivates the classification. What is the intuition that enables us to say with confidence that purely procedural matters do not enter into the "law" that individuals have a right to know before they act. I suppose the answer is that the rules of procedure do not bear on the morality of acting. Whether evidence of prior spousal abuse is admissible against O.J. Simpson has nothing to do with the morality of killing his wife. We could formulate a principle this way:

> Individuals have a right to know that which could make a moral difference in their choosing to engage in the action or not.

We should remind ourselves that the topic is the permissibility of retroactive legislation. Ex post facto laws are not permissible if they infringe on what individuals have a right to know when they act. They have a right to know, the principle holds, those matters and only those matters that bear on the morality of their actions. For example, a physician has the right to know the local definition of death before he treats a body as dead and begins to remove an organ for purposes of transplantation. Whether society perceives a moribund patient with a flat EEG reading as dead surely does indeed make a moral difference in deciding whether to harvest organs from the body. As a result, it would clearly be unfair to a physician who relied on the definition in force at the time of his action to have the definition of death changed retroactively. Doing so would convert an action that was morally indifferent into a homicide punishable as murder.

A physician might properly rely on the local definition of death in reaching a decision whether to make an incision into a body and remove its organs; but could you imagine someone calculating whether to commit murder or not on the basis of whether evidence of prior spousal abuse could be admitted against him? If the culprit decided to kill because the evidence of prior abuse would not be admissible against him, he would hardly be relying on a factor that could make a *moral difference* in choosing to engage in the action. Now how do these reflections assist us in classifying the statute of limitations as substantive or procedural?

What do we think of the person who reflects upon the possibility of killing in the following way: "If I commit this crime now, I am subject to prosecution, at most, for the next twenty years. This is a risk worth running." Deciding to kill on the basis of this consideration would hardly be morally superior to killing on the assumption that evidence of prior spousal abuse would not be admissible at trial. Engaging in highly immoral acts in the calculated hope of getting away with them is hardly worth the protection of the law. It would be equally suspect for the actor to adopt the substantive interpretation of the statute of limitations and conclude that if he commits the crime, he would be guilty for only twenty years. The statute of limitation has many purposes, including setting a limit on the state's power of investigation and prosecution and avoiding trials on the basis of stale, unreliable evidence. It would be difficult to say that among these purposes was providing an incentive to commit murder in the hope of getting away with it.

On the basis of these reflections we can conclude that the statute of limitations is procedural and that, therefore, it was constitutionally permissible for the German legislature retroactively to abolish the twenty-year statute of limitations on murder.[6] It is worth noting, however, that the German Constitutional Court distinguished between cases in which the twenty-year period of limitation had run and those in which it had not. In cases where the period of limitations had run, the suspect had the right to rely on the new state of affairs created by the passage of time. He had no right to rely on the statute at the time of acting, but after twenty years of exposure to the state's punitive authority, he was entitled to resume his life without fear of prosecution.

Some courts might disagree with this distinction developed by the German Constitutional Court. For example, the Hungarian Constitutional Court concluded in 1992 that the post-Communist Parliament had no authority whatsoever to alter the statute of limitations in force during the Communist period. It did not matter whether in the particular case the prescriptive period had run or not. In whatever form it took, legislative intervention in this area appeared, at least to the judges of the Hungarian Constitutional Court, to violate the constitutional provision entrenching the rule of law in the post-Communist legal system.[7]

1.2 The Burden of Proof: Half A Loaf

The distinction between substance and procedure comes into play in many contexts other than the permissible retroactivity of legislation. It is not easy to fathom, for example, whether the burden of proof should be treated as a matter of substance or procedure. First, we have to pause to think about the meaning of the term "burden of proof" and closely related concepts.

The burden of proof addresses the question: Who wins the trial on a particular issue in the event the jury (or other trier of fact) cannot decide one way or another on that issue. Suppose the defendant asserts self-defense in a homicide case. The jury is convinced that the defendant killed the victim and did so intentionally, but it cannot resolve the question whether it was done in self-defense. The evidence on that evidence is simply inconclusive. In cases of this sort, where there is no way to decide clearly one way or the other, the burden of proof resolves the tie. If the state has the burden of proving the absence of self-defense, then the defendant should under these circumstances be found not guilty. If the defendant has the burden of proof on the issue, then the result is just the opposite: self-defense is regarded as not proven and therefore the defendant should be guilty of murder. What is at stake, therefore, is not proof but persuasion. The question is: Who has the burden of persuading the judge or jury on a particular issue. If you bear the burden and you fail to persuade, you lose on the point. Therefore, the burden of persuasion is more aptly labeled "the risk of nonpersuasion." It is obvious that allocating the risk of nonpersuasion of proof between the state and the defendant can have a radical impact on the outcome of the trial.

Some European lawyers might maintain that the risk of nonpersuasion is irrelevant to European legal thinking, the reason being that the judge—and not the parties—always bears the burden of investigating and establishing the facts. Yet in the nineteenth century, the same mode of "inquisitorial" trial prevailed in Europe and it was quite common to allocate the risk of nonpersuasion to the defense.[8] The burden of investigation and of fact-finding does not dictate any particular decision about whether the state or the defendant should bear the risk that a particular issue, such as self-defense, remains unclarified at the end of trial.

At first blush, the burden of persuasion appears to be a purely procedural institution. A more careful look at the various burdens as they are known in common law trials suggests, however, that they carry substantive meaning. For the sake of clarity, we should distinguish between "the burden of persuasion" and two related concepts—the "burden of going forward" and the "standard of proof."

The "burden of going forward" imposes either on the state or on the defendant the duty of providing sufficient evidence for the court to take the question seriously as subject to debate. For example, if the defendant comes into court and simply says, "The decedent tried to kill me," that would hardly be enough. The defendant must raise enough evidence to generate a debatable issue, one on which reasonable people might disagree. If the defendant does not meet this burden, the judge will simply rule against the defendant on the matter; for example, self-defense will not be considered an issue in the case. The state also has the burden of going forward on those matters that it must prove to the satisfaction of the jury. In a homicide case, for example, the prosecution must raise a debatable issue about whether the defendant directed his deadly attack against a living victim. If the state does not meet this burden, the judge will dismiss the indictment and terminate the trial.

Both jury trials in common law systems and judge trials in Continental civil law jurisdictions recognize a burden of going forward.[9] In a jury trial, the burden finds its practical expression in the judge's decision to grant or deny jury instructions on the particular question. If the defendant does not meet the burden of going forward on self-defense, the judge will deny jury instructions, which means that for all practical purposes the issue is regarded as not existing in the trial. In bench trials on the European Continent, the judge must write an opinion analyzing the issues raised in the case. If the defendant does not bring forth evidence to support a particular claim, the judge need not analyze that issue in the opinion finding the defendant guilty or not guilty. Silence in the opinion, then, is equivalent to silence in the jury instructions. In both cases, the judge's silence testifies to a decision that the defendant has not produced sufficient evidence to raise a debatable issue for resolution at trial.

The second related concept, "the standard of proof," differs further from the burden of proof. When the prosecution bears the burden of persuasion, it must prove these facts "beyond a reasonable doubt." If the jury has a reasonable doubt on the particular question, it should find for the defendant—in other words, the prosecution bears the risk of a reasonable doubt at the end of the case. This is the strictest standard of proof.

Less strict than "proof beyond a reasonable doubt," the burden of proving the issue "by a preponderance of the evidence" requires a showing that the fact is probably more true than false. Proof "by clear and convincing evidence" requires something more than proof by a preponderance and less than proof beyond a reasonable doubt. The assumption behind these diverse standards is that we can speak of proof in quantitative terms.

A sports analogy might be helpful (American lawyers like to think of trials as competitions akin to sporting matches). If the different standards were arrayed on a football field with yard lines numbered from one to 100, and we thought of bearing the burden of proof as analogous to moving up the field with the ball, the strictest standard of "beyond a reasonable doubt" would require taking the ball at least to the 99th yard line. The standard of "clear and convincing evidence" might be equivalent to the 70th yard line. And the lowest standard of "preponderance of the evidence" would coincide with the 51st yard line. This metaphor is useful as well in explaining the duty of going forward, which designates a rather low standard of bringing the ball, say, to the 10th yard line.

In civil cases [private legal disputes], the standard of proof for both plaintiff and defendant is usually no more than a preponderance of the evidence and occasionally proof by clear and convincing evidence. The idea that the standards of proof in criminal and civil [private law] trials lend themselves to quantitative measurement marks an important difference between common law jurisdiction and most Continental courts. Beginning with the French revolution, European lawyers have come to use the standard of *intime conviction*—a subjective standard requiring the judge's personal conviction. Consequently, Continental lawyers purport to use the same standard of proof in criminal and civil [private law] trials.

This accounts for a common law procedural option that strikes Continental lawyers as odd. In common law courts and only exceptionally in Continental courts, a finding of not guilty in a criminal trial in no way hinders a subsequent action at private law for damages. This is precisely what happened in the trials of Bernhard Goetz and O.J. Simpson, both of whom were acquitted of the serious criminal charges levied against them, but were then forced to stand trial again for tort damages.[10]

The reason that this phenomenon puzzles Continental Europeans is that they typically use the same standard of proof for both criminal and tort cases. A finding of not guilty in the criminal trial represents a final judgment of the legal system that the defendant is not liable for the acts charged. The finding is considered *res judicata*—"a thing determined"—for purposes of the private law trial. The failing of the prosecution is binding, therefore, on the injured victim who might wish to sue for damages. This is not true in the common law system. A judgment of not guilty in the criminal trial means merely that the prosecution had not carried the ball to the 99th yard line. If the jury thought, say, that the proof carried the case only to the 80th yard line, another jury in a tort case could well find that the injured plaintiff introduced sufficient evidence to pass the required 51st yard line. This is all the plaintiff must do to recover for tort damages.

What matters, in the Continental view of the trial, is not imaginary lines on a football field, but the judge's response to the evidence and personal conviction of guilt. As a result of this single concept of proof, most Continental lawyers sense a contradiction if the defendant is acquitted on criminal charges and then tried again on a complaint for compensation in tort law.

Another major difference between the common law and the Continental traditions is that the common law has struggled for centuries with the question: Who should bear the burden of proof on issues raised by the defense? Notable among these controverted issues are self-defense and insanity. Many jurisdictions in the United States require the defense to bear the burden on either or both of these issues.[11] This shifting of the burden to the defense on "defenses" almost never occurs in Continental courts.

Now what are the implications in common law courts of shifting the burden of persuasion? Is this purely a procedural rule? Or does it also have substantive implications? There are at least two ways that the legal system can strengthen or weaken a particular defense. It can add qualifications that make it more difficult for the defendant to prevail on the defense. For example, in a case of self-defense, suppose the existing rule on self-defense holds that any time the defendant believes, in good faith, that he is about to be attacked, he may use deadly force in his defense. The courts tighten the defense, as they did in the Goetz proceedings, by insisting that the defense apply only if the defendant maintains a reasonable belief that he is about to be attacked.[12] If his belief is unreasonable, he has no valid claim of self-defense. Adding the requirement of reasonableness undoubtedly makes it more difficult for the defendant to prevail on a claim of self-defense.

Alternatively, the state has the option of tightening the defense by shifting the burden of proof on the issue to the defendant. This would mean that the defendant would have to prove by a preponderance of the evidence that he did act in self-defense. Combining these options, we can list, in order of preference to the defendant, the following versions of self-defense:

Versions of Self-Defense

I.　The best option for the defense is a "subjective" standard that enables the defense to prevail anytime he or she acts in good faith *coupled with* the requirement that the prosecution disprove claims of self-defense by proof beyond a reasonable doubt.

II.　The worst option for the defense is an "objective" standard that limits self-defense to cases in which the defendant acts with reasonable belief in the conditions for the defense *coupled with* a rule requiring the defense to establish the defense by a preponderance of the evidence.

III.　Arrayed between these two extremes are two middle positions:

> A) An "objective" standard that limits self-defense to cases in which the defendant acts with reasonable belief in the conditions for the defense *coupled with* the requirement that the prosecution disprove claims of self-defense by proof beyond a reasonable doubt.

> B) A "subjective" standard that enables the defense to prevail anytime he or she acts in good faith *coupled with* a rule requiring the defense to establish the defense by a preponderance of the evidence.

One departure from the best standard for the defendant implies a shift in the burden of persuasion (IIIB). The other requires the defendant to have a reasonable belief that he is about to be attacked (IIIA). There is no way to rank these two versions because whether one or the other is worse for the defense depends entirely on the facts of the particular case. There are some situations—events that occur behind closed doors—about which it is hard to know exactly what happened and therefore the shift in the burden of persuasion would be devastating for the defense. There are other cases, such as the *Goetz* case itself, where the shooting occurs in public and therefore the primary problem is not what happened but assessing whether the defendant's fear of violent attack was reasonable or not.

Now we restate the question with which we began this inquiry: Is the allocation of the burden of persuasion a procedural rule or a substantive rule? The answer is not easy, for we see that the allocation of the burden has an impact on the balance of advantage between prosecution and defense that resembles toughening or weakening the substantive rule of self-defense. From a functional point of view, rules allocating the burden of persuasion have the same impact as changes in the substantive law.

There are some situations in which allocating the burden is clearly a technique for modifying and therefore softening substantive legal reforms. For example, the Model Penal Code advocates a new defense of mistake of law and to soften the blow for those opposed to the innovation, the Code recommends imposing the burden of persuasion on the new defense on the defendant.[13] There is no apparent reason for this shift except the politics of law reform. Another example is the proposal to move from strict liability, in which proof of the defendant's negligence is not required, to insisting on proper evidence of the defendant's negligence, but with the added twist of requiring the defendant to bear the burden on the issue.[14]

Does it follow that by analogy to changes in the statute of limitations (before the prescriptive period has run), the state may retroactively change the burden of persuasion? Recall the question we asked previously: Does the defense have a right to rely on law in force at the time of his action? It would seem odd to say that the defendant may not rely on the statute of limitations but he may rely on the requirement that the prosecution bear the burden of proof. On the other hand, we could make the argument of functional equivalence with the substantive law in regard to the statute of limitations as readily as we can in regard to the burden of proof. I confess that I am not sure of the right answer to this quandary. To be sure, we are beginning to see how difficult and subtle the distinction between substance and procedure turns out to be in these borderline cases.

1.3 The Distinction in Context

To add to our difficulties in fathoming the distinction between substance and procedure, we must note that the chameleon-like distinction takes on different hues in the context of different legal problems. Common law judges must decide, for example, which issues to decide for themselves and which issues to send to the jury. The guiding principle is that the judge resolves questions of law, and the jury decides questions of fact. The distinction between law and fact correlates with that between the major and minor premise in the syllogism of legal guilt, and these two premises dovetail, more or less, with the distinction between substance and procedure.

This view of "substance" turn out to be broader than any theory we have encountered so far. Judges decide what the statute of limitations and the burden of persuasion should be, and juries decide whether the factual preconditions are present for concluding either that the prescriptive period has run (when did the crime occur?) or that the burden has been met (how much evidence is there and how convincing is it?). This approach to the concept of substantive law—namely, as equivalent to the "law" the judge must determine—sweeps too wide and therefore provides little guidance to the quandaries we considered earlier.

The legal context influences our perception of substance and procedure. Consider a notable example from the field of private legal disputes: the *Erie* doctrine in the federal courts of the United States.[15] To understand this doctrine, a few words about the jurisdiction of the U.S. federal courts are in order. In the area of private disputes, the federal courts hear cases either arising under federal law, including the Constitution, or cases based on diversity of citizenship, which for these purpose means suits between residents of different states. In these so-called diversity cases, the courts apply the "common law" of torts, contracts, and other fields of private law. At a certain point in the early twentieth century, the courts became skeptical about whether the common law remained a unified whole. If the federal "common law" turned out to be different from the "common law" in the state courts, many plaintiffs would go to federal court just to take advantage of the federal rule. The loss of unity in the common law resulted, eventually, in the Supreme Court's holding that in diversity-of-citizenship cases, the federal courts should apply the "substantive" law of the state in which they were sitting. This made sense intuitively. The purpose of diversity jurisdiction was not to provide an alternative body of law but merely to guarantee a neutral forum for citizens of different states. Accordingly, the court would use its own procedures but would hear the case as it arose under the local law of the state.

Applying this distinction between state substantive law and federal procedural law required, of course, the courts to contemplate the distinction between substance and procedure. A few years after its *Erie* decision the Supreme Court had to decide whether the New York statute of limitations should be classified as one or the other. The Supreme Court took the occasion of that decision to formulate a general theory about resolving these problems of classification.[16] Because the purpose of the *Erie* decision was to ensure the same outcome in the state and

federal courts, the purpose of classifying issues as substance or procedure should be the same.

The question is whether such a statute concerns merely the manner
and the means by which a right to recover, as

> recognized by the State, is enforced, or whether such statutory limi-
> tation is a matter of substance . . . namely, does it significantly affect
> the result of a litigation for a federal court to disregard a law of a State
> that would be controlling in an action upon the same claim by the
> same parties in a State court?[17]

There we have it. Procedural rules are those that concern "merely
the manner and the means by which a right . . . is enforced" and substantive rules are those that "significantly affect the result." A few lines
later in the opinion, the Court coins the expression that has caught on
as the "holding" of the case: substantive rules are those that "determine
the outcome of a litigation."[18] That has come to be known as the "outcome-determinative" test.

Unfortunately, virtually all rules "determine the outcome" of litigation. To be sure, the statute of limitations and the burden of persuasion fall under this expansive concept of substance. But so do many
minor rules bearing, say, on the law of evidence. Yet this test might be
right for its context—namely, reconciling federal and state law and
avoiding the temptation of "forum shopping," but it would not work
well as a test for the scope of the prohibition against ex post facto legislation or as a medium for distinguishing the scope of the "law" that
the judge rather than the jury should decide.

The distinction between substance and procedure comes into play
as well in the conflicts of laws (the field known in Europe as "private
international law"). If a dispute between private parties arises in one
state or country and then is heard in another, the forum that hears the
dispute will apply its own procedural rules. That makes sense: you come
to my court, you use my rules. Also true, however, is that under the
traditional approach to the conflicts of laws in fields of torts and contracts, the forum would apply the substantive law of the state or country where the dispute had arisen. It is perfectly normal, therefore, for
California to try a case under its own procedural law but under the
substantive law of New York or France.

It is worth noting that in criminal law, the jurisdiction of the court
determines the applicable substantive law. It is very rare that one court
will apply the substantive law of another. Why is it possible in contract
and tort disputes, but not in criminal cases, to determine liability under
the law of another jurisdiction? The reason, I believe, is that in criminal
cases, the state where the crime occurs is intimately involved with the
resolution of the suspect's guilt or innocence. Crimes typically leave
victims and social anxiety in their wake. Resolving the consequences

of the crime invokes local interests in a way that accidents and contractual problems do not. For this reason, criminal trials do not lend themselves to export.[19] They stay in the community where the crime occurred.[20]

When legal disputes are exported, however, the receiving court must decide how much of the substantive law of the foreign jurisdiction it is willing to apply. The same problems arise with regard to classifying issues like the statute of limitations and the burden of proof that we have seen in other contexts. Here, however, the tendency of the receiving court—in contrast to the *Erie* jurisprudence—is to take a very constricted view of substantive law. With few exceptions, the statute of limitations and the burden of persuasion are treated as procedural: the receiving court applies, therefore, its own law. The "outcome-determinative" test does not fare well in this context because the possibility of an outcome in California, different from, say, in New York or Mexico, is not so disturbing. The principle is that the courts will recognize the norms of a foreign jurisdiction as governing the plaintiff's claim, but it need not recognize every foreign rule that would influence the trial, had it been held where the claim arose.

These, then, are the five different contexts for seeing the distinction between substance and procedure at work:

1. *Legality:* The scope of the prohibition against ex post facto laws

2. *Proof:* The allocation of the burden of persuasion between the prosecution and the defense

3. *Law and fact:* Decisions about which issues should be determined by a judge and which by a jury

4. Erie *doctrine in the United States:* Federal courts hearing cases arising under the substantive law of the state in which they sit

5. *Conflicts of law:* One court hearing a dispute arising under the substantive law of a foreign jurisdiction

To summarize our thinking about substance and procedure, let us recall the different ways of thinking about the the statute of limitations:

Context	Classification of Statute of Limitations
Legality	Procedure (for sure)
Erie doctrine	Substance (for sure)
Conflicts of law	Procedure (generally)

As we have seen as well, the burden of persuasion poses its own problems of classification because of the functional similarity between shifts in the burden and changes in the substantive rule. Deciding what is law for the judge to resolve and what is fact for the jury to find, provides it own distinctive take on the distinction between substance and procedure.

This study in the way in which one fundamental legal distinction plays itself out in different legal contexts could generate the wrong message. One might think these decisions of classification were simply arbitrary and politically motivated. But that would be the wrong lesson to grasp from this inquiry. The impact of context on legal analysis is not arbitrary. There are good reasons why the distinction comes out one way when the concern is legality and another way when the inquiry is achieving harmony between state and federal courts sitting in the same city.

The deep message that unites this chapter with the others that follow is that the basic distinctions of criminal justice transcend the enacted law of particular states and countries. The local statutory law does not determine the boundary that runs between substance and procedure or the way the boundary adapts to the changing context of the inquiry. The message of this chapter illustrates the overarching theme of this book. The basic distinctions of criminal justice require philosophical and conceptual analysis. On these matters, you cannot simply look up the law in the books. You have to think about the problem and clarify in your own mind the construction of the concepts that makes the most sense.

Notes

1. U.S. Constitution , art. I, sec. 9, cl. 3

2. German Basic Law §103(II); Mexican Constitution art. 14; Portugese Constitution art. 29(1); European Convention on Human Rights §7(I).

3. See Judgment of Constitutional Court, October 24, 1996, 1997 Neue Juristische Wochenshrift 929. For a critical assessment of the Court's allowing a breach of the prohibition against retroactive liability, see Jorg Arnold, *Einschränkung des Rückwirkungsverbot*, 1997(5) Juristische Schulung 399.

4. See authorities cited in note 2 supra.

5. It is worth noting the difference between the two Latin maxims. *Ex post facto* laws are statutes enacted after the occurrence of the crime. The maxim *nulla poena sine lege* is violated if the court, imposes liability, in the absence of a statute, simply as a matter of common law development. Common law crimes, so far as they still exist in England and the United States, violate the maxim *nulla poena sine lege* but do not infringe on the constitutional prohibition against *ex post facto* laws.

6. BVerfGE 25, 269 (Decision of the Constitutional Court 1969).

7. Resolution of the Constitutional Court of Hungary, No. 11/1992 (III.5) AB.

8. George P. Fletcher, *Two Kinds of Legal Rules: A Comparative Study of Burden-of-Persuasion Practices in Criminal Cases*, 77 *Yale L. J.* 880 (1968).

9. It is important to keep in mind the difference between the terms "civil trial" and "civil law jurisdiction." "Civil trials" litigate matters of private law. Today virtually every state or country has a "civil code" and this code regulates private legal transactions, such as torts, contracts, property, etc. "Civil law" systems are those found on the European Continent. The terminology is misleading and I would not use it if it were not so well entrenched.

10. On the trial of Bernhard Goetz, see generally George P. Fletcher, A Crime of Self-Defense: Bernhard Goetz and the Law on Trial (1988). There are many books on the Simpson trial. Two of the most informative and legally insightful are Alan Dershowitz, Reasonable Doubts (1996), and Jeffrey Toobin, The Run of His Life: The People v. O.J. Simpson (1996).

11. For a detailed discussion of this problem, see sections 6.1–6.2.

12. See A Crime of Self-Defense, chap. 3.

13. MPC §2.04.

14. The leading case in Canada on this point is Regina v. City of Saulte Ste. Marie, 3 Dominion Law Reports 3d 161 (1978) (in cases of strict liability the defendant must bear the burden of persuasion on the defense of "due diligence").

15. Erie R.R. Co. v. Tompkins, 304 U.S. 64 (1938)

16. Guaranty Trust v. York, 326 U.S. 99 (1945).

17. Id. at 109.

18. Id.

19. Another exception to the principle of "exporting" disputes to other jurisdictions is divorce law. Apparently, the community and the state are involved in the maintenance of marriages in the same way they must attend to the aftermath of crime.

20. See U.S. Constitution, Sixth Amendment, which provides: "the accused shall enjoy the right to a speedy and public trial, by an impartial jury of *the State and district wherein the crime shall have been committed.*" For an interpretation of this amendment in line with the argument of the text, see George P. Fletcher, With Justice for Some: Victims' Rights in Criminal Trials, 169–176 (paperback ed. 1996).

2

Punishment versus Treatment

All systems of criminal law represent a shared commitment to acquitting the innocent and punishing the guilty. This shared commitment confers upon them a single unifying purpose that centers on the institution of punishment. Without punishment and institutions designed to measure and carry out punishment, there is no criminal law. It is fair to say, then, that the institution of punishment provides the distinguishing features of criminal law.

The problem is: What is punishment? Not every form of coercion, not every sanction, constitutes punishment. Not even coerced confinement provides an adequate signal that the criminal law has come into play. One can lock people up for many reasons—for example, quarantine for disease, commitment for mental illness. Not all seizures of the person are equivalent to the old fashioned punishment of flogging. Grabbing a person to prevent him from committing suicide is neither assault nor punishment but rather beneficial coercion. Understanding criminal law, therefore, requires that we probe the distinction between punishment and forms of coercion, expressing a benevolent desire to aid the person affected. With some risk of oversimplification, I refer to all these alternative, beneficial uses of coercion as "treatment."

The elaboration of the difference between punishment and treatment depends largely on the context and purpose of legal analysis. The argument tracks, therefore, the analysis in chapter 1 on the distinction between substance and procedure. Fathoming the contours of punishment depends not on the positive law of particular states but on the results of philosophical and conceptual inquiry.

2.1 Two Constitutional Perspectives: Impact versus Motive

For purposes of constitutional analysis, the concept of punishment is of great importance. Most contemporary constitutions provide greater procedural protection in criminal trials than in civil or administrative hearings. In the United States, a proceeding is criminal in nature if and only if the defendant faces "punishment" as a sanction.

In the United States, the special protection for criminal trials includes the provisions of the Fifth and Sixth Amendments to the Constitution: among others, the privilege against self-incrimination, protection against double jeopardy, the right to assistance of counsel, and the right to a jury trial. As a test for when a threatened sanction is criminal in nature, the Supreme Court unhesitatingly invokes the concept of "punishment" as the relevant criterion.[1] That a sanction is inflicted in the criminal courts for a violation of a state or the federal criminal code is sufficient to classify the sanction as "punitive," but there are recurrent problems in assessing the punitive nature of other sanctions, such as administrative commitment, expatriation, deportation, fines for custom violations, and the deprivation of social security benefits.[2] That Congress or another legislative body has labeled these sanctions as civil in nature does not control the constitutional issue. The question is ultimately conceptual or philosophical. The courts must answer the question whether, no matter what the legislature has said, the sanction is inherently "punitive." If it is, then regardless of the legislative label, the process is criminal and the constitutional guarantees apply. As the statutory law cannot demarcate the line between substance and procedure, it cannot resolve the question whether a sanction constitutes "punishment" and therefore requires a criminal proceeding, with full constitutional protection.

One of the best candidates for punishment is physical confinement. Since the early nineteenth century, we have used prisons as our standard mode of punishment. Sometimes confinement is dictated for social protection, sometimes for the purpose of treatment, for the therapeutic benefit of the person confined. The juvenile court movement early in the twentieth century conceived of homes for juveniles as a form of benevolent intervention, designed only to help wayward young people avoid a life of crime. Because the purpose of confining juveniles was considered to be treatment, for the good of the juvenile, rather than punishment, the proceedings that led to the confinement of juveniles was thought to be exempt from the constitutional protection that surrounded criminal trials.

In the 1960s, civil libertarians mounted a broad attack against the idea that beneficent motives could exempt coercive techniques from constitutional controls. The argument was that a locked door is a locked door, whatever the motive. Specifically, with regard to the juvenile court movement, the Supreme Court concluded that however "euphemistic the title . . . ," a home for juveniles was "an institution of confinement in which the child is incarcerated for greater or lesser time."[3] In the leading case of *In re Gault*,[4] the Supreme Court took significant steps to expand the constitutionally required protection in state juvenile court proceedings. Henceforth, the Fourteenth Amendment due process clause would require that juveniles enjoy the privilege against self-incrimination, that they receive the assistance of counsel, and that they be able to exercise the right to confront witnesses against them. The euphemisms of treatment and rehabilitation paled in contrast to the reality of incarceration.[5] Yet the Court resisted the arguments of those who sought to equate the confinement and treatment of juveniles with the punishment of criminals. Though many elements of due process apply to juvenile courts, not all of the protections of the Sixth Amendment are required. The right to a jury trial, for example, is not included within the constitutionally required procedures in juvenile cases.[6]

Also, in the 1960s, the prison rights movement mounted a general attack against indeterminate sentencing, a general practice of sentencing convicted persons to undefined terms in prison, with parole authorities entrusted with the responsibility of setting a release date.[7] This practice was thought to be justified by the need to provide a program of treatment that would meet the individual needs of the individual confined. The attack on indeterminate sentencing stressed two values: (1) the importance of equality in sentencing from court to court, and case to case, and (2) the right of the prisoner himself to know at the beginning of his term when he is likely to be released. The outcome of this campaign is that most states abolished indeterminate sentencing and the federal government issued its sentencing guidelines to achieve greater equalization of sentences in the federal courts.[8]

Implicit in this critique of indeterminate sentencing was an attack on the rehabilitative ideal, the aspiration of treating and reforming prisoners instead of punishing them. Because the goal of rehabilitation cloaks the coercive power of the state in benevolent motives, the denial of liberty is considered less problematic.[9] Good motives by the state, then, can generate a low-visibility threat to individual autonomy and liberty.

In the debate about juvenile court and indeterminate sentencing, two different perspectives vie for supremacy. According to one point of view, if the state's *motive* is therapeutic, the confinement is nonpunitive and its imposition is exempt from the procedural niceties of jury trials, the participation of counsel, and the confrontation of witnesses. According to the conflicting point of view, the decisive consideration is the *impact* of the proceedings on the interests of the defendant. This, then, is the matrix of the debate: motive versus impact.

By and large, the advocates of "impact" have been ascendent.[10] The civil commitment of the dangerously insane is no longer the procedurally casual process it once was. A motive to provide treatment no longer suffices to label a sanction as treatment instead of punishment. Depriving even an allegedly insane person of liberty requires a full-scale hearing and other due process protections.[11]

But it would be wrong to conclude that "motive" is entirely passé as a rationale for justifying the power of the state. A good example of the continuing influence of good motives is the interpretation of the concept of "search" under the law of search and seizure. According to the Fourth Amendment to the U.S. Constitution, the "people" have a right to be secure "against unreasonable searches and seizures." If the police violate this right and seize evidence, the "exclusionary rule," as developed by the Supreme Court,[12] prohibits the use of the illegally seized evidence at trial.

The threshold question for applying the exclusionary rule is whether the police seized the evidence in the course of a search. The police and other governmental officials intrude in many ways in our privacy, and not everything they do constitutes a search. For example, if an employee of the city-owned gas company enters an apartment to read the gas meter and while he is there he happens to see a bag of heroin in plain view, his taking the contraband and turning it over to the police does not violate Fourth Amendment. Why? Because entering a private apartment for the purpose of reading the gas meter does not constitute a "search" in the constitutional sense. In this context a neutral "motive" triumphs over the effect of violating someone's private physical space.

The general rule is that when police or other state officials enter someone's home, their intervention constitutes a search only if their purpose is to look for evidence of crime or to arrest a suspect. If police have other motives, such as rescuing someone in danger, their entry is immune to constitutional criticism. Figuring out exactly what motivates the police in a particular case is not so easy. This became a burning question at the outset of the O.J. Simpson saga. Early in the morning of June 13, 1994, after the discovery of the dead bodies, detectives Mark Fuhrman, Philip Vannatter, and two other officers entered the Simpson estate in Brentwood, California. In the course of walking around the estate, they found evidence that linked Simpson to the crime, notably the bloody glove that Detective Fuhrman found on the ground. If they had entered the estate for the purpose of arresting Simpson or to look for evidence related to the double homicide, their entry was clearly a search under the Fourth Amendment. Under the complicated rules governing search and seizure and the necessity of warrants, their search—if that is what it was—was clearly unconstitutional. And if it was so labeled, the bloody glove would not have been admissible at Simpson's trial.

At the preliminary hearing in July 1994, Municipal Court Judge Kathleen Kennedy-Powell held that the dominant purpose of the search was, as the police officers alleged, to determine whether there were other possible victims in need of assistance.[13] That motive—analogous to the desire to help rather than punish juveniles—exempted the intrusion from the scope of the constitutional protection. That decision has triggered extensive criticism, but the critics have focused largely on the tactics of the Simpson trial. The more basic point is that the legal principle governing the debate might have been wrong: it might be better to stay away from police motives altogether and to treat the entry as a search on the basis of its impact on the privacy of the homeowner Simpson.

It would be a mistake, however, to think that motives never play a role in the constitutional analysis of punishment. A whole array of sanctions are regarded as "civil" in nature and therefore exempt from the implications of imposing punishment. Among the most troubling of these are deportation, disbarment, and impeachment, for in all three of these cases, the state seeks to impose a sanction on an individual for a crime or a misdemeanor. The sanctions are directed to their status. If they are aliens, they are subject to deportation for having committed certain offenses. If they are lawyers, they are subject to disbarment. If they hold public office, they are subject to impeachment.

Impeachment of the U.S. President, in particular, looks very much like punishment. The House of Representatives must issue the indictment or the impeachment for "Treason, Bribery, or other high Crimes and Misdemeanors."[14] The trial takes place before the Senate, and a two-thirds vote is sufficient to convict.[15] Yet removal from office is not the same as punishment. Its purpose is not to expiate or atone for the crime. The purpose of all these status-related sanctions—deportation, disbarment, and impeachment—is simply to deprive an individual of a status that enables him or her to constitute a continuing social threat.

Classifying a proceeding as criminal carries implications for the double jeopardy clause. If deportation, disbarment, and impeachment are criminal in nature, then the person affected cannot subsequently be prosecuted in criminal court for the crime that led to the loss of status. As provided in the Fifth Amendment: "Nor shall any person be subject for the same offence to be twice put in jeopardy of life or limb." This provision is read broadly to include a prohibition against subjecting a person "for same offence to be twice put in jeopardy" of criminal punishment. Once a person is punished, therefore, he or she cannot be punished a second time. If impeachment and removal from office are considered "punishment," therefore, the person affected cannot be tried in criminal court again for the same offense.

The Constitution itself provides that those removed from office "shall nevertheless be liable and subject to Indictment, Trial, Judgment and Punishment, according to Law."[16] This provision might convince many jurists that impeachment and removal from office are in the nature of criminal punishment; without the additional language, subsequent prosecution and punishment would presumably violate the prohibition against subjecting someone twice to a "criminal" trial and thus violating the prohibition against double jeopardy.[17] But this reading is not self-evident. The constitutional language might simply seek to avoid doubts about the matter. The question whether impeachment is punishment or not cannot be resolved simply by looking up a statute, even a constitution. The problem is conceptual or philosophical in nature.

In the course of arguing that impeachment is not punishment, I introduced a problematic consideration. The purpose of these status-deprivation sanctions is, I argued, not to punish but to protect society in the future. "[Their] purpose is not to expiate or atone for the crime."[18] Now of course one may ask: So what? Why is the purpose of punishment relevant? What about the theory that only impact matters? In order to answer this question, we need to turn in some detail to different theories about the purposes or rationale of punishment.

2.2 The Purposes of Punishment

Not everyone would take the purpose of punishment to be expiation or atonement for the crime. Indeed one major school of thought, taking its lead primarily from Jeremy Bentham's eighteenth-century utilitarianism, finds the justification for criminal sanctions in the good that they engender. The predicted *benefits* of condemning the particular defendant as a criminal and depriving him of his liberty outweigh the *costs* imposed on the imprisoned convict and his or her family.

Among these benefits are general deterrence, special deterrence, rehabilitation, and the incapacitation of offenders. General deterrence is based on the prediction that punishing one criminal will influence others not to commit the same crime. Special deterrence means that the punished offender will be deterred from future offenses after his release. Rehabilitation implies that as a result of treatment during incarceration, the convicted offender will be cured of the impulse to engage in criminal activity. Incapacitation means that during his confinement, the offender will not pose a threat to people outside the prison.

General deterrence has a great moral appeal. We would like to think that making criminals suffer contributes to a more orderly society.

But the evidence of effective deterrence is hard to come by.[19] In the particular case, it is almost impossible to predict the incremental value of punishing one more offender, or punishing a repeated offender, one more time. Special deterrence is also speculative. It is not clear how much the particular offender is likely to be affected or deterred by a term in the penitentiary. High recidivism rates suggest that in contrast to the ideal of rehabilitation, prisons serve more to harden the antisocial inclinations of criminals than to convert them to a law-abiding way of life. Admittedly, incapacitation works: during the term of imprisonment the convicted offender is less of a threat to people on the outside. Of course, he may commit crimes against others incarcerated with him, but these costs are not usually counted in the calculus of benefits deriving from imprisonment.

All four of these goals—general deterrence, special deterrence, rehabilitation, and incapacitation—are grouped under the general heading of "social protection" as the purpose of punishment. Not one of them suggest that the purpose of punishment is to atone for or expiate a crime that has disturbed the moral order.

It is hard to deny the value of protecting society against criminals. But if social protection becomes the exclusive rationale for punishment, we confront two serious problems. First, how do we reconcile this concept of punishment with our constitutional analysis that the motive of benefiting society, standing alone, fails to explain the difference between punishment and other closely related sanctions? Second, focusing on the good that might follow from punishment could well lead to ignoring the justice of punishing the particular suspect. Many tyrannical regimes have propped themselves up, at least in the short run, by inflicting punishment indiscriminately and thereby deterring disobedience by weak-hearted dissidents.[20] The goal of rehabilitation is particularly insidious because the coercive power of the state is cloaked by benevolent motives; if the suspect is "sick" and in need of treatment, it seems totally irrelevant whether on a particular occasion he "happened" to commit a crime.

Looking to the good that will follow from punishment distracts the attention of the judges from the particular offense that the defendant has committed. Not only does the point of requiring an actual offense become unclear, but the appropriate length of imprisonment comes to depend more on the projected dangerousness of the offender (or on the need for treatment) than on the gravity of the offense triggering the conviction.

The genesis of social protection as a rationale for punishment lies in the utilitarian theory developed by Beccaria[21] and Bentham:[22] The suffering of the prisoner is justified as necessary to achieve the greater good of improving the welfare or happiness of society. Immanuel Kant perceived this "theory of happiness" or "eudaemonism" as justifying differential punishment for the same crime—depending on the social needs of the moment. He responded in outrage:

> The principle of punishment is a categorical imperative, and woe to him who crawls through the windings of eudaemonism in order to discover something that releases the criminal from punishment.[23]

Kant insisted that punishment is an imperative both of morality and of justice. And "if justice goes, there is no longer any value in men's living on earth."[24] Retributive theories are generally thought to be more closely aligned with the imperative to seek justice in the criminal process. Many retributivists defend this commitment to do justice on the ground that it incidently serves to affirm the dignity of the offender.[25] Retribution, it is said, recognizes the criminal as a responsible human actor, someone who deserves punishment for his crime.

The core of the retributive view, however, is that punishment speaks to the wrong represented by the criminal act. It is here that we can begin to make sense of the idea that punishment should expiate the crime and restore the moral balance in the universe. As nineteenth-century German philosopher G. W. F. Hegel argued, the punishment cancels the wrong and restores the Right.[26] Or as the modern French social critic Michel Foucault interpreted punishment prior to the rise of the modern prison, executing or abusing the body of the offender reenacted the crime on his or her body, presumably to expunge the evil represented by the crime.[27] One might balk at the metaphysics of these arguments about the operative effect of punishment, but the notion that the suffering of the offender can negate the suffering caused by the offense continues to resonate in our intuitions of justice.

The contemporary American philosopher Herbert Morris has developed a modern version of this argument by stressing the imbalance of benefits and burdens generated by a criminal offense.[28] Those who obey the law incur burdens that offenders refuse to take upon themselves. To rectify this imbalance the offender must suffer an appropriate punishment. His refusal to conform generates the proverbial "debt" that must be paid. This argument makes some sense with regard to crimes that tempt many of us, such as illegal parking, or even cheating on our income tax. Yet it is less plausible to argue that we all suffer a burden in abstaining from the core crimes of murder, rape, arson, robbery, and burglary.

Social protectionists respond to these views, deriving from Kant and Hegel, with a mixture of disdain and disbelief. The idea of making criminals suffer for the sake of a transcendental ideal of justice makes many moderns cringe. How could anyone seriously propose a program of punishment that disregarded human welfare? There is no single line in the literature as pithy as Kant's "woe-to-him-who-crawls" rejection of the utilitarian view of punishment. But Bentham comes close with his contemptuous dismissal of the traditional view of human rights: The idea of "natural rights is simple nonsense; natural and imprescriptible rights, rhetorical nonsense—nonsense on stilts."[29]

The debate has circled around these themes for 200 years. There are those who believe that punishment should be imposed *retrospectively*, solely as an imperative of justice, as a way of addressing, negating, and overcoming the criminal act committed. Others hold that the aims of punishment are at least partly *prospective*: the purpose of imposing suffering on the offender should be to improve the welfare of society. The first camp derides the moral insensitivity of the second; the second camp accuses the first of indifference to human welfare.

The constitutional analysis of punishment seeks a middle position in this philosophical debate. The concept of punishment serves as a test for applying the procedural protections of the Sixth Amendment and recognizing the bar of the double jeopardy clause of the Fifth Amendment. As a constitutional touchstone, punishment is neither exclusively retrospective nor prospective in nature. The goals of social protection and promoting the public interest in safety may be relevant as policies of punishment, but they are insufficient to classify a sanction as either punishment or as nonpunitive treatment. The criminal law represents only one way to further the public interest. Deportation, disbarment, and impeachment aim to protect the public, but they are not constitutionally punitive. An adequate account of punishment must take note of the traditional metaphysics of retribution: that somehow the punishment must address the crime and seek to negate its occurrence.

2.3 The Conceptual Analysis of Punishment

A response to the claim that punishment implies retributive motives might go something like this. The argument so far has shown only that the *constitutional* concept of punishment requires some attention to the state's punitive motive. A purely *conceptual* account of punishment might come out differently. For example, the distinguished twentieth-century British philosopher H. L. A. Hart sought to give a purely conceptual account of punishment. He attempted to specify the features of those cases that we ordinarily call "punishment" in English discourse. These are worth quoting in full:

1. Punishment must involve pain or other consequences normally considered unpleasant.
2. It must be for an offense against legal rules.

3. It must be of an actual or supposed[30] offender for his offense.

4. It must be intentionally administered by human beings other than the offender.

5. It must be imposed and administered by an authority constituted by a legal system against which the offense is committed.[31]

There appears to be nothing in this list that invokes a motive to expiate or atone for the offense, and therefore it appears that if Hart is correct, his purely conceptual account of punishment might avoid the retributive implications we have noted in the constitutional analysis. The question is whether this purely conceptual account can explain what we mean by punishment.

Hart's criteria help us eliminate some metaphoric applications of the notion of punishment. Suppose that a father kills his child by driving drunk and crashing into a tree. He confesses to the police, but the prosecutorial officials refuse to prosecute on the ground that the death of his son is already sufficient "punishment" for his wanton drinking. Though the first three of Hart's criteria would be satisfied, the latter two would not be. No human beings, no official authority, can impose the "punishment" of a son's dying in an automobile accident. Yet this is hardly a counterexample to Hart's theory; saying that the father was punished by his own acts seems to be simply a metaphor—an extension of the core concept.

Let us take a closer look at a key clause among Hart's five conditions for punishment: that the sanction be imposed "for an offense against legal rules." The problem is that there are many sanctions imposed for the violation of legal rules. These include tort liability for negligence in violating a statutory norm, fines for late payments of taxes, injunctions imposed for unfair labor practices in violation of national labor legislation. Yet none of these constitutes a sanction that we would readily identify as punishment. This clause of Hart's five-part test obviously sweeps too wide and includes too many instances of sanctioning.

It may be that Hart's test can help us understand the rudimentary difference between civil commitment, compulsory military service, and quarantine, on the one hand, and criminal punishment on the other. The former does not presuppose the violation of any legal rule; the latter does. Yet the truly difficult problems in determining the scope of the criminal law—notably the cases of deportation, disbarment, and impeachment—are left unresolved.

By focusing on the phrase "for an offense," however, we might be able to adapt Hart's criteria to reach the result we found to be required by the constitutional analysis of punishment. Strictly speaking, deportation for a heinous criminal act is not imposed *for* the criminal act; it is carried out for the sake of protecting the public. Disbarment and removal from office exhibit the same ambiguity. These sanctions may be imposed *in response* to criminal behavior but they are carried out *for the sake of* protecting the public. These prepositions matter. A sensitive construction of the phrase "for an offense against legal rules" leads to the conclusion that punishment must have the purpose of establishing a conceptual link between the crime and the punishment. The word "for" requires this link to emerge from the act of punishing.

The connection between the punishment and the crime might be symbolic, as in Foucault's thesis that punishment inflicted on the body reenacted and therefore expiated the crime.[32] Or the connection between them obtain in the consciousness of the offender, as, for example, if the punishment is designed to bring home to the offender the nature of his criminal act.[33] In either sense, eliciting a connection between the punishment and the crime is what it means for the punishment to be imposed "for an offense against legal rules."

We have come full circle in the argument. Our interpretation of Hart's phrase "for an offense" captures the element of motive that characterized the constitutional theory of punishment, namely, that the purpose of the sanction must be to expiate or atone for the crime. That requirement is expressed more generally in this context as meaning: the primary purpose of punishment cannot be social protection (as in the cases of deportation, disbarment, and impeachment) but must be to express a connection between the offender's suffering a punishment and the victim's suffering the crime. The search for a conceptual account of punishment leads invariably, it seems, to the inclusions of elements of the state's motive and retributivist thinking.

2.4 Punishment: Public and Private

Individuals, situated equally in society, can wreak vengeance against each other. They can give tit for tat and try to get even. But they cannot, strictly speaking, exact punishment from those who offend against them. As suggested in Hart's fifth requirement, punishment presupposes a neutral authority. Private individuals do not have this authority with regard to each other. True, parents can punish their children, and God can punish human beings for their sins. Teachers can impose penalties on students. In these hierarchical relationships, private individuals do exhibit the kind of authority required for punishment.

If hierarchical authority is a necessary condition for punishment, the implication is that individuals cannot "punish" if they act simply for personal revenge. To express their legitimate authority, they must invoke interests that go beyond their limited private sphere. Our judges punish publicly, in the name of the community and the state. God punishes as the "judge of all the universe."[34]

This requirement of a higher interest expresses an important point about the nature of crime. Crimes intrude upon the public sphere as well as damage private interests. True, the offender may harm a distinct individual, but the act of killing, stealing, burglary, or rape violates and unnerves the community as a whole. The crime generates a general fear of violence among those who learn about it. Because crime itself is an assault upon the public, it makes sense to think of punishment itself as an expression of public authority.

The rise of public prosecution illustrates this point. The public prosecutor seeks punishment of the guilty in the name of the People, the State, or, in England, the Crown. In the United States and in most parts of the common law world today, the public prosecutor claims exclusive authority to seek punishment for crimes committed against private individuals. The victim may have an action under private law for monetary damages as a result of harm suffered in the crime, but only the State or the People can demand punishment.

The public nature of punishment is expressed in the rationale and structure of retributive punishment, which differs both from the purely private nature of corrective justice and the public nature of distributive punishment. Corrective justice seeks to redress the imbalance that the wrongdoing generates between victim and offender. The victim loses and the offender gains by engaging in self-interested wrongdoing. Corrective justice equalizes this maldistribution of advantage by forcing the offender to make a monetary payment to the victim, a payment that is called *compensation*.

So far as punishment brings the offender down to the level of the victim, punishment has a corrective function. It equalizes the suffering of the two sides. Some might object, however, that this is not a genuine form of corrective justice because the offender's suffering does not in fact eliminate or correct (it only imitates) the victim's suffering.

The distinctive feature of punishment is that it also has a distributive dimension. Distributive justice means that the benefits and burden of living together in society are distributed to each according to his due. Unless there is a sound basis for punishing some offenders more than others, distributive justice mandates equality in the distribution of the burden that punishment represents. Because the state is responsible for distributing the burdens of fines and imprisonment (not to mention the death penalty), it is critical that the state abide by criteria of distributive justice. This obligation implies that it may not discriminate in selecting some people and not others to suffer for their crimes.

For this reason the leading philosopher of retributive punishment, Immanuel Kant, stressed the imperative of maintaining strict equality among offenders.[35] It is patently unjust, in Kant's view, to punish some offenders less because they are willing to cooperate in some way with the state. Kant would turn over in his Koenigsberg grave if he knew about the modern American and growing European practice of plea bargaining, under which the prosecution makes special deals with certain suspects in return for their providing evidence against other suspects. Kant was so firm in his commitment to equality among offenders that he regarded any deviation from equality for the sake of practical advantage as illustrative of the principle: "if justice goes, there is no longer any value in men's living on earth."[36]

The corrective side of punishment stresses the equalization of suffering as between victim (or victim's family) and offender. The distributive side focuses on the importance of equal and just distribution of sentences to those and only those who are guilty of committing crimes.

As Kant was committed to the principle of equality among offenders, he also recognized the importance of victims and their interests in the criminal process. In an often (and unfairly) derided passage, he develops an argument for taking the victim's perspective in punishment.[37] He imagines that a society is about to disband, but it has a problem: there are still murderers, condemned to die, languishing in prison. What should the society do about them? Kant insists that the murders should be executed "so that each has done to him what his deeds deserve and blood guilt does not cling to the people."[38] Yet executing them seems to be pointless because no good could possibly follow. This is the challenge posed by Kant's argument.

The notion of a society's disbanding should be treated as a thought-experiment, very much like the idea of a society's coming together in a social contract. Neither of these events ever occurred in history, but they are useful constructs for testing our intuitions about the conditions of a just social order. The biblical reference to blood guilt recalls an ancient rationale of punishment that takes the victim's suffering as its point of departure. The view in biblical culture, as one leading scholar argues, was that a manslayer acquired control over the victim's blood; the slayer had to be executed in order to release the blood, permitting it to return to God as in the case of a natural death.[39] The failure to execute the murderer meant that the rest of society, charged with this function, became responsible for preventing the release of the victim's blood.

We may interpret the notion of gaining control over the victim's blood as a metaphor for the criminal's gaining dominance over the victim or the victim's family. This idea of criminal dominance remains with us, in other forms, today. Criminal conduct establishes the supremacy of the criminal over the victim and, in the case of homicide, the victim's family. This is obvious in some crimes, such as rape, mugging, and burglary, where victims characteristically fear a repeat attack by the criminal. It is also true in blackmail, where the offender induces services or money in return for silence and is in a position to return at any time and demand additional payments.[40] Instilling fear and this form of subservience is a mode of gaining dominance. Punishment counteracts domination by reducing the criminal to the position of the victim. When the criminal suffers as the victim suffered, equality between the two is reestablished. One function of punishment, then, is to express solidarity with the victim. It is a way of saying to the victim and his or her family: "You are not alone. We stand with you, against the criminal."

Whatever the biblical metaphysics of gaining and releasing control of blood, the point relevant today is that the failure to punish renders the rest of society, those charged with a duty to punish, complicitous in the original crime. According to the ethics of the Bible, those who "stand idly by"[41] are charged with blood guilt. Similarly today, we are inclined to see the failure to punish as a form of complicity that falls on those who abandon the victim to his or her "private" tragedy. When society and its officials look the other way, their indifference continues the criminal's dominance over the victim. When we fail to prosecute and punish a known violent offender, we all become complicitous in maintaining the victim's state of subservience.

Admittedly, this rationale for punishment hardly works to justify the institution of punishment at its initial historical stages. Other arguments of principle are necessary to justify the conscious creation of a system of retributive punishment. Once the institution is in place, however, a tradition of punishing crime takes hold, and it acquires a logic of its own. The practice of punishing crime provides an opportunity for the victim's cocitizens to express solidarity and to counteract the state of inequality induced by the crime. When they refuse to invoke the traditional response to crime, citizens disassociate themselves from the victim. Abandoned, left alone, the victim readily feels betrayed by the system.

The connection between punishment and solidarity has become apparent in the last few decades in the numerous countries that have overcome dictatorial regimes and have begun the transition to democracy. The first notable example was Argentina, which in the mid-1980s began a program of prosecuting the generals who were responsible for the mass-disappearances in the period of the military junta. The victim's families themselves—led by *Las Madras*—insisted on prosecution as a means of vindicating their dignity as citizens. Since the shift of government from President Alfonsin to President Menem, the leaders of the junta have been pardoned.[42] Those connected to the victims must endure the sight of those responsible for their suffering now leading the good life as free citizens.

The transition to democracy in Eastern Europe has led to repeated demands to punish the leaders of the Communist governments that were responsible for evil deeds, ranging from encouraging Soviet intervention in Budapest in 1956 and Prague in 1968 to shooting escaping East German citizens in the 1980s. Procedural barriers, such as the statute of limitations, prevent many of these prosecutions. Yet the Germans have been insistent about prosecuting border guards for shooting escaping citizens.[43] They have also ruled that those who gave the orders to shoot must also be held as perpetrators in the shooting.[44]

Also, in the United States, the symbolic significance of the victim has come center stage. The most dramatic example is the deep resentment among African-Americans of the 1992 Simi Valley acquittal of the four Los Angeles police officers who brutally assaulted Rodney King. Those who identified with the victim King felt betrayed by the failure of the jury to convict. The same sense of betrayal was evident among Orthodox Jews after the acquittal by New York juries of Lemrick Nelson for the slaying of Yankel Rosenbaum in 1992 and of El Sayyid Nosair for the killing of Meir Kahane in 1990. The extraordinary outpouring of anger after the 1995 acquittal of O.J. Simpson reflects the same pattern of identification with the victims of violent crime.[45]

Clearly, justice requires attention to the victim as well as to the defendant. Yet there is considerable confusion in some quarters about victims' rights. It is important to distinguish actual victims from those—indeed all of us—who might be victims in the future. Those who have actually endured criminal assaults merit our solidarity. Those who complain that they cannot walk the streets for fear of crime are in no special position relative to other citizens. It is a mistake to group these potential victims with actual victims.

Opponents of victims' rights object that we really do not know who is a victim until we know whether the defendant is responsible for an alleged crime against the alleged victim. It is all a matter of allegation until the evidence comes in and establishes the defendant's guilt. There is something to this point. If there is no crime, no wrongdoing, there is no victim. Yet in a homicide case we might well know that there are victims—Ron Goldman and Nicole Simpson or Yankel Rosenbaum or Meir Kahane—without knowing who is responsible for the deaths. Or the offender might have created a victim, even though he might not be personally accountable for the crime. President Reagan was a victim of John Hinckley's attack in 1981, even though Hinckley was acquitted by reason of insanity.[46] Thinking about who is a victim and why turns out to be a very important guide to the analysis of certain difficult questions in the theory of responsibility. This is a matter that we take up in chapter 5 on the distinction between general wrongdoing and personal responsibility.

The danger in focusing exclusively on victims' rights is that so far as it is designed solely to satisfy the victim, punishment reduces itself either to vengeance or compensation. In the end punishment must maintain its public character. It is not purely a private institution. It is imposed in the name of the People or State against actions that threaten the well-being of the entire society.

We started this chapter by probing the distinction between punishment and various forms of beneficial coercion I called treatment. We see, in the end, that the concept of punishment must fend off confusion from many directions. It must hold its own against those who try to obliterate the distinction between punishing crime and imposing other sanctions for the sake of protecting the public. The concept must also secure its place in opposition to purely private institutions, such as wreaking vengeance and securing compensation for injury. The concept of punishment must straddle the delicate line between the public and the private, between the motive of protecting society and the motive of promoting the welfare of victims. The task of thinking lawyers is keep their focus on this delicate line and to cultivate the correct conceptual account of punishment.

Notes

1. Kennedy v. Mendoza-Martinez, 372 U.S. 144 (1963); Helvering v. Mitchell, 303 U.S. 391 (1938).

2. See generally Comment, *The Concept of Punitive Legislation and the Sixth Amendment: A New Look at Kennedy v. Mendoza-Martinez,* 32 U. Chi. L. Rev. 290 (1965). On deportation, see Fong Yue Ting v. United States, 149 U.S. 698 (1893).

3. In re Gault, 387 U.S. 1, 27 (1967).

4. 387 U.S. 1 (1967).

5. The same tension between motive and impact shapes the debate about the intrusions that constitute "searches" under the Fourth Amendment. Cf. Plitko v. State, 11 Md. App. 35, 272 A.2d 669 (1971) (good-faith inventory search consistent with Fourth Amendment) with Mozzetti v. Superior Court, 4 Cal. 3d 699, 484 P.2d 84, 94 Cal. Rptr. 412 (1971) (impact of search prevails over motive, Fourth Amendment applicable).

6. This reservation in *Gault* was affirmed in McKeiver v. Pennsylvania, 403 U.S. 528 (1971).

7. See e.g., In re Lynch, 8 Cal. 3d 410, 503 P.2d 921, 105 Cal. Rptr. 217 (1972) (potential life sentence for second offense of indecent exposure unconstitutional as cruel and unusual punishment); In re Rodriguez, 14 Cal. 3d 639, 537 P.2d 384, 122 Cal. Rptr. 552 (1975) (Adult Authority had a statutory duty to set a release date for sex offender serving an indeterminate, potentially life term; the time spent must be proportionate to the crime).

8. U.S. Sentencing Guidelines Manual (1995).

9. My mind was first opened to this issue by reading *The Rehabilitative Ideal,* in Francis Allen, The Borderland of Criminal Justice (1964). Cf. Morris, *Persons and Punishment,* in Herbert Morris, On Guilt and Innocence 31 (1976). The issues were kept alive by C.S. Lewis, *The Humanitarian Theory of Punishment,* 6 Res. J. Judicata 224 (1953).

10. See the quote from *Gault* in the text *supra* at note 3.

11. E.g. Addington v. Texas, 441 U.S. 418 (1979) (hearing required before involuntary civil commitment); Heyford v. Parker, 396 F.2d 393 (10th Cir. 1968)(right to counsel).

12. Mapp v. Ohio, 367 U.S. 806 (1960)

13. See Scott Turow, Simpson Prosecutors Pay for Their Blunders, The

New York Times, October 4, 1995, at A21: "If veteran police detectives did not arrive at the gate of Mr. Simpson's home thinking he might have committed these murders, then they should have been fired."

14. U.S. Constitution, art. II, sec. 4.

15. U.S. Constitution, art. I, sec. 3, cl. 6.

16. U.S. Constitution, art. I, sec. 3, cl. 7.

17. U.S. Constitution, Fifth Amendment. For a recent case confronting the problem of punishment under the double jeopardy clause, see United States vs. Ursery, 116 S.Ct. 2135 (1996) (convicting first for drug offense and then applying in rem forfeiture provision did not constitute double "punishment" under the Fifth Amendment).

18. See text *supra* after note 15.

19. See generally Robert Martinson, *What Works? Questions and Answers about Prison Reform*, 36 Public Interest 22 (1974).

20. Whether punishment actually suppresses dissidence depends on the particular historical situation. Arbitrary conviction and punishment did not work well in the former Soviet Union. See Telford Taylor (with G. Fletcher, A. Dershowitz *et al.*), Courts of Terror (1976).

21. Cesare Becarria, Dei Delitti e Delle Pene (1764), translated as "An Essay on Crimes and Punishment" (1st English ed. 1775).

22. See Jeremy Bentham, An Introduction to the Principles of Morals and Legislation (J. H. Burns and H. L. A. Hart, eds., 1970).

23. Immanuel Kant, The Metaphysics of Morals 141 (Mary Gregor trans., 1991).

24. Id.

25. See H. Morris, supra note 9, at 31.

26. Georg W.F. Hegel, The Philosophy of Right 69 (T.M. Knox trans., 1962).

27. Michel Foucault, Discipline and Punish: The Birth of the Prison 3–16 (1977).

28. H. Morris, supra note 9, at 34–36. A distinct argument is that punishment expresses respect for the offender's choices as a person. Id. at 48–49.

29. Jeremy Bentham, Anarchical Fallacies, in 2 The Works of Jeremy Bentham 501 (John Bowring ed., 1962).

30. Note that Hart admits the possibility of punishing the innocent.

31. Hart, *Prolegomenon to the Principles of Punishment* in H. L. A. Hart, Punishment and Responsibility 4–5 (1968).

32. See note 27 supra.

33. Cf. Robert Nozick, Philosophical Investigations 374–80 (1981).

34. This is the way Abraham refers to God in Genesis 16, 19.

35. Kant, supra note 23, at 141.

36. Id.

37. Id. at 142.

38. Id.

39. David Daube, Studies in Biblical Law 122–23 (1947).

40. For more careful development of this theory in the context of blackmail, see George P. Fletcher, *Blackmail: The Paradigmatic Crime*, 119 U. Pa. L. Rev. 1617 (1993).

41. Leviticus 19:16.

42. See Jaime Malamud-Goti, *Punishment and Human Dignity*, 2(1) S'vara: A Journal of Law, Philosophy and Judaism 69 (1991).

43. See decision of the German Constitutional Court, supra note 3.

44. For further details on these legal deliberations, see chapter 11 at pp. 199–200.

45. For more detail on these cases, as well as consideration of women and gays as victims, see generally With Justice for Some.

46. See Washington Post, June 22, 1982, A1.

3

Subject versus Object

The distinction between subject and object runs through the criminal law and provides a useful perspective on our conception of whom we are prosecuting and on what we are punishing for. A subject is someone who acts, and an object is someone or something that is acted upon. Do we prosecute suspects and punish offenders as subjects or as objects? That question is never posed directly in the doctrines of the criminal law but it underlies many current disputes about defining and determining who is liable for crime.

To be protected in their dignity, human beings must be treated as subjects, not as objects. Immanuel Kant expressed this idea by interpreting the moral law to yield the following practical imperative: "So act as to treat humanity, whether in thine own person or in that of any other, in every case as an end withal, never as a means only."[1] We may use objects as means; but we must respect human beings as subjects, as ends in themselves. One clear implication of Kant's prohibition against treating human beings as means to an end is the rejection of deterrence as a sufficient rationale for punishment. Punishment must respect the offender as an end in himself, as a responsible agent called to account for his wrongdoing.

Legal systems vary in the extent to which they show respect for offenders and suspected offenders as subjects rather than objects. One primary mode of expressing this respect is found in the rule that punishment is imposed only for human actions, that is, for the crimes committed by human beings when they act as subjects. The requirement is called the "act requirement," and it is as close to a universal requirement of criminal justice that exists. This is our first topic of investigation. Later in the chapter, we shall turn to the field of procedure and consider the extent to which the criminal suspect should be seen as a subject rather than as an object of the proceedings. In other words, is the suspect someone who appears as a player and an actor in the trial? Or is the suspect and the alleged crime merely the object of the court's investigation? The distinction between subject and object emerges both in structuring the substantive criminal law and in designing procedures for fair trials.

3.1 The Requirement of Human Action

All legal systems concur that punishment is imposed only for human action or a "human act." It is considered barbaric to punish animals for causing harm,[2] or to impose punishment on those whose bodies are the mere instruments of harm. Suppose A takes the hand of B and uses it to slap C. It seems clear that the only possible wrongdoer in this situation is A. B's hand is the instrument of the crime, but B is not a subject or an actor in the slapping. If the state punished B for having the misfortune of having his hand used as the instrument of crime, it treats B as an object rather than a subject.

The "act" requirement has led to some confusion, however, because of a long practice of defining action by looking at its most superficial manifestation: the movement of the limbs. Of course, movement alone cannot constitute action. If my hand moves, it does not follow that I have moved my hand. If A takes B's hand and slaps C, B's hand moves but he is not acting. The tempting resolution of this quandary is to say that only those movements count as action that are traceable to the volition or will of the actor. Thus we encounter the popular formula defining a human act as "a willed muscular contraction."[3] A leading American writer, Michael Moore, recently endorsed this practice by defining human acts as "willed bodily movements."[4]

There are many problems with this reliance on the joinder of movement and will as the touchstone of human action. One of them is the philosophical question: How do we know whether when the actor's hand rises, the actor has exercised his will relative to raise his hand? It seems that the only way to perceive the will is to see it in action, which means to perceive action first and then to explain the action as the manifestation of will. It seems that we then get trapped in a definitional circle. We define action as a manifestation of the will but we know that the will is operative only if we first perceive action in the movement of the actor's limbs. For purposes of legal thought, the more pernicious influence of defining actions as "willed bodily movements" is that the absence of movement seems to represent a serious problem for the act requirement. The argument goes like this:

1. Movement is a necessary condition for action.

2. When individuals do not display movement, they cannot be acting.

3. Therefore doing nothing and letting death or other harm occur cannot constitute a crime.

This is the problem, known the world over, of punishing omissions. We need to fathom precisely what the problem is.

3.2 Acts and Omissions

Consider the famous textbook example of the bystander who can save a drowning child but decides not to do so. It is widely believed—and it follows from the above syllogism—that there would be something just or conceptually untoward about punishing the bystander. After all, he merely "omits" to save the child, and that is not quite the same as laying hands on it and holding its head under water. Drowning the child is murder and everyone agrees that murder should be severely punished, but merely standing by as the child drowns is regarded as an omission. Even though the bystander could easily have saved the child, many lawyers and legal theorists think that it would be wrong to punish the bystander for his coldheartedness.

Because the bystander seems to do nothing to hasten the child's death, his passivity is called an omission. And punishing omissions, or "doing nothing," supposedly runs afoul of the act requirement. But note one important feature of the bystander's doing nothing. He is not unconscious, and he is not oblivious to the plight of the drowning child. He chooses to do nothing to help the child. It is not that he necessarily chooses to do "nothing at all," for he may choose to do something else, like read the newspaper, rather than save the child. Human agency is built into the example. The problem would not even be interesting unless we assumed that the bystander chose to remain passive, despite an unrestrained option to intervene and rescue the child.

It is clear, then, that the lack of human agency is not the problem expressed in the widespread anxiety about punishing omissions. There is agency and in this sense action in choosing nothing or choosing to do something other than rescuing someone in need. Yet if we took seriously the definition of action as "willed bodily movement," we might think the problem of omissions is the problem of human action. Omissions are supposedly not acts, for though they might be willed, they do not consist in a "muscular contraction." As Moore puts it, "Omissions are the absence of any willed bodily movements."[5] They are "literally nothing at all."[6]

Defining omissions as the absence of action is problematic for several reasons. First, not everything we fail to do is properly described as an omission. Every time a physician treats one patient, he fails to treat a million others who might require treatment at that very moment. It does not follow that he omits to give treatment to these others in need. Every time I give charity to one cause, I fail to give to many others. It does not follow that I thereby "omit" to help the others. Whether one omits to render aid depends on contextual factors that make the rendering of aid expected and normal. If my doing something would be a great surprise—say quitting my job or committing suicide—then it is implausible to say that every moment I do not do these things, I am "omitting" to do them.

In addition, approaching omissions as a problem of "negative" action or the opposite of action puts too much weight on the definition of acting. The mistake is assuming that the two are conceptually connected.

The thesis, then, is very simple. The problem of punishing omissions has nothing at all to do with the act requirement. What, then, is the problem? Why do we even distinguish between acts and omissions?

In fact, there are two entirely distinct problems typically grouped under the standard textbook analysis of "omissions." One problem is whether crimes defined by action verbs such as killing, burning, maiming, assaulting, and raping can be committed by people who stand and let events run their course. Thus in the case of the bystander who lets the baby drown, the question is whether he can be held accountable for killing the child. There is not now and there has never been a separate crime of letting a person drown. The charge is murder or manslaughter and the verbs used to define this crime are always "killing" or "causing death." In the French literature, this problem is aptly called the problem of "commission par omission."

The second problem is punishing, by special statutory prohibition, various activities that can be described as failures to act. Consider the failure to register for the draft, the failure to pay income tax, or the common failure to pay social security tax on household employees. The most hotly disputed form of "failure" offense is the failure to render aid at the scene of an accident. Most European countries have first aid statutes of this sort;[7] most American states do not. The important feature of these crimes is that the failure is the gist of the crime. There is no need for a further consequence. When an obligatory first aid statute does apply, it imposes a relatively small penalty on everyone at the scene who fails to give easily rendered aid before emergency assistance arrives. These statutes do not impose liability for homicide in the event that the victim of the accident dies.

There are different reasons for regarding these two sorts of omissions as problematic. Let us look at each category in turn.

Commission by Omission

In the case of commission by omission, the problem is statutory interpretation and the danger implicit in extending the verb "killing" to encompass cases of "letting die." That is a rather serious issue, but it has nothing to do with the question of motion versus nonmotion. There are many cases of motion that are not killing, and, I dare say, some cases of nonmotion that are. Suppose that one of the guards at Buckingham Palace, renowned for their ability to remain still without moving, enters into a conspiracy with outsiders to kill the Queen. He signals to his coconspirators that they should bomb a certain portion of the palace by his remaining motionless an extra five seconds after the other guards begin to change their posture. This would be enough to render him complicitous in the death of the Queen, if the plot succeeds. He contributes to her death by signaling that the bombing should proceed.

The defender of the traditional view that omissions are the absence of motion might reply: Yes, but the guard cannot do it alone. Nonmotion cannot cause anything in and of itself—and least of all death. But surely, unexpected nonmotion could be the cause the death: A car refuses to move from the path of the motorcade; a pilot becomes motionless and refuses to guide an airplane in flight. There are numerous examples of this sort that trade on the unexpected nonmotion of one thing relative to other things in motion. Some people think that a passive figure, someone who is motionless, cannot be a cause of any harmful consequence,[8] but I have yet to see a convincing argument made against the plausible position of Hart and Honoré that failing to do the expected can be the "cause" of resulting harm. For example, the failure to water a plant, when the contrary is reasonably expected, may "cause" the plant to die.[9]

There might be many cases, then, in which death results from (is caused by) a failure to render care. A mother's failure to feed her child is readily treated as the affirmative act of neglect or starvation, and thus virtually every Western legal system would include this case within the ambit of criminal homicide. Whether the mother remains motionless as the baby dies is totally irrelevant.

The more difficult cases are those that we would call "letting die" rather than "killing." A woman falls sick and her lover fails to call for medical help. He lets her die when he could have intervened and staved off death.[10] Whether he is liable depends, in the common view of the courts, on whether he has a duty to aid her. Imposing these duties raises serious problems of legality, for in fact all of these duties, in all legal systems, are judicially generated. There is no Western legal system that exhaustively regulates, by statute, the situations that generate a duty that will, in breach, support a conviction for criminal homicide.[11] The Model Penal Code provides that "liability for the commission of an offense may not be based on an omission . . . unless a duty to perform the omitted act is imposed by law."[12] "Law" in this context means case law, not statutory law. Therefore the punishment of commission by omission raises serious problems under the principle *nulla poena sine lege* [no punishment without a prior *statutory* prohibition]. [13]

Offenses of Failing to Act

When a statute requires action of a particular sort, it poses no problem of legality,[14] but for some, it might pose a problem of intruding too much upon our liberties. We do not hear this objection too often about the statutory duty to file an income tax return or the duty to report for jury service. The only area of controversy seems to be the duty to render first aid at the scene of an accident. Most people, in my impression, stop and render aid. Even in a callous city like New York, passersby will stop and give assistance when their safety is assured. There might be a case for expressing the communitarian judgment that rendering aid is the right thing to do. There is a danger, however, that a statute of this sort would be understood as imposing the kind of duty that would support liability for homicide. German courts are very clear that violating the duty-to-aid provision is insufficient for homicide.[15] In view of our casual attitudes toward the principle of legality, however, a duty to aid statute could be a basis for judicial misunderstanding.

The question remains whether there is something fundamentally wrong about statutes that require us to act in order to aid others instead of simply abstaining from causing harm. The statutes in question demand beneficial actions rather than prohibit intrusions against others. This demand on us supposedly violates our autonomy or liberty. But I should think that whether a statutory demand or prohibition is more noxious depends more on its content than on the form (active or passive) of the duty imposed. Regulations that prohibit smoking in university buildings are very intrusive upon the liberties of smokers; the newly evolved custom requiring smokers to ask permission before they light up is not so intrusive. Laws prohibiting homosexual sodomy are rather intrusive (if enforced). Promoting a culture of safe sex (an affirmative duty to use condoms) is less intrusive. These examples should be enough to call into question the assumption that demanding action somehow offends liberty in a way in which prohibiting action does not.

It may be less intrusive to require people to abstain from killing than it is to require them to avoid the occurrence of a natural death.

But this increased difficulty has nothing to do with the distinction between motion and nonmotion. The problem with affirmative duties is that they fall due at a time and place over which we have no control. All of a sudden you find yourself next to the pond with the proverbial drowning child. You must act now. It matters not that you are not in the mood to be a good samaritan, that you have something better to do. There is nothing quite so unpredictable and insistent as having the circumstances determine when and how we must act.

Beyond all these explanations, we still encounter a taboo surrounding the "problem of punishing omissions." One explanation may be that in the absence of action, it appears that we might be punishing individuals for their thoughts alone. Thus we run up against a sensitive taboo in criminal justice. Everyone seems to agree that it would be a perversion of the institution to punish in the absence of action—for thoughts alone. The question is whether punishing omissions poses this problem. It seems as though it might, for if an omission is the absence of "willed bodily movements," as Moore claims, there is nothing there to punish but the thought of doing nothing. Several decades ago Herbert Morris pointed out that we do not punish for passivity alone but for an omission that permits the occurrence of a harmful event, typically the death of someone in distress.[16] The crime of the omission expresses itself, therefore, in an untoward event in the external world. But this is not the case with regard to crimes of violating a statutory duty to act, and therefore in the latter cases the problem remains.

Suppose we had a statutory requirement to vote, as do many countries. If I were punished for not voting, would I be punished for thoughts alone? It is not the thought of not voting that triggers liability, but actually not voting. But not voting, it is said, is nothing, and therefore, all there is to punish is the thought that accompanies the not voting. But if not voting were "nothing," why would anyone think of sanctioning it? Like other punishable failures, not voting occurs in the context of others' complying with the demand. It is the wrong of free riding on those who maintain the democratic system. And not voting is hardly the absence of bodily movement. The point of not voting is not simply to "do nothing" but to engage in a variety of activities that seem more important than going to the polls.

This digression into the "problem of omissions" was prompted by the seeming connection between action defined as "willed bodily motion" and omissions as the absence of bodily motion. The problems associated with omissions turn out to be of a different order. One problem is the extension of norms governing actions such as killing to passive noninterventions, such as letting die. The other is the determination when it is legislatively appropriate to punish certain instances of failure. Neither of these problems raises the problem of treating people as subjects rather than as objects. Liability for omissions—as for ac-

tion—presupposes agency as a human subject. But if we can leave behind the implications of defining action as "willed bodily movement,"
we still face the problem of giving an adequate account of action as a
human subject.

3.3 Alternative Approaches to Human Action

It is important to ask the question: What is the point of defining human
action? Do serious problems arise in criminal cases that call for a definition of action? In general, we assume that people who look like they
are acting are in fact acting, unless some factor intervenes to suggest
the contrary. If we learn, for example, that despite the appearance of
purposive and calculated action, the actor in fact is hypnotized or is
sleepwalking,[17] we may have second thoughts. In these cases, we might
wonder whether the action is self-generated. Is the actor under the
control of someone else, such as a hypnotist, or is he laboring under
some malady such as a brain tumor that itself generates the harmful
action?

   These alternative cases are those in which the appearance of action
is deceptive. The "bodily movements" turn out to be akin to a natural
phenomenon. In this inquiry about whether action is present, the abstract definition of action is of little value. The decisive factors are the
specific grounds for treating bodily movement as a natural phenomenon rather than as the assertion of a human agent.[18]

   But even the listing of specific considerations that can negate the
quality of action in bodily movements fails to solve the problem of
action. For in each case we must ask the question whether, despite the
hypnosis, sleepwalking, brain tumor, or other source of overwhelming
pressure, the actor *really* is acting or not. There seems to be no alternative in this approach to referring back to the question whether in the
particular context, the action is the product of the actor's will (or determination or assertion or effort or volition). Yet all the synonyms we
can devise for the notion of the actor's will fail to resolve the problem
of circularity: We can only know whether the will (or determination
or assertion or effort or volition) is operative if we first perceive human
action in events we are trying to explain.

   The problem of defining human action differs fundamentally from
litigating insanity as an excusing condition. A claim of insanity presupposes human action. The M'Naghten formula of insanity generates an
excuse if the defendant does not know "the nature or quality of his
act."[19] More contemporary standards stress the actor's ability to control
his actions as well as his cognitive understanding of the harmful action.[20] The assumption is that there is an "act" about the nature and
quality of which the actor is ignorant. Insanity is an excuse, but when
there is no action there is nothing to be excused. For this reason, there

is little dispute that if doubts are raised about whether the event causing harm is attributable to the defendant as an action, the prosecution must prove beyond a reasonable doubt that the defendant has acted. If the claim is one of insanity, there is debate in many jurisdictions about whether the defendant should prove his claim of excuse for harmful action. Admittedly, the line might not always be sharply defined between denying human action and affirming action but labeling it insane, however, the conceptual distinction remains important.[21]

Because the problem of human action is so subtle, most criminal codes sensibly avoid the problem. The codes do contain formulae for assessing sanity and insanity, but they leave the task of fathoming human action to scholars with a philosophical bent. The Model Penal Code (MPC) boldly breaks from this pattern and tries to define action as it seeks to define other concepts typically thought to be beyond the definitional power of legislatures.[22] Yet in this area, the definitions of the MPC merely repeat the bias of the literature that action consists in willed bodily movements.[23]

Even if the nature of human action does not lend itself to a definition that is both precise and useful, the question is rich with moral and ideological overtones. Our approach to human action determines the kind of discipline that criminal law represents.

Two factors intersect in our thinking about human action. One is the degree of contextualization or abstractness in our perception of human conduct. The other is the extent to which we think of understanding human action as a special mode of humanistic understanding or whether we apply to action mechanistic terms of explanation, such as those of physical cause and effect.

The standard definition in the textbooks—action as "willed bodily movement"—is both mechanistic and abstract. The will is the mechanical cause, and the action is the effect. The will is the lever that moves the body into action. The beauty of this formula is that it is simple. The perception of action is abstracted from the complexity of surrounding circumstances.

One alternative approach retains the mechanistic view of action but broadens the perception of causation to include the environment and the actor's psychological history. Human action is explained, therefore, as a natural outgrowth of the context: the totality of factors in the environment dictate the action. This is the way environmental determinists tend to think of human action.

The humanistic approach toward understanding action requires that we abandon the idea of scientific *explanation* of action as the product of causal forces. The humanistic view stresses the way human beings *understand* other people to be acting when they do act. This difference is signaled in German as that between *verstehen* (understanding) and *erklaeren* (explaining).[24]

To understand the implications of intersubjective "understanding," think about how we know that the motionless guards at Buckingham Palace are in fact acting, that they are not paralyzed but committed to remaining motionless. There are numerous cues in the environment that suggest deliberate standing at attention—their uniforms, the group formation, their location in front of the castle, the time of day, the regularity of their behavior. All of these are suggestions that we pick up from the environment of action, from its context.

Take the same guard, dress him in street clothes, and station him alone in the middle of a forest. A passerby would not know whether he was paralyzed, hypnotized, or a robot with occasionally blinking eyes. The context is critical to our understanding that either bodily movement or passivity are the product of human agency. Note that the environment and the context are not the means of explaining the behavior but of perceiving and understanding it.

This, then, is the humanistic and contextualized approach to action. It is the opposite of the mechanistic and abstract view that action should be defined as "willed bodily movement."[25] The conflict between these views of human action generated an enormous rift in postwar German criminal theory. In the early 1930s, Professor Hans Welzel began to develop a humanistic theory of "acting" that in the postwar period became the cornerstone of an entire theory of criminal responsibility.[26] Welzel attacked the received notion of acting, which at that time corresponded to the common law view that the will causally produces action. Welzel argued that acting was teleological, goal-directed activity. Human acting could not be understood simply as willed bodily movements without perceiving the aim of the action. Human action, Welzel argued, was intrinsically purposive, not merely the external manifestation of an inner mechanism. Welzel dubbed his theory the "finale Handlungslehre," which is captured in English as the "teleological theory" of human action.

Welzel developed an aversion to the mechanistic and causal theories of psychology that had gained ascendancy in German thought in the late nineteenth century. His target was the preoccupation with the causal mode of understanding in the criminal law. As a result, he referred to the opposing theory of human action, namely, that acts were products of the will, as the "causal theory" of acting. He rejected any view that held that the will or any set of desires caused the external bodily movements identified as acting. His teleological concept of acting escaped the flaws of the causal perspective by holding that a human act could be comprehended only so far as we, in the context of action, could perceive the agent's goal. Action was not blind, he insisted, it was "seeing."[27]

The essence of Welzel's argument, and by and large it is correct, is that we do not perceive someone as acting unless we also perceive that the person is after something. Another way of making this point is that we always see particular acts, rather than some general phenomenon called acting. We see people breaking into houses, putting sugar in coffee, and loading revolvers. Of course, we also perceive a range of human activity that is of no particular relevance to the criminal law— walking down the street, dancing, and driving automobiles. The notion of "purpose" might not be entirely appropriate in this latter set of cases, for the activity is often engaged in as an end in itself.[28]

Welzel's theory could be restated, perhaps with profit, not as a theory of acting, but as a theory about the relationship of acting and intending. The proposition that an act cannot be understood apart from its purpose implies that an act should not be separated from the actor's intention. Intending a result is implicit in the nature of acting, at least in the array of cases of morally and socially significant conduct. Welzel objected strongly to the view that intending an act consisted in an inner experience that mirrored the external act.[29] Intending and acting are bound up together; the two dimensions of the same phenomenon should not be disassociated and treated separately in the analysis of criminal liability.

Welzel's theory of acting and intending coincides with other strains in modern philosophy. It dovetails with Wittgenstein's sustained attack against the mentalist bias in philosophical psychology. Intending, Wittgenstein argues, is not an inner experience, a mental state, an event, or consciousness—or any of those other things that lawyers are wont to say.[30] Acting intentionally is a way of acting.[31] Perceiving that others are acting and intending is implicit in a way of life in which we are all reared. To learn that language of "intending" is to learn when the circumstances warrant saying that someone intended to hit another rather than to say that the contact was accidental or absent-minded. The most appealing aspect of Welzel's theory of acting is that it overcomes the false dichotomy between acting and intending that pervades theoretical work in the criminal law.

The general significance of the theory of human action in the criminal law derives from the assumption that "an act" is required for liability. Thus the debate about the nature of acting is in effect a debate about an element that everyone takes to be essential to criminal liability.

3.4 Subject and Object in Criminal Procedure

In the substantive criminal law, all legal systems express a strong commitment to treating suspects as subjects. This commitment is expressed primarily in the act requirement. We prosecute and condemn only those who have committed crimes as subjects, as responsible actors. All legal systems display an aversion to punishing people simply because their bodies, as objects, were the locus of harmful impulses.

In the field of criminal procedure, we encounter a more subtle conflict of values. Treating a suspect as an object means, in this context, that the suspect is a full participant in the proceedings, an actor in his own drama, a player on the stage of his own trial. The opposing point of view stresses the crime as the object of investigation. The resulting mode of investigation treats the suspect as a passive object of inquiry rather than a subject shaping the proceedings.

The adversarial system of the common law countries stresses the defendant as subject and director of his own trial. The inquisitorial tradition on the European Continent focuses on the crime and the defendant as objects of investigation. These positions are stated as polar opposites; in reality the differences are matters of emphasis. Some legal cultures veer more toward structuring the trial so that the defendant is a subject; others, toward treating the defendant as an object.

Many specific legal differences lend themselves to explanation as the difference between seeing the defendant as subject and treating him as an object. In the common law system we—unlike our European counterparts—insist that in order to stand trial, the defendant must be sufficiently sane to understand the charges against him and to participate in his own defense. If the suspect does not comprehend the trial, he cannot be a player, a subject making decisions that affect his fate. After the Second World War, for example, the U.S. federal government charged the famous poet and German-sympathizer Ezra Pound with treason. His lawyers interposed that he was not sufficiently sane to stand trial and as a result he was hospitalized (imprisoned?) indefinitely in St. Elizabeth's Hospital in Washington, D.C. If Pound and his alleged treason had been the object of investigation, there would have been no particular reason why, when the courts thought he was mentally ill, they should have stopped his trial and incarcerated him. If Pound had been charged in France or Germany, he would have been put on trial, represented by counsel, whether he understood what was going on or not.

The idea that the defendant must participate in and potentially direct his own trial leads to two other distinctive features of our procedural tradition. In common law systems, we allow the defendant to plead guilty and, in effect, waive the official inquiry into the truth of the charges. This is a mysterious idea to those trained in the European inquisitorial system, which assumes that the state must determine the truth of all charges before sending a convicted person to jail.

Also, in common law systems we permit defendants to decide for themselves, even in serious felony cases, whether they are better off seeking representation by counsel or defending themselves.[32] Abraham

Lincoln reputedly said that if a lawyer defends himself he has a fool for a client. The point applies even more dramatically to someone who is not legally trained. As hard as it might be for Europeans to believe, we even allow defendants facing the death penalty to defend themselves.[33] We assume that the defendant, acting alone, is autonomous and capable of deciding his own fate. Continental European legal thinkers believe that a person untrained in the law can neither defend himself properly nor make a responsible decision to stand alone against the state's prosecutors.

Admittedly, in some areas, it is difficult to know precisely what it means to be a "subject" of the trial as opposed to an "object" of investigation. The American Fifth Amendment accords the defendant an absolute right to remain silent during a criminal trial. Forcing the defendant to answer questions would, it is thought, violate his privilege against self-incrimination. If a defendant chooses to exercise his privilege to remain silent, he forgoes an opportunity to be an active participant. When O.J. Simpson sat almost quietly for the course of his nine-month trial, he created the impression that he was a passive observer of the inquiry into his guilt.[34] Of course, behind the scenes, Simpson did a great deal to shape the defense his lawyers presented. The important principle is that no one can be forced to be an active player at his own public trial.

The common law systems express some ambivalence, however, toward the ability of a suspect to manage his own defense, particularly during the stage of interrogation. The tendency of recent years has been to maintain that suspects subject to police interrogation cannot decide autonomously whether they should cooperate with the police or not. In the 1950s and early 1960s, the U.S. Supreme Court repeatedly declared confessions given while in custody to be coerced and therefore involuntary. The Court relied upon the image of a powerless suspect subject to the wiles and intimidating techniques of the police. In one of the key precedents of this period, Justice Frankfurter claimed that police interrogation came too close to the model of inquisitorial investigation. He wrote: "ours is an accusatorial and not an inquisitorial system—a system in which the State must establish guilt by evidence independently and freely secured and may not by its own coercion prove its charge against an accused out of his own mouth."[35] The image is not one of the suspect in charge but of the state's bearing down on the suspect and treating him as an object of manipulation. The outcome of this way of thinking about police interrogation was the Supreme Court's famous ruling in *Miranda*,[36] which accords to every suspect the right to be represented by counsel (either privately paid for or a public defender) at the time of police interrogation.

Paradoxically, a criminal suspect, once read his *Miranda* right, can waive his right to representation by counsel and seek to cooperate with

the police interrogation. It is not so easy to understand how the un-
tutored who need legal representation in the police station can make
a rational decision, on their own, about whether to waive their right
to counsel. We seem to fluctuate in common law systems between a
conception of a strong criminal defendant, master of his own defense,
and a picture of a weak defendant in need of a lawyer to be able to act
autonomously.

Though expressed differently in substantive law and procedural institutions, the distinction between subject and object provides an important window on the respect for human autonomy in the criminal
law. The requirement of agency or action as a condition for liability
means that we punish only individuals who autonomously violate the
law. The emphasis on the criminal suspect as a subject of the proceedings carries this idea of a suspect's autonomy further into the structuring of the criminal trial and the assessment of responsibility. The opposing mode of proceeding, once entrenched in the inquisitorial
methods of the European Continent, underscores the state's duty to
determine liability and to punish offenders. The more the state takes
charge, the less room remains for the suspect's role as a subject shaping
the trial. Wherever a legal system falls on this spectrum, ranging from
treating the suspect as master of the trial to regarding the suspect as
object of the state's investigation, the distinction between subject and
object provides the best vantage point for understanding the issues at
stake.

Notes

1. Immanuel Kant, Fundamental Principles of the Metaphysics of Morals
46 (Thomas Abbot trans. 1949).

2. But it is not necessarily "barbaric" to punish legal entities for crimes
committed by the people who constitute the entity—e.g., states, corporations,
etc. For further discussion of this issue, see section 11.4.

3. Oliver W. Holmes, Jr., The Common Law 54 (1881); Restatement
(Second) of Torts §2. For a critique of this account of acting, see Herbert Morris,
Book Review, 13 Stan. L. Rev. 185 (1960).

4. Michael Moore, Act and Crime 28 (1993). See also Douglas Husak, A
Philosophy of Criminal Law 174 (1987) (concluding that the criterion of bodily
movements "has been vigorously attacked, no satisfactory alternative has
emerged to take its place").

5. Moore, supra note 4, at 28.

6. Id.

7. E.g. StGB art. 323c; French Penal Code art. 63; Spanish Codigo Penal
619.

8. Moore may take this position. See Moore, supra note 4, at 277–78.

9. H.L.A. Hart & Tony Honoré, Causation and the Law 35–38 (2d ed.
1985).

10. E.g. People v. Beardsley, 150 Mich. 206, 113 N.W. 1128 (1907).

11. The new Spanish Codigo Penal comes close in article 11, which provides a "duty" to intervene in cases where there is a "contractual or legal" obligation to do so or the actor has created the risk by his previous action.

12. Model Penal Code § 2.01(3)(b).

13. On the meaning of this provision, see chapter 1 at pp. 14–17.

14. Note the Model Penal Code § 2.01(3)(a) recognizes that "liability for commission of an offense" by an omission is acceptable if "the omission is expressly made sufficient by the law defining the offense." That the code wastes words on this redundant provision (it's all right to punish omissions if a statute says so) testifies to our confusion about the area.

15. W. Stree in Schönke/Schröder, Strafgesetzbuch:Kommentar §13, comment 57 (T. Lenckner, P. Cramer, A. Eser, W. Stree eds. 25th ed. 1997).

16. Herbert Morris, *Punishment for Thoughts*, 49 Monist 342, 346–48 (1965).

17. See Fain v. Commonwealth, 78 Ky. 183 (1879) (sleepwalking); Regina v. Charlson, [1955] 1 W.L.R. 317 (brain tumor).

18. This is the line of reasoning that H. L. A. Hart used to advance his theory of acts as "defeasible ascriptions." Hart, *The Ascription of Responsibility and Rights*, in A. Flew, Logic and Language 145 (First Series 1968 ed.). The problem with this view is that it lacks a criterion for determining when a particular ground will defease the ascription of action. To find a criterion, one is led back to the variations of "the will."

19. M'Naghton's Case, 8 Eng. Rep. 718 (H.L. 1843).

20. See MPC §4.01 (lacks "substantial capacity . . . to conform his conduct to the requirements of law.")

21. E.g. People v. Marsh, 170 Cal. App. 2d 284, 338 P.2d 495 (1959) (acting under hypnosis).

22. For example, the MPC tries to capture one of the most difficult conceptual problems of all, the concept of causation. See MPC §2.03.

23. The Model Penal Code §2.01(2)(d) indirectly relies on this formula by holding that a bodily movement is not an act if it "is not a product of the effort or determination of the actor."

24. See G.W. von Wright, Explanation and Understanding (1971).

25. I will leave it to the reader to ponder whether it would be possible to have a theory of action that would be humanistic but nonetheless abstracted from circumstances. Does the traditional theory of "free will" satisfy these requirements?

26. For the early papers, see H. Welzel, *Kausalität und Handlung*, 51 ZStW 703 (1930–31); H. Welzel, *Studien zum System des Strafrechts*, 58 ZStW 491 (1938) (an acceptable teaching during the Nazi period!); the best repository of the theory's development and fluctuation are the eleven editions of H. Welzel, Das Deutsche Strafrecht (11th ed. 1969), hereafter cited as Welzel.

27. Welzel 33.

28. Welzel is fully aware of this point and sees no difficulty in regarding activity itself as the end of acting. Welzel 36–37.

29. Welzel 43 (criticizing Mezger's view that the actor's intention was but "mirror image" (*Spiegelbild*) of the act).

30. L. Wittgenstein, Philosophical Investigations §580 ("An 'inner process' stands in need of outward criteria.").

31. Ibid. ("The intention with which one acts does not 'accompany' the action any more than the thought 'accompanies' speech.").

32. Colin Ferguson defended himself against charges of going on a killing spree on the Long Island Railroad. He was convicted and sentenced to 200 years in prison. See The New York Times, March 23, 1995, B1.

33. Faretta v. California, 422 U.S. 806 (1975).

34. I am indebted to Albin Eser for calling this point to my attention.

35. Rogers v. Richmond, 365 U.S. 534 (1961).

36. Miranda v. Arizona, 384 U.S. 436 (1966).

4

Human Causes versus
Natural Events

Crimes typically occur when an offender brings about harm to the significant interests of a victim.[1] Think about the standard felonies of the common law: homicide, assault, rape, mayhem, arson, robbery, larceny, burglary. All of these crimes leave palpable harms in their wake: someone is killed (homicide), attacked (assault), sexually violated (rape), or disfigured (mayhem). A dwelling house is set afire (arson), property is taken violently or with a threat of violence (robbery), something is taken stealthfully (larceny), or a private home is invaded with felonious intentions (burglary). These are harms that unnerve the community as well as leave the victim in a state of irreversible damage.

A special requirement of causation attends a subset of these harms. Murder or more generally homicide does not occur unless a human actor causes the death of another human being. That is, the offender must *kill* the victim. The offender's actions must be the force that brings about the death. Suppose Alice intends to kill Bill and drives to Bill's house ready to commit the crime; just as Alice is about to knock on Bill's door, Bill dies of a heart attack totally unrelated to Alice's criminal plan. Alice does not kill Bill. She does not cause the death. Bill's death is a natural event. It is not caused by human hand.

Of course, if Bill became frightened upon seeing Alice and then had a heart attack, Alice's coming to the door might have been the cause of Bill's death. It all depends, as we shall see, on the likelihood that Bill would have had a fatal heart attack at that moment without Alice's coming to the door.

This is the distinction between *natural events* and *human causes*. The former are of no interest to the criminal law; the latter—the harmful consequences of human actions—satisfy the minimum condition of criminal liability.

The distinction between *causes* and *events* is central to the structure of the criminal law. The first section of this chapter explains the kinds of offenses that invite an inquiry into causal relationships.

4.1 The Domain of Causation

There are, in fact, two kinds of offenses. In one category, causal questions are relevant; in the other category, they are not relevant. To understand why this cleavage runs through the criminal law, think about the difference between these two sets of relationships between actions and harms:

Crime	Action	Harm
homicide	shooting	victim dies
arson	setting fire to house	house burns down
rape	forcing intercourse	victim violated
larceny	taking object	victim dispossessed of object

Note that in the first two of these offenses, murder and arson, the harm may occur either as a result of the action or as a distinct event. People die and houses burn down. The occurrence of the event does not implicate a human being. But as to the second two crimes, rape and larceny, the very description of the harm implies that a human being (or some other agent of action) brought about the harm. Women and men cannot be violated without someone's bringing about the relevant harm. Sexual penetration (in the relevant sense) does not occur as a natural event. Similarly, people are not "dispossessed" of their belongings without some agent's effectuating the dispossession.[2] People lose things, and sometimes their belongings are destroyed. Loss and destruction occur as natural events as well as a consequence of human action. But "dispossession" is different: it occurs only when some agent takes away the belongings of another.

The distinction at work in these cases marks a basic cleavage in the criminal law. We may refer to the first group, including murder and arson, as crimes of *harmful consequences*.[3] The second group, including rape and larceny, are characterized by the harm's being bound with action. They may be called crimes of *harmful actions*. The crimes that we have considered so far classify themselves as follows:

Crimes of harmful consequences: homicide, arson, mayhem, assault[4]

Crimes of harmful actions: rape, robbery, larceny, fraud

The problem of distinguishing between human causes and natural events—the topic of this chapter—is limited to crimes of harmful consequences. The reason for this limitation should be obvious. It follows logically from the definitions of "harmful consequences" and "harmful actions." The harm required in the latter category cannot occur as a natural event and therefore the very act of perceiving the harm implies a human being as the causal agent. But the harms of death, physical injury, and destruction of property might occur in nature—without human causation—and therefore we encounter a special problem in determining whether in fact the harm is attributable to human or natural causes. If the former, the harmful consequence becomes the business of the criminal law; if the latter, the natural event is beyond the law's concerns.

Crimes of harmful action—for example, rape, larceny—rest on an immediate connection between the harmful action and the relevant harm. But crimes of harmful consequences are characterized by a causal gap between action and consequence. After the action occurs, one can never be sure that the harm will ensue. This causal gap between action and harm can cover vast stretches of space and time. Pushing a button can result in the death of someone on the other side of the planet. Pulling the trigger now means that someone might die of bullet wounds a year or two years from now. Nothing like these spatial and temporal gaps exists in the crimes of harmful action. Forcing intercourse implies rape here and now. Taking away the belongings of another entails dispossession on the spot. Of course, there might be long-term human consequences of these crimes, but these effects are not essential to saying that a crime has occurred.

The spatial and temporal gap in crimes of harmful consequences opens the field to the problems of causation. "Causation" is the name we give to the complexities that can break the link between action and consequence; when causation is absent, the harmful consequence is but an event, no longer attributable to the suspect.

The distinction between crimes of harmful consequence and crimes of harmful actions yields an important insight about the way harmful results may come about without the actor's being criminally liable for the harm. In both areas the harm may result from the innocent failure of the actor to realize that his actions would bring about the harm. The nature of the innocence, however, differs. In the case of harmful consequences, the actor may cause the harm *by accident*; he or she may not foresee that his or her actions will produce the harm in question. For example, a hunter might not realize that his well-aimed shot would ricochet in a particular way and hit an innocent bystander. The death of the bystander is due to an accident. Alice might not realize that her coming to Bill's house and knocking on the door would frighten him and cause a fatal heart attack.

By contrast, the crimes of harmful action do not lend themselves to commission by accident. You cannot rape by accident. You cannot steal or rob by accident. You cannot defraud another by accident. What you can do in these latter cases, however, is generate the relevant harm *by mistake*. A man can be mistaken about a woman's consenting to intercourse. A person who takes an object can be mistaken about its ownership (the standard example is taking an umbrella that in fact belongs to another); if he thinks the object belongs to him, he does not take it with the intent to deprive the owner of his property. In other words, his mistake negates his intent to steal. He commits the harm, by mistake, of dispossessing the owner. In these cases of mistake, the actor would probably not be guilty—at least if the mistake is totally without fault on his part. But this problem requires detailed analysis, a task reserved for chapter 10.

The important point to note is that the problems of accident and mistake characterize different kinds of crimes. Accidents are limited to crimes that require causation. Mistakes may technically occur in all crimes but are of greater significance in crimes of harmful action. Why is this? Accidents are instances of causation out of control. Only where causation occurs across time and space can we encounter a problem of accidental consequences.

To summarize the argument of this section, we can formulate the following proposition:

Causation is a problem only where accidental harm is possible.

Accidental harm is possible in crimes of homicide, arson, mayhem, assault (harmful consequences) but not in the crimes of rape, robbery, larceny, fraud (harmful action).

4.2 How to Approach Causation

The prevailing theory of causation in the criminal law, both in Germany[5] and the United States,[6] is the expansive test: an event X causes an event Y if, but for X, Y would not have occurred. This test, conventionally known as the *sine qua non* or "but for" test, poses a counterfactual conditional question: What would have happened if X were absent? Would Y have happened anyway?

Of course, there is no way of knowing for sure whether Bill would have died, even if he had not seen Alice's coming up the stairs and knocking on the door. There is no way to roll back history and to run the sequence again with one factor changed. Yet this is precisely what we have to imagine in order to apply the "but for" test. We have to imagine the unfolding of events in an imaginary world: the world in which everything is the same, except for one difference. If we are testing whether X is a cause of Y, we have to have imagine the events leading up to Y with X missing: if we can say confidently that without X, Y would not have occurred, then X is a cause of Y.

The "but for" test captures an important truth about causation; if Bill's death would have occurred regardless of Alice's actions, then we cannot say that Alice caused the death. We apply this rule of thumb in cases of failing to avert death as well as affirmative acts leading to death. If a swimmer would have drowned, no matter what measures the lifeguard might have taken, we cannot say that the lifeguard's ignoring the plea contributed to the death. The lifeguard cannot be said to have caused the death unless he could have prevented it.

Problem One: Alternative Sufficient Causes

Yet the "but for" test suffers from three major deficiencies. The first of these strikes at the heart of the maxim: if Y would have occurred without X, then X is not a cause of Y. The best example is the problem of merging fires.[7] Suppose that both Joe and Karl set fires that converge and destroy the plaintiff's house. Either fire alone would have been sufficient to destroy the house. Therefore both Joe and Karl can point the finger at the other and say: He was the cause; I was not the cause because the harm to the plaintiff's house would have happened even without my fire. This is a serious challenge to the "but for" test for in fact if that test is applied, neither Joe nor Karl is responsible for the damage to the plaintiff's house.

A tantalizing version of the same puzzle is posed in the following story. Joe wants to kill Paul and therefore on the eve of Paul's setting forth on a hike across the desert, Joe sneaks into Paul's room and replaces the water in his canteen with scentless and colorless poison. Karl also wants to kill Paul and therefore later the same evening he sneaks into Paul's room and drills a small hole in the bottom of Paul's canteen. Paul leaves the next morning without noticing the hole in his canteen. After two hours in the desert he decides that it is time to drink but by now the canteen is empty. Without other sources of water he dies of dehydration in the desert. Who is responsible for the death? Karl can claim that if he had not drilled the hole in the canteen, Paul would have died of poison. But Joe can maintain that in view of Karl's subsequent action, replacing the water with poison was an irrelevant act.

These scenarios illustrate the limitations of counterfactual thinking in assessing causation. In these cases, where there are alternative sufficient conditions, the question should be not what would have happened, but what in fact did happen. Can one perceive causal power operative in the narrative as it is told? In the story of Joe's and Karl's combined fire, the answer seems to be clearly yes. Together they generate a single fire that in fact destroys the house. Their roles with regard to Paul's death are more nuanced. Their actions do not converge to create a single source of danger; rather their efforts succeed and displace each other. Karl creates the state of affairs of Paul's trying to drink from an empty canteen—even though this is hardly more dangerous than the canteen full of poison would have been. Yet in fact Paul dies as a result of his canteen's being empty, and Karl brought about that condition. Whether Joe is also a cause is more dubious, and indeed it is only by reintroducing counterfactual thinking (if Karl had not intervened, Paul would have drunk the poison) that Joe becomes a candidate for causal responsibility. In these cases of independently sufficient causes, the better approach seems to be to avoid counterfactual questions. In place of this logical and scientific account of causation we fall back on the simpler question whether ordinary observers would perceive causal power operative in the facts.[8]

Problem Two: Proximate Cause

The second objection to the "but for" test is that it sweeps up so many causal factors that some additional factor is required to eliminate far-flung effects from the range of liability. It may be true that for want of a nail, the kingdom might be lost. The blacksmith who fails to nail in the horseshoe unleashes a crescendo of consequences: the horse falls, the rider is killed, the battle is lost, and the kingdom is conquered.[9] Should the blacksmith be blamed for it all? The question is whether we should limit the responsibility of the blacksmith by holding that he did not cause the fall of the kingdom or, alternatively, that he could not have foreseen the fall and therefore, though he caused it, he was not at fault or culpable for the unfortunate consequences of his actions.

The tendency in modern legal thinking is to cut off responsibility at the level of causation. To cope with the far-flung effects of a cause that satisfies the "but for" test, common lawyers have introduced the term "proximate cause." Therefore, as it is commonly said, the analysis of causation comes in two stages: first, whether the factor in question satisfied the "but for" test of causation and second, whether it satisfied the requirement of "proximate causation."

Some lawyers rely on the metaphor of the stream to explain the concept of "proximate cause."[10] There are two ways that a stream can dissipate its force. It can lose its flow in the sands. Or, it can be overwhelmed and submerged in an intersecting tributary. So it is with causation. As the streams dissipates into the sand, causal energy loses its power and merges with background forces. The blacksmith's oversight remains technically a cause of the empire's fall, but the want of a nail would hardly stand out among the multitude of economic and political factors that spell military defeat.

As the stream can be overwhelmed by a larger flow, causal forces are sometimes superseded by new causes. Defense lawyers often try to mount the argument that their clients seemingly fatal blow to the victim did not cause the victim's death because after being shot or stabbed, the victim received negligent medical care. The defense tried this argument in the trial of Bernhard Goetz: Darrell Cabey was supposedly paralyzed for life not because of the gunshot wound that Goetz delivered to Cabey but because of the subsequent negligent care in the hospital.[11] The same argument came forward in the trial of Lemrick Nelson for having allegedly stabbed and killed Yankel Rosenbaum.[12] Rosenbaum was taken to the hospital and as the argument goes, if he had received proper care for his wounds he would have survived. There the negligent medical care is like the intersecting tributary that overwhelms and dominates the original causal stream.

Though often tried, these arguments about "negligent intervening causes" almost always fail. The complications that occur in the hospital are seen as part of the background circumstances that worsen the original wound. In these situations, Goetz's shooting and Nelson's alleged wounding were the causal factors that remained in the foreground. This distinction between background and foreground factors captures the theme of this chapter. When a factor recedes into the background, it is a natural event, not a cause that generates criminal liability.

To grasp the subtlety of these notions of background events and foreground causes, compare these cases of negligent treatment in the hospital with a hypothetical situation in which the argument of "supervening cause" is likely to succeed. Suppose Jack negligently runs down the mob boss Gabe. While Gabe is recuperating in the hospital, his nemesis in the criminal underground, Mike, finds him in the room and executes him, mob style, with a rope around the neck. In this situation the party responsible for Gabe's death appears to be Mike, not Jack. Jack's negligence merely explains why Mike finds his victim in the hospital rather than at home. In other words, Mike's actions emerge in the foreground as the responsible cause and Jack's bringing about the car accident recedes into the background. There is good authority for the conclusion that Jack would not be liable for Gabe's death.[13]

Now what is the difference between medical negligence in treating Darrell Cabey and Mike's executing Gabe? Is it a matter of probability? Of foreseeability, as lawyers say? Some prominent judges, notably Justice Benjamin Cardozo, have reasoned that analyzing proximate cause is nothing more than assessing "the eye of vigilance" and the degree of foreseeability.[14] But this seems to be an oversimplification. The perspective of probability ignores the key factor in the situation, namely, that the wound injuring Darrell Cabey in the hospital was merely negligence. The mode of Mike's killing Gabe was intentional and willful. It could well be the case that the intentional killing of a mob boss in the hospital was more probable, more foreseeable, than the hospital staff's negligent treatment after a gunshot wound. Yet increasing or decreasing the probability of the intervening cause would not change the analysis. What, then, is the difference between a negligent and an intentional intervening cause?

To express our intuitions in this context, we have to invoke some rather imprecise ideas. I would rely on the metaphor of "causal energy." When Mike enters Gabe's room and lays his hand on his intended victim, he invests more personality, more energy, into the unfolding of causes and events. This greater input of personal force brings his actions into the foreground. In our perception of Gabe's demise, Mike becomes the responsible cause. It is also worth noting another difference between the stories of Darrell Cabey and of the hypothetical victim Gabe. Goetz injured Cabey intentionally, though arguably in self-defense.[15] Jack's initial injury of Gabe is merely negligent. This means that at the outset of the story, Goetz invests more energy into Cabey's suffering than does Jack in the negligent accident that lands Gabe in the hospital. Goetz's causal contribution is stronger at the outset and it survives intervention by the negligent hospital staff. Jack's contribution at the outset is less substantial and it is overwhelmed by Mike's committed and willful intervention.

It should be noted that intentional intervening causes are more likely to be recognized in tort than in criminal cases. Most of tort law is about responsibility for negligently causing harm. Most of criminal law is about responsibility for intentional invasions into the interests of others. This means that at the outset of the analysis in criminal cases, we have a stronger contribution by the alleged offender. That stronger contribution is likely to survive against intervening causes.

The difficulties of getting precise about cause has lead some theorists to argue that proximate cause is just a value judgment, a matter of policy.[16] This argument is less threatening in the field of torts than in criminal law. Tort law proceeds without a principle of legality, of prior warning of potential liability. If proximate cause in murder cases were simply a value judgment, however, we would encounter serious problems of principle. Would it be right to convict someone of one of our most serious offenses, the only offense subject to the death penalty in the United States, simply because judge or jury made a value judgment that he ought to be held responsible for the far-flung consequences of his attack on the victim? Admittedly, we have not yet addressed the theory of legality. Until we assay the field in chapter 12, we shall leave the matter of proximate cause with our concerns properly noted. It is clear that great issues of justice and of legality inhere in our analysis of when we hold individuals accountable for the remote consequences of their actions.

Problem Three: Omissions

If the implications of the "but for" test are followed through, there is no important difference between the causal role of acts and of omissions. The implication is that a failure to intervene and prevent a suicide causes death in the same sense as strangling the victim to death. A doctor's failing to aid a stranger in need causes death in the same sense that injecting air into a patient's veins causes death. It follows as well that for every crime there are a large if not infinite number of factors that could have prevented its occurrence. The fact that no one killed B the day before A's assault is as much a "cause" of death as A's actually killing B. This is the third major objection to the theory of "but for" causation.

One way of coping with this objection is simply to deny that omissions can be causes. This view, which has some support in the history of philosophy, draws on the popular idea that causes must be operative forces in the circumstances leading to the harm.[17] This view holds that omissions are not forces; they are "literally nothing at all."[18] To use language already introduced, omissions display no "causal energy." In this example we see a clear contrast between the quasiscientific "but for" test, which implies that all omissions are causes, and the view of the ordinary observer, which stresses our shared perception of causal forces at work.

The debate about whether omissions are causes brings us into a field of subtle differentiation. In one sense omissions are not causes, and in another sense they are. First, I will explain why letting someone die is not a "cause" in the same strong sense that killing someone is. Letting someone die represents the failure to allocate resources to save the person. It is possible to respect the liberty of others and fail, hardheartedly, to allocate resources to save their lives. By contrast, terminating life represents a direct interference with the most basic interest of another human being. There is no way that killing is compatible with respect for the liberty and autonomy of another person. Admittedly, this view has come in for criticism recently in the field of assisted suicide, but if we leave aside this special case, there is no doubt that killing takes on contours entirely different from letting someone die.

The criminal law operates on the assumption of a general prohibition against all cases of direct killing. There is no need, in particular cases, to prove a special duty not to kill. Everyone falls under the general duty not to terminate the life of another. Yet in cases of letting someone die, there is no liability unless the person who could have saved the life of another was under a duty to do so. These duties are based on a variety of factors, including family relationships, undertakings to assist, communities of shared risk, and professional obligations. The important point is that in cases of letting die as opposed to direct killing, only those who come under a special duty to aid are responsible for the death.

If those who killed and those who let others die both "caused" death in the same way, we would have trouble explaining the differentiation in the law. All those who cause death should be treated in the same way. Yet in fact we do not hold accountable those who merely allow or let others die, unless there is a special duty to render aid. It is clear, then, that the law does not rigorously follow the "but for" test, for if it did, it would treat as causal agents all those who could have saved the life of the deceased and did not.

But if the law took the view that omissions were not causes at all, we would run into problems making sense of our practice of holding liable for homicide those who, under a duty to aid, knowingly let the victim die. The ambivalence of the Model Penal Code illustrates the problem. It is not easy to reconcile these three provisions:

1. Section 210.1(1) conditions criminal homicide on "causing the death" of another human being.

2. Section 2.01(3)(b) restates the traditional rule that liability for commission of an offense by omission turns on whether a "duty to perform the omitted act is . . . imposed by law."

3. Section 2.03(1)(a) commits itself to the orthodox "but for" rule, namely, that "conduct is the cause of a result when it is an antecedent but for which the result in question would not have occurred." The term "conduct" is defined earlier as an "action or omission."[19]

Rule 3 holds that all cases of letting die are instances of causing death. But if that were true, they would all qualify as criminal homicide under rule 1, in which case rule 2 would be entirely superfluous.[20]

It should be clear from the discussion of the foregoing three problems that at least two conceptions of causation interweave in our legal discussions. On the one hand, we encounter the pervasive "but for" theory, which captures an important truth about the distinction between causes and events. When a harmful occurrence would have taken place anyway, regardless of the suspect's contribution, then it is a natural event. It is not "caused" by the criminal suspect. On the other hand, we work with an intuitive understanding of causation as a force displaying energy in the world. We see this in the analysis of (1) alternative sufficient causes (merging fires), (2) proximate cause and intervening causes, and (3) liability for omissions. The former "but for" test stresses the counterfactual condition question: What would have happened if the suspect's actions were absent? The latter focuses on what in fact transpires: we see the fires merge and burn down the house, we perceive the intervening intentional killing in the hospital in the causal foreground, and we have trouble recognizing omissions, cases of letting die, as instances of "causal energy."

It seems that the ordinary thinking of lawyers is in conflict. We are drawn simultaneously to quasi-scientific analysis that treats any necessary condition as a cause (the "but for" test) and to the ordinary prescientific view of causation as energy or force that brings about a result. The former has the vice of being out of touch with the reality of the way we think about causation (e.g., all omissions are causes), and the latter posits mysterious metaphysical energies that drive the world (as a result no omissions are causes). To complement this conflict we should consider a recent philosophical account of causation that has gained prominence in the work of H. L. A. Hart and A. Honoré.[21]

4.3 Causation in Ordinary Language

Like so many of the other terms used in criminal law, causation is a concept that figures prominently in our day-to-day efforts to make sense of the world. If we wish to build a system of criminal law on the basis of our ordinary concepts, then we must attend to the way the concept functions in our daily lives. This means that we must examine our reasons for making causal inquiries and pay close attention to the way we ordinarily speak about "causing" harm.

One important feature of causal inquiries is that we do ordinarily inquire about the cause of normal or continuing states of affairs. We speak about the cause of death, but not about the cause of life. Why not? Death at a particular moment is unplanned and unexpected and therefore we wish to know why it happens. But a healthy person's remaining alive does not stimulate our interest in explaining the world around us. Things would be different, of course, if we expected someone to die in an airplane crash and she survived. Then we might appropriately ask: How did she survive? To what does she owe her added days of life? (Note that we still have some difficulty framing our questions with the word "cause.") This difference between life and death demonstrates that causal inquiries are not always appropriate. When inappropriate causal questions are raised, as if someone should ask you the cause of your being alive today or the cause of the water still being in the ocean, we are likely to be puzzled about the point of the question.

It would be difficult to give a complete account of when causal inquiries are appropriate, but one obvious category is precisely the range of accidents, unexpected events, and untoward acts that preoccupy the law. We probably find it odd to ask: What caused him to wear clothes to the office? But we would never find it odd to inquire: Why did he take off his clothes and harass his secretary? Why did he breach his contract? What prompted her to kill her child? Any death, any unexpected destruction of property, any injury to a human being— these are the stuff of causal inquiries.

If we see the "results" that lend themselves to "causal" questions as a special class of events, we should not be surprised to learn that causes, too, are different from ordinary and routine events. Every cause must satisfy the "but for" criteria. The water's being in the ocean is a cause for the shipwrecked sailor's drowning in it. Apart from the minimal qualification of being conditions, "causes" are like the "effects" that they explain. Among all the necessary conditions for a particular event, according to the theory developed by Hart and Honoré, the "causes" are those conditions that make the difference under the circumstances. They are the abnormal and unexpected factors that stand out from the background and help to explain the particular result. There are some factors that might be causal in one situation and not in another. For example, we would not say that the presence of oxygen in the air was the cause of a forest fire (even though "but for" the oxygen the fire would not have occurred). Yet there might be situations, such as in laboratory experiments, in which the presence of oxygen is unexpected and therefore the oxygen would be properly discerned as a causal factor.

This emphasis on the normal and the expected injects criteria of convention into the perception of causation. If smoke alarms in the home are highly unusual, we could hardly explain the death of the children in a home fire by saying that the family did not have a smoke alarm (we might as well explain the death by saying the fire department failed to have a station next door). Yet if every other house in the city has an alarm, we might well explain the death of the children by pointing to the absence of an alarm that could have saved their lives. The rule of convention means that what was not a cause might cease to be more than a necessary condition. Indeed, this is the way we are inclined to think about literacy in relationship to success in the world; literacy might previously have been sufficient to assure success, but it is now at most a necessary condition. This degree of fluidity and uncertainty in the concept of causation makes one wonder whether this common-sense concept of causation is well suited to function as a basic building block in a theory of criminal liability.

4.4 Ideology and Causation

It is clear that in fact we do not follow our ordinary perceptions of causation in making judgments about criminal liability. Our perceptions and our analysis of causes are shaped by moral assumptions about the nature of the criminal law. This is particularly noticeable in our attitudes toward the victim's participation in the circumstances producing the crime.

With regard to the role of the victim, the differences between torts and criminal law are dramatic. The injured party's contributory fault plays an important part in the structure of tort liability. Defendant swings a stick in an effort to break up a dog fight. The dogs move around, the defendant and plaintiff move with them. Eventually the stick hits the plaintiff in the eye. Now we could focus narrowly on this interaction and see it just as an act of aggression against a passive victim. Defendant's swing injures the passive plaintiff and the plaintiff should collect compensation. But we could also see the interaction as a failure of the parties, taken together, to prevent the injury. Since the mid-nineteenth century, American tort law has treated the victim of negligent injury as jointly responsible for the minimization of harm. When the stick makes contact with the eye, it turns out that the bearer of the eye as well as the bearer of the stick might be seen as the causally dominant party.[22] The victim's role is assessed under the doctrines of contributory negligence, comparative negligence, and assumption of risk.

Tort law today goes so far as to assume the relative contributions of defendant and victim are subject to precise quantification. Under the doctrine of comparative negligence, applied today both in Europe and common law jurisdictions, the victim's contribution to the injury need not be assessed as all or nothing. It may be a percentage that is then used to reduce the defendant's monetary responsibility. If the defendant's negligent act is adjudged only 60 percent responsible for the accident, the defendant pays only 60 percent of the damages.

Against the backdrop of these assumptions in private legal disputes, we can appreciate the ideological changes wrought by criminal jurisprudence. The guiding principle of criminal justice is disarmingly simple: the victim's contributory fault is irrelevant to liability. If the victim is mugged while jogging at night in Manhattan's Central Park, the defendant could hardly defend by claiming that "she assumed the risk." It was irrelevant in the trial of Bernhard Goetz that when he entered the subway car on that fateful day he choose to sit next to the four "boisterous" youths who would ask him for money. The irrelevance of the victim's fault cuts across the criminal law. Pickpockets cannot interpose that their victims should have kept a closer eye on their wallets. Even in cases of criminal negligence, the defendant cannot defend on the basis of the victim's contributory fault. The role of the victim in precipitating crimes has engaged the interest of sociologists, but the phenomenon has no bearing on the proper analysis of criminal liability. The question is: Why?

The criminal law shields victims against their own imprudence. They are entitled to move in the world at large with as much freedom as they enjoy behind locked doors. They can walk in the park when they want, sit where they want in the subway, and wear skimpy clothes without fearing that they will be faulted for precipitating rape. This is what it means to be a free person endowed with rights, and the criminal law protects this freedom by not censuring those who expose themselves, perhaps with less than due care, to risks of criminal aggression. The blame properly attaches to the mugger, thief, and rapist, regardless of the victim's role in the interaction leading to the crime.

Criminal law represents a distinct ideology about the way aggression occurs. Criminals impose these aggressive impulses on victims. Tort stands for a different view. Tortfeasor and victim interact in ways that generate harms. It is difficult to say that either of these is definitively right or wrong. They are two different perspectives on the same reality.

The important point to keep in mind about distinguishing human causation from natural events is that these categories are rife with conflicting methods and divergent moral assumptions. Some scholars advocate the "but for" test that sweeps too wide. Other writers insist either on the view that causes must possess energy that operates on the world or that the notion of causation should be limited to the way we speak about causation in ordinary language. On top of these methodological debates we find layered our conflicting moral assumptions about the roles of different fields of law. In criminal law, at least, we remain committed to the view that victims do not cause their own suffering. Their participation is but the background event against which the criminal wreaks his harm.[23]

Notes

1. See the definition of harm as a "setback to interests" in Joel Feinberg, The Moral Limits of the Criminal Law: Harm to Others 33–34 (1984).

2. Note that the agent in these cases need not be a human agent. One could imagine an animal "raping" a human being, or "stealing" food from a human owner.

3. I developed this concept as one of three patterns of criminal liability in George P. Fletcher, Rethinking Criminal Law 235–241 (1978).

4. American tort law distinguishes between assault and battery. Battery requires physical harm, assault is an attempted battery. If we were following this usage, we would put battery in the column of harmful consequences (physical injury) and assault in the column of harmful actions (the threat of injury is harmful because it is threatened by a human agent). The common law of crimes has blurred this distinction and treats "assault and battery" as a single crime.

5. T. Lenckner in Schönke/Schröder, Strafgesetzbuch §13, prelim. note 73, at 132. For a thoughtful critique of the "but for" test in German law, see Naucke, *Über das Regressverbot im Strafrecht*, 76 ZStW 409 (1964).

6. MPC §2.03(1)(a).

7. Dan Dobbs, Robert Keeton, & David Owen, Prosser and Keeton on the Law of Torts 266–67(5th ed. 1984).

8. This distinction between "scientific" thinking and "ordinary observing" is reminiscent of Bruce Ackerman's analysis of these ideas in a different context. See Bruce Ackerman, Private Property and the Constitution 156–67 (1977).

9. The origins of this famous parable are elusive.

10. See Palsgraf v. Long Island R.R., 248 N.Y. 339, 347, 162 N.E. 99, 101 (1928) (Andrews, J., dissenting).

11. A Crime of Self-Defense at 67–69.

12. On the Nelson trial generally, see With Justice for Some at 86–106.

13. Dobbs, Keeton, and Owen, supra note 7, at 287 ("The real problem . . . [is] one of social policy.") The Model Penal Code introduce a criterion of "just bearing on the actor's liability." MPC § 2.03(2)(b) & 3(b).

14. See Justice Cardozo's famous opinion in Palsgraf v. Long Island R.R., supra note 10.

15. Note that the self-defense argument prevailed in the criminal case but was rejected in the civil case, where the jury awarded Cabey $43,000,000 in compensatory and punitive damages. See George P. Fletcher, Justice for All—Twice, The New York Times, April 24, 1996, A21.

16. Dobbs, Keeton, and Owen, supra note 7, at 273 (5th ed. 1984).

17. Cf. Hans-Heinrich Jescheck and Thomas Weigend, Lehrbuch des Strafrechts 618 (5th ed. 1996) (denying the causal effect of omissions because omissions lack a "real source of energy").

18. See the view of omissions held by Michael Moore, discussed supra at pp. 66–68, 71.

19. MPC §1.13(5).

20. One way to solve this problem is to hold that rule 2 imposes a requirement of duty in addition to the fact of causing death and thereby satisfying the definition of criminal homicide under MPC §210.1. I am indebted to my colleague Harold Edgar for this suggestion.

21. See Hart and Honoré, supra note 9.

22. These facts are drawn from the important tort precedent Brown v. Kendall, 60 Mass. (6 Cush.) 292 (1850).

23. Recent German scholarship has begun to pose the question whether in some situations the victim should take responsibility for avoiding situations in which harm may occur. One of the initial moves came in Knut Amelung, *Irrtum und Zweiful des Getauschten beim Betrug*, 1977 Goldtdammer's Archiv fuer Strafrecht 1. For a critical assessment of the emphasis on prevention by victims, see T. Lenckner in Schönke/Schröder, § 13, prelim. comment 70b.

5

The Crime versus
the Offender

When defense lawyer Clarence Darrow was defending two young men accused of a brutal and senseless murder, he appealed to the jury to direct their condemnation to the crime instead of the accused criminals. They should hate the evil done, he said, but not those who did it. Judging crime, he argued, did not preclude compassion for those charged as offenders. With his plea for understanding, he managed to rescue the two defendants, Nathan Loeb and Richard Leopold, from a threatened death sentence.[1]

The distinction between the *crime* and the *offender* recurs in both scholarly as well as rhetorical reflections on the criminal law. The precondition for this general distinction is the analysis of the global phenomenon of crime into distinct issues. Once the crime is broken down in this way, we can contemplate grouping the distinct issues into those relevant to the offense in the abstract and those relevant to the offender as a concrete person. The analysis of crime into distinct issues is part of the daily practice of criminal justice. Let us consider, then, the array of distinct issues that can arise in a homicide trial. As to the following, we should inquire whether each question bears on the crime or on the offender:

1. Was the alleged offender a juvenile or an adult at the time of commission?

2. Did the alleged offender engage in an act that led to the death of the victim?

3. Was the victim a human being (this could be important in abortion and infanticide cases)?

4. Was the victim alive at the time of the alleged offender's act?

5. Did the alleged offender cause the death of the victim under the "but for" test?

6. Did the alleged offender's causing the death of the victim meet the requirements of "proximate causation?"

7. When the alleged offender acted in a way that caused the death of the victim, did the former intend the death of the latter?

8. If the alleged offender did not intend the death of the victim, did he act with reckless disregard of the victim's life?

9. Did the alleged offender premeditate and deliberate about the death of the victim?

10. At the time that he caused the death of the victim, was the offender provoked by the victim's or a third person's behavior to act as he did?

11. At the time that he caused the death of the victim, did the offender fear that by virtue of the victim's aggression, his own life or safety or the life or safety of another was in serious danger (i.e., did he act in self-defense)?

12. At the time that he caused the death of the victim, did the offender fear that a third person would kill him or his family or otherwise cause them great harm (i.e., did he act under duress)?

13. At the time that he caused the death of the victim, did the offender suffer from a mental illness that either prevented him from knowing that he was doing the wrong thing or that precluded his controlling his behavior (i.e., was he insane at the time of acting)?

14. When the defendant shot and killed the victim, was he mistaken about the conditions for invoking the claims above in issues 4, 11, 12, or did he think that he was entitled to kill in order to eliminate suffering in the world?

In some jurisdictions, it might be relevant as well whether the decedent had consented to his own demise.[2] In some cases, arising under wartime conditions, the defense might assert that the defendant acted under military orders. We can leave aside for these purposes all the procedural issues, such as the statute of limitations and the competence of the court. These procedural matters speak neither to the nature of the crime nor to the guilt of the offender. Rather they address the problem of how the state should go about holding the offender liable for the crime.

The impulse to distinguish between the crime and the offender derives from the simple observation that some of the issues listed above bear on the nature of the crime and others bear exclusively on the offender's personal responsibility or culpability for the crime. Put another way, some of the issues focus on the crime in the abstract, considered apart from the personal characteristics of the alleged offender; others bring into relief personal qualities of the suspect in an effort to determine whether if the crime was committed, the suspect can fairly be held accountable for it.

In very general and tentative terms, we can say that all the questions about the act causing the death of a live victim bear upon the nature and gravity of the crime. The psychological makeup and personal peculiarities of the suspect do not enter into this assessment. Yet the broad distinction between the objective features of the act and the subjective features of the offender generates some difficulty in classifying the issues bearing on intention, recklessness, premeditation, and deliberation (issues 7, 8, 9). These issues, which determine the level of homicide and the degree of punishment, implicate the subjective attitudes of the offender, but still they do not require an assessment of the offender as a person with peculiar traits and propensities.

The paradigm of agent-specific questions are those bearing on the exemptions permitted for infants and the insane (1, 13). Typically, infants in a certain range, say ages 16 to 18, are exempt from punishment only if, in the court's judgment, they lack the maturity to be held responsible.[3] The assessment of insanity, of course, requires a personalized judgment about the particular offender's mental condition and the way it bore on the commission of the crime.[4]

The question of provocation (10) represents a borderline issue. The test is used in many legal systems to distinguish between murder and manslaughter.[5] Murder is (intentional) killing without provocation; manslaughter is killing under provocation. Knowing where provocation fits in the scheme of grading the severity of homicide does not tell us whether the issue bears on the crime or the criminal. As we shall see, controversy persists about the proper interpretation of provocation. Additional controversy is posed by the proper classification of self-defense (11), duress (12), and various kinds of mistakes (14). These topics recur in the remainder of this chapter and indeed throughout the rest of this book.

In working out this distinction between the qualities of the *crime* and the characteristics of the *offender*, two sets of words tend to group themselves around these two analytic poles. Consider the following correlations:

Crime: Wrong, wrongfulness, wrongdoing, offense,
              criminality, actus reus

Offender: Attribution, imputation, responsibility, account-
              ability, blameworthiness, culpability, mens
              rea.

The purpose of this chapter is to explore the meaning of these terms as they are used to explicate the differences between aspects of the crime and attributes of the offender. We start with the notion of "wrong" as a guide to the concept of crime.

5.1 *The Basics of Wrongdoing*

The word "wrong" stands out among the terms associated with the concept of "crime" or "offense," as understood in abstraction from the offender. In Blackstone's usage, torts are private wrongs because the impact of the wrong is limited to the interests of a private person.[6] Crimes are public wrongs, for in addition to the particular victim the public as a whole is injured in its sense of security and well-being. The word "wrong" is used here in the popular, nonlegal sense. You have to go beyond the written law and the conventions of the legal culture to answer the question: What exactly makes a crime wrong? There are divergent answers, which can be understood by probing the difference between *wrongfulness* and *wrongdoing*.

The concept of "wrongfulness," like the German notion of *Recht-swidrigkeit*, highlights the conduct standing in violation of a rule of law, specifically a rule of *Recht* [*Rechts-widrig-keit* means "contrary-to-lawness"].[7] The implication is that anytime a rule comes into being, conduct in violation of the rule will be, or could be, wrongful. The rule might have a moral or theological foundation,[8] or it might simply be enacted as statutory law. Although most of the rules of the criminal law have moral or theological roots, this is not true about many modern offenses that are merely preventive (or "prophylactic") in nature. A good example are prohibitions against possessing certain articles—such as guns, counterfeit bills, or pit bulls—that might accidentally cause injury or might be dangerous if they came under the control of less well-intentioned people.

It is useful to have a special term to refer just to that species of wrongfulness in which the wrong derives exclusively from the violation of a statutory rule. There might be nothing wrong at all with possessing certain items (say, as a collector), except that the legislature has said: Thou shall not have these things. The common law developed the term *malum prohibitum* to refer to this class of offenses. We could also refer to these cases of *mala prohibita* as "statutory wrongdoing." The wrong consists in defiance against the state. In contrast, crimes that are also moral or theological wrongs are *malum in se*—"wrong in themselves." These core wrongs of the criminal law are not wrong just because they are prohibited; they would stand for evil whether the legislature said so or not.

The term "wrongdoing" generally has a focus different from "wrongfulness." "Wrongdoing" corresponds to the German term *Unrecht* or to the common term in tort law "tortfeasance." A "tortfeasor" is literally a "wrongdoer." The wrong in this sense of the word derives not from the violation of a rule but from a characteristically dangerous and feared way of doing harm to others. The wrongs that, in this sense, drive the criminal law, are associated with the basic verbs for wronging others: killing, stabbing, poisoning, stealing, robbing, burglarizing, assaulting, mutilating, raping. Each of these value-laden verbs carries with it a particular image of aggressive violence. The notion of wrongdoing captures them all in a single idea of action invading the protected interests of others.

Wrong*fulness* stands for the logical dissonance between behavior and the rules of criminal law. When this dissonance arises, the act is categorically wrongful. In contrast, wrong*doing* is expressed in degrees. Murder is worse than burglary, which is worse than larceny, and a theft of great value is worse than a theft of lesser value. The harm to the victim weighs heavily in determining the degree of wrongdoing. When there is no harm, as in the case of attempts or other inchoate offenses,[9] the risk of harm or the proximity of the action to causing harm informs the degree of wrongdoing.

The difference between wrongfulness and wrongdoing tracks the general distinction between law based on rules and law based on paradigms. The notion of wrongfulness starts with a rule and then inquires whether conduct, under a given description, violates—or is logically incompatible—with a given statement of the rule. The notion of wrongdoing relies less on words and more on images. We have a shared image of the danger associated with "stabbing, poisoning, stealing, robbing, breaking in . . . , etc." Each of these ways of wronging another calls forth a particular picture of aggression. A child could easily draw you a picture of stabbing, poisoning, or stealing, but it would be hard pressed to explain to you in words the boundaries of the crimes of homicide or theft.

These two methods of generating law—rules and paradigms—underlie the contributions of legislation and judicial development of the law. Legislation proceeds in rules and words that demarcate the boundaries of the rules. Courts proceed by identifying a core image of crime and punishing it. That precedent, then, becomes the paradigm for the offense. In other words, it becomes the model for measuring whether new and unanticipated cases conform to the crime or not. If, to be as imprecise as the courts are, it is "sufficiently like" the paradigm, it falls under the criminal prohibition. If it is "sufficiently different" from the paradigm, it is not covered by the crime.

A good example of paradigmatic development of a crime is theft. If the book of Exodus is a good guide, the ancient crime of theft focused primarily on the taking away of barnyard animals that were necessary for survival. The taking and carrying away of specific animals, for example, oxen and sheep, became the paradigm of the offense.[10] Then, the question came up whether the crime would cover the taking of domestic animals, such as cats and dogs.[11] Or would it cover the simple borrowing of a horse? Or, at a later stage, the question arose whether the traditional crime could encompass the appropriation of electrical impulses—electricity, cable TV signals, and the like. Working out all these questions required a process of thinking by analogy: Was the new case essentially like or different from the paradigm—our shared picture—of the offense?

At a late stage of evolution—not until 1916 in England—legislators formulated a general "rule" defining larceny. The crime required the "taking from possession and carrying away of a thing with the intent permanently to deprive the owner of his property."[12] The same questions arise under this statutory definition as under the paradigm-driven, case-by-case elaboration of the crime. But now there is a precise verbal formula to guide the thinking of judges. They must decide whether electricity is a "thing" and whether joy-riding in an automobile represents a taking with the intent "permanently" to deprive the owner of his property.

Some observers of the legal process might doubt whether these are really two distinct modes of legal development. Those who think in paradigms must appeal implicitly to rules. And those who try to ponder the meaning of words in rules fall back on shared images of the essential wrongdoing in committing the offense in question. Though the two mental processes may overlap, it is useful to distinguish between them.[13] One proceeds deductively from rules. The other proceeds analogically from shared paradigms.

The tension between wrongfulness and wrongdoing runs deeper than the methodological differences that derive from thinking deductively from rules or analogically from paradigms. The critical feature of wrongful conduct is that a rule—any rule—suffices to label conduct as wrongful. Once the legal system recognizes the capacity of legislatures to establish new rules, it generates the possibility of offenses that are merely *mala prohibita*. The nature of wrongdoing then shifts from paradigmatic forms of aggression against a victim to defying the authority of the state.

If we look at the criminal law historically, the drive to respond to evil and to punish wrongdoing stands out as the force that shapes the law. At the core of wrongdoing lies the shared perception of aggres-

sion—of an invasion against the victim's interests. Punishing wrongdoing becomes necessary to vindicate the interests of the victim as well
as to restore the moral order disturbed by the crime. As the criminal
law has matured in the last few centuries, however, the movement has
been away from paradigms of wrongdoing toward rules laying down
the definition of offenses. In all the jurisdictions of the Western world,
the legislature has gained the upper hand over the courts. And with
legislative dominance has come the method of law-making in which
legislatures specialize: formulating rules that define offenses. The violation of state-supported rules has displaced the violation of the victim's
interests as the rationale for punishment. The purpose now of punishing offenders is rarely seen as an effort to restore the moral order of
the universe. The primary purpose of punishment today, even for retributivists, is to defend the authority of the state and to uphold the
rules that systematically ensure the interests of all those affected by
crime.

Yet the ancient idea of crime as wrongdoing, as a paradigmatic
wrong against a victim, continues to shape the rhetoric of prosecutors
and the passions of the public. We must meld these sentiments with
the recognition that the state now has the authority to enact prohibitions that are purely preventive in nature or which express the moral
views or sexual taboos of a politically influential subgroup in the society. In modern systems of criminal law we must live with an uneasy
accommodation of wrong*doing* (the violation of victims's interests) and
wrong*fulness* (the violation of rules). It will be convenient to use the
terms interchangeably, though this will require some tolerance for the
resulting ambiguity.

Before leaving the subjects of wrongdoing and wrongfulness, we
should explain why self-defense (11) should be considered an issue
bearing on wrongdoing rather than on the personal culpability of the
offender. In its modern understanding, self-defense is a justification.[14]
It converts the nominal wrong of killing an aggressor into an action
that is, on balance, compatible with the legal order. Yet in killing an
aggressor in legitimate self-defense, there is still something untoward,
something not quite right. This is why one is inclined to say that homicide in self-defense is still homicide (it's not like killing a fly), but that
the extraordinary circumstances of self-defense preclude a finding of
wrongdoing or of wrongful conduct. The implicit rules governing
wrongful homicide include the absence of self-defense and other possible justifications. Besides self-defense and its variations like defense
of others, the only possible justification for homicide today is capital
execution according to a valid death warrant issued in accordance with
a judicial sentence.[15]

The formula that emerges, therefore, is that conduct is wrongful if

(A)   it violates the rules defining the offense, and

(B)   there is no applicable conflicting principle that generates a justification for the conduct.

In the language of wrongdoing, the two-step analysis is similar:

(A)   The conduct conforms to a paradigm of wrongdoing.

(B)   There are no extraordinary circumstances that locate the case outside the paradigm of wrongdoing.

Judith Jarvis Thomson devised a suitable terminology to capture the distinctions between three types of conduct.

I.   *Perfectly legal,* i.e., no infringement of any legal prohibition. (under normal circumstances; walking, breathing, killing a fly)

II.   An *infringement*: Killing in justifiable self-defense

III.   A *violation:* Killing without justification.[16]

The notion of a "violation" is equivalent to our use of the terms wrongdoing and wrongfulness. It is important to maintain these distinctions for they capture important nuances in our perception of criminal conduct. Killing a fly is not an infringement. Killing a human being in self-defense is an infringement but not a violation. In order to maintain this critical difference in our perceptions, we must retain the vocabulary that enables us to express the difference.

In the next chapter we shall look at the full range of possible claims of justification and in chapter 8 examine in great detail the difference between the two most important claims of justification, self-defense and necessity.

5.2 The Basics of Attribution

Once we know that a crime—described as wrongdoing or wrongful conduct—has occurred, the next question: Who did it? Who is responsible? The inquiry requires us to localize the crime in the person or a particular offender. The "attribution" captures the idea of bringing home the crime to the offender and holding the offender responsible for the crime.[17] *Attribution* signifies an active social and legal process. Attributing or imputing the wrongdoing to a suspect means that we hold him or her accountable, answerable, liable, and punishable for a particular instance of wrongdoing.

Once we know to whom the crime should be attributed, we describe these parties as accountable or responsible. They must give an "account" of themselves or "respond" to the occurrence of the crime.

If the wrongdoing is attributed or imputed to them, they are "culpable" or "blameworthy" for the wrongdoing. They are "liable" when they are subject to deserved punishment for their wrongdoing.

The basic proposition of criminal justice is this:

> There can be no criminal liability without wrongdoing attributed to a particular actor.

This proposition is both logical and moral. Crimes are not obviously responsible for themselves. As a logical matter, the wrongdoing must be localized in a suspected offender before we can even think about a criminal trial and holding someone accountable. The proposition is also moral for it is wrong to charge someone for a crime unless the prosecution can establish that wrongdoing has occurred and that it is attributable to a suspect.

The use of the term "attribution" conceals an ambiguity. There are in fact three issues of attribution that occur in the inquiry about guilt for criminal wrongdoing. The first inquiry is whether a human act arguably in violation of the law can be imputed to a particular person. Is it his or her act that prompts our inquiry about criminal guilt? This is the question that concerned us in chapter 3. Next is the question whether a particular harmful consequence can be attributed to the actor. Is the harm of her or his doing? This is the problem assayed in chapter 4. And finally, the third inquiry is whether the action producing harm can be attributed to the suspect as a culpable or blameworthy action.

Two broadly different approaches have emerged to solve the last and most difficult inquiry about attribution. Each of these two approaches gives a different twist to the terms "culpability," "blameworthiness," and "mens rea." The interpretations are radically different, to be sure, but they are masked by a single set of terms to describe the questions they pose and the solutions they offer. I shall refer to these as the "psychological" and "moral" theories of attribution.

The psychological theory inquires whether the crime is mirrored in the consciousness of the suspect. The key question, then, is whether the suspect has chosen to commit the crime or is at least aware and foresees that his actions will result in the crime. The theory of attribution at work here seems to be that if the crime is mirrored in the consciousness of the actor, then he is accountable or responsible for that which his actions produce. The reflection of the criminal act in the actor's psyche brings it home: the wrongdoing becomes the crime of *that person*. The suspect's state of mind, therefore, is the key to attribution. The terms "culpability" and "mens rea" are interpreted accordingly to imply that if the actor has the appropriate mental state, he can be held accountable for his action or the "actus rea." This approach to attribution is common in many legal systems, including the common law system and the Model Penal Code (MPC).[18]

The contrasting "moral" approach to attribution stresses the fairness and justice of holding a particular suspect accountable for a criminal act. The question is not whether the crime is mirrored in the mind of the actor, but whether, regardless of the images that transpire in the actor's consciousness, he or she can be fairly blamed for committing the wrongful act. The approach is not descriptive but evaluative. Attribution of the wrongful act is not posited solely on the basis of particular facts but on the basis of a social and legal evaluation of all the facts bearing on whether the actor can be properly blamed for the crime.

The factors that negate responsibility and attribution in this broader sense enjoy a particular label: they are called "excuses." A good excuse implies that the act may be wrongful, but the actor is not to blame for the crime.

We have already noted three possible excuses: Insanity, infancy, and duress or personal necessity. The first two are based on shortcomings in personal capacity. If because of mental illness or defect the actor cannot appreciate the wrongfulness or criminality of his action, then he is not to blame and not to be held personally accountable for having engaged in the wrongful act. The judgment of infancy is similar, at least with respect to the margin of years in which the court must assay the personal capacity of the youth.

Duress and personal necessity are excuses that derive from the pressure of circumstances. If the suspect is subject to terrifying intimidation from a third party that leads him to commit the crime, then the question of blame requires evaluation of the question: Could we, as a society, have fairly expected the suspect to resist the intimidation? A common example of the latter is the risk of starvation facing shipwrecked sailors or hikers trapped in a landslide. If under these circumstances those in desperate need kill and cannibalize their victims, it makes sense to condemn the act of killing as wrongful, but it makes less sense to hold the desperate offenders personally blameworthy for having done the wrong thing.[19]

The central question in this second approach to attribution is what we can fairly expect of each other in civilized society. Can we expect that individuals, even those suffering from mental illness or those caught under circumstances of overwhelming pressure, always abstain from doing the wrong thing? In a society with little tolerance for human nature as it is, one would expect to find little room for excuses. This was the case under Communist governments in the former Soviet Union and in Eastern Europe. The ideological drive to create a new Communist person implied minimal indulgence for human weakness. Surprisingly, the common law has also taken a strict view on the possibility of excusing those who, for reasons of personal weakness, yield to the pressure of circumstance and engage in wrongful conduct.

German criminal theory has taken the lead in developing a theory of excuses. In an oft-cited passage in his Philosophy of Law, Kant poses the case of the shipwrecked sailor who, lost at sea, saves his life by pushing another person off the only available plank. Our intuitions tell us that we should not punish this person who acted in order to save his own life. The question is why. Kant writes:

> In other words, there can be no *penal law* that would assign the death penalty to someone in a shipwreck who, in order to save his own life, shoves another, whose life is equally in danger, off a plank on which he has saved himself. For the punishment threatened by the law could not be greater than the loss of his own life. A penal law of this sort could not have the effect intended, since a threat of an evil that is still *uncertain* (death by judicial verdict) cannot outweigh the feat of an evil that is *certain* (drowning). Hence the deed of saving one's life by violence is not to be judged *inculpable (inculpabile)* but only *unpunishable (impunible)*, and by a strange confusion jurists take this *subjective* immunity to be *objective* immunity (conformity with law).[20]

This passage initiated a tradition of receptivity toward excuses in German law. The first code enacted by Bismarck's Reich, the Criminal Code of 1871, included § 54, which recognized an excuse of personal necessity. Mindful of the admonition at the end of Kant's analysis, German theorists have been careful to treat excuses as the basis merely for a subjective or personal immunity—namely, for a denial of attribution to a particular subject who claims the personal immunity. They avoid the assertion that excused conduct conforms, in some objective sense, with the legal norm. In other words, excused conduct is still wrongful—contrary to law—but not properly subject to punishment.

My claim is that all cultures of criminal law posit theories both of wrongdoing and attribution. They may not use this precise language, but the theories are implicit in the doctrines they use. Take, for example, the common law's reliance on the maxim: *Actus non facit reus nisi mens sit rea.* [There can be no criminal liability without the joinder of *actus reus* and *mens rea.*] In this formula the *actus reus* stands for the wrongful act, and *mens rea* for the criteria of attribution. In other words: there can no criminal liability without culpable (or blameworthy) wrongdoing.

This proposition does not resolve, however, the conflict between the psychological and moral theories of attribution. And in fact, both theories run through the common law. The practical difference between them is whether excuses are seen to negate *mens rea* (culpability or blameworthiness) or whether excuses are regarded as "defenses," as claims of confession and avoidance. According to the Model Penal

Code § 2.02, excuses do not negate the "kinds of culpability" required for commission of an offense. Claims of duress, insanity, and mistake of law lie outside the boundaries of culpability.[21]

In many common law decisions, however, we find judges treating insanity and other excuses as factors negating *mens rea*.[22] There may be some practical virtue in maintaining ambiguity between these conflicting approaches toward attribution, or it may be that in common law thinking on these matters, the structuring of issues has simply never received the intellectual attention that it deserves.

My own view, which I will defend later, is that the correct approach to attribution is the moral theory, and that is the way in which I will present the distinction in elaborating why it is practically important in the theory of criminal law. To be clear that this is the theory I advocate, I will use the term "blameworthy" to express the principle of moral attribution. The basic propositions that we have posited, therefore, are:

1. There is no criminal liability without blameworthy wrongdo-ing.
2. Claims of justification negate wrongdoing.
3. Claims of excuse negate blameworthiness.

5.3 The Operative Significance of the Distinction

The distinction between wrongdoing and blameworthiness guides us through a number of structural quandaries. Foremost among these is determining the kinds of attacks against which self-defense is permissible. The general rule, followed by most legal systems, is that self-defense is available against unlawful or wrongful attacks. The question, then, is how should we interpret the requirement that the attack be unlawful or wrongful. Must the attack itself be an instance of blameworthy, punishable behavior? What if the aggressor is excused, say, on grounds of duress or insanity?[23] Some theorists think that self-defense should be available only against culpable, unexcused attacks. Others insist that the attack need only be wrongful, that it be a violation of the norms of proper and lawful conduct, regardless whether the aggressor is personally culpable for the attack.

The purpose of force used in self-defense is not to inflict on the aggressor the pain he deserves as a blameworthy wrongdoer. The defender does not attack as a surrogate for the state for the purpose of inflicting punishment on the aggressor. Rather the purpose of the defense is simply to uphold the norms of lawful conduct by nullifying the wrongful attack. Therefore, it makes sense that a wrongful attack should generate a complete right of self-defense, whether the aggressor is excused or blameworthy.

The distinction between wrongdoing and attribution also enters into the analysis of complicity for the crimes of others. It is often the case that the perpetrator of harm is not punishable for the aggressive action. The question then arises whether those who aid the perpetrator can be held be accountable for an offense. Consider two different situations:

I. Alan sees that Cole is about to attack Betty. Alan hands Betty a knife with which to defend herself, but does so with the intent not just to defend Betty but to use the occasion to harm Cole. Is Alan liable for assault against Cole?

II. Alan intimidates Betty to attack Cole with a threat of harm against Betty's children. Alan assists Betty's attack by handing her a knife. Betty attacks Cole. Is Alan liable for the harmful consequences to Cole?

Here are two similar situations in which Betty, the perpetrator of the actual attack, is not guilty. In the first case she has a good claim of self-defense, and in the second, a good defense of duress. In both situations Alan acts with a guilty intent, but the question is whether there is some violation of law for which Alan can be held accountable. In other words, is there an instance of wrongful conduct that can be attributed to Alan? Well, one might say, there is his act of handing the knife to Betty. But handing someone a knife, even with the intent that the recipient use the knife to assault or kill, is not itself a crime. The only crime—the only offense or wrongdoing—occurs when Betty uses the knife. The question, then, is whether Betty's conduct amounts to a crime that can be attributed to the one who helps her, namely, Alan. This, as we shall see, is the nature of complicity in criminal actions— one person becomes liable for contributing to the wrongdoing of another. The meaning and rationale of complicity must await full exploration in chapter 11.

If Alan can be guilty as an accomplice only if a crime—an instance of wrongful conduct or wrongdoing—is attributable to him, then it makes all the difference what kind of defense Betty enjoys. Does the defense negate the wrongfulness of his assaulting Cole? The answer derives clearly from the conceptual research we have already rehearsed. As a justification for using force, self-defense negates the wrongfulness of Betty's actions against Cole. As an excuse, duress does not negate the wrongfulness of Betty's use of force. It follows that in the first case, Betty's actions are not wrongful; they are justified as a matter of self-defense. In the second case, Betty's actions are merely excused on grounds of duress; the attacks remain wrongful. The implication is that in the second case but not in the first, Alan's assisting in a wrongful attack implies criminal responsibility.

Two consequences follow from identifying the use of aggressive force as wrongful. First, the victim of the force (in this case Cole) may use self-defense to repel the attack. And further, anyone who assists or encourages the wrongful attack becomes criminally liable as an accessory to the attack. The steps in this argument are summarized as follows:

1. What kind of defense is at issue? An excuse or a justification? [Assumption: justifications negate wrongdoing; excuses do not.]

2. According to whether the defense is an excuse or a justification, the attack subject to defense is wrongful or not.

3. If the attack is wrongful, the victim may respond with defensive force; and further, providing assistance to the attack implies criminal liability as an accessory.

These propositions summarize the logic of distinguishing between wrongdoing and culpability (or attribution). This is not the only context, however, in which the distinction plays a significant part. Anytime we attempt to state the criteria for an excuse, for example, we will find it useful to refer to wrongdoing as a category independent of and logically prior to the set of excuses. For example, section 4.01 of the MPC defines insanity, in part, as a wrongdoer's lacking "substantial capacity . . . to appreciate the criminality [wrongfulness] of his conduct." The drafters could not decide whether "criminality" or "wrongdoing" better captured the point, but they agree that the insanity consists in the failure to appreciate this logically prior dimension of criminal conduct. Similarly, in section 2.04(3), the MPC's version of mistake of law is based on "a belief that the conduct does not legally constitute an offense." To avoid circularity, this language must be read to mean that whether the conduct constitutes "an offense" requires an answer "yes" or "no" before we assess the actor's beliefs about whether his conduct is unlawful or lawful (an offense or not).

Another way to express this critical point about the distinction between wrongdoing and attribution is to invoke the distinction between conduct rules and decision rules, as illuminated by Meir Dan-Cohen.[24] In general, conduct rules defining wrongful conduct are addressed to the public at large as well as to judges; decision rules on attribution are directed exclusively to judges. It is the job of judges and juries acting on judicial instructions—not of individual citizens—to decide whether wrongful conduct is attributable to a given person. Because excuses, including duress, insanity, and mistake of law, bear on attribution of wrongdoing, the person who asserts the excuse cannot be expected to know whether the excuse applies or not. The distinction between conduct and decision rules is of great value. It explains, for example, why vagueness in defining legal norms is sometimes considered a constitutional defect and sometimes not. Vagueness undermines the ability of individuals, not educated in law, to follow the dictates of conduct rules. Because it is not the task of individual citizens to apply decision rules to their own conduct—this is the task of judges and juries—vagueness in the criteria of attribution is a less serious problem.[25]

5.4 A Problem in the Borderland: Putative Self-Defense

The value of the distinction between wrongdoing and attribution seems fairly clear. Less obvious is the classification of particular issues in one category or another. We might agree that claims of justification bear upon wrongdoing and claims of excuse on attribution, but it is not always self-evident whether a particular issue recognized in law is an excuse or a justification. The problem is well illustrated by the complexity of analyzing the mistaken perception of the factual conditions required for a claim of justification. A good example is the mistaken judgment that one is about to be attacked and that deadly force is necessary to avert the attack. These might well have been the mistakes that Bernhard Goetz made when he shot four youths in the subway.[26] He claimed that they were about to attack him and that he had no reasonable alternative but to shoot to protect himself. Yet no one knows what the four youths would have done had Goetz not shot, and there is no way of proving that more was necessary to contain the danger than merely drawing and pointing the gun.

In the Continental literature, this defense is labeled "putative justification," and in particular in the Goetz situation, putative self-defense. Self-defense presupposes an actual attack, but putative self-defense applies simply on the basis of belief, or reasonable belief, that a feared aggressor is about to attack. The claim of putative self-defense is based on dissonance between the truth of the matter and the defender's perception of the situation. The analogous claims of putative consent and putative necessity are based, respectively, on the mistaken assumption of consent, say, sexual intercourse and the mistaken assumption that the greater good justifies the nominal violation of the law.

There are at least three distinct approaches to the problem of putative self-defense or indeed to any putative justification. One approach is to assimilate the claims of putative justification to claims of actual justification, as exemplified by the language of the Model Penal Code § 3.04 and the state codes enacted under its influence. The reasonable perception of an attack is treated as equivalent to an actual attack for purposes of self-defense as a justification. Yet it is not entirely clear why the mistake need be reasonable; voices are often heard for the so-called subjective view of justification,[27] which would treat as sufficient a good faith belief in the conditions of justification, regardless whether this faith is reasonable or not. This is a controversy we will take up in chapter 8.

Alternatively, one might argue that a mistake about the conditions of a justification is just like a mistake about the object of the required intent. The mistake negates the intent required for commission of the offense. Thus, the House of Lords concluded in a controversial decision that any mistake, reasonable or not, about a woman's consent would negate the intent required for rape.[28] If you assume that the intent required for rape is "the intent to have intercourse with a nonconsenting female," then indeed a man cannot formulate this intent if he believes, however irrationally, that the object of his sexual aims has consented to intercourse. There are many who would advocate an analogous intent for homicide. It would read: You are guilty of homicide if you engage in an act causing death and you intend to kill a human being *who is not an aggressor*. A mistake about whether the apparent aggressor was indeed an aggressor would negate the intent required for criminal homicide.

A third way of approaching a putative justification focuses on the possibility of excusing rather than justifying the use of force. The argument is that a mistake about the conditions of justification constitutes an excuse parallel to the excuses of insanity, personal necessity, and duress. The mistake allegedly negates the voluntariness of the act in the same way that overwhelming pressure undercuts the voluntariness of choice. This was Aristotle's argument about mistake:

> Therefore that which is done in ignorance, or though not done in ignorance is not in the agent's power, or is done under compulsion, is involuntary. . . . those done in ignorance are *mistakes* when the person acted on, the act, the instrument, or the end that will be attained is other than the agent supposed. . . . [29]

The basis of Aristotle's argument is that wrongful conduct can be attributed to an actor only if he engages in the conduct voluntarily. Certain kinds of mistakes, he maintained, negate the voluntariness of the conduct and therefore the culpability of the actor for the wrongdoing. This seems like a plausible argument for treating mistakes about the conditions of justification as excuses.

Yet there are some who concur with the MPC and argue that these cases of putative self-defense are justified. The basis of the argument is that those who are plausibly or reasonably mistaken have good reasons for their actions. They do not act involuntarily in any ordinary sense of the term. It is more plausible, therefore, to treat their actions as sound from a social point of view. Kent Greenawalt has offered us the most sustained and sophisticated defense of this position and therefore I turn to a detailed analysis of his argument.[30] I examine the argument here in the language of justification and excuse. The reader should keep in mind that by definition, claims of justification negate wrongdoing, and excuses negate attribution and culpability.

Greenawalt imagines a case of putative necessity in which Roger intentionally destroys property in order to prevent the spread of a forest fire.[31] The decision to blast a fire break in one place rather than another depends on the actor's predicting the way the fire is going to spread, and that in turn depends on his assessment of wind movements. "Employing the most advanced techniques" for making this judgment, Roger thinks that the wind is going to blow one way and in turn it blows the other way. His destroying the property is for nought. And yet Greenawalt reasons that although this conduct turns out to be wasteful, it was reasonable and therefore justified at the time of decision. How is this case different, one might ask, from a reasonable judgment that a companion in an elevator is about to attack or a reasonable judgment that a female companion really wants sex even though she protests to the contrary?

Greenawalt has no qualms about saying "the risk Roger took was justified" and infers that his action was therefore warranted and justified.[32] The strategy of the argument is to shift from whether the invasion of the victim's interests was justified to the question whether the risk that the actor took—regardless of the impact on the victim— was reasonable and therefore justified. In the end, then, the question whether putative justification is equivalent to actual justification depends on how much we value the victim's perspective in the theory of justification and wrongdoing. Following the Model Penal Code, Greenawalt argues for a theory of justification that depends entirely on the world as the actor reasonably perceives it. What actually happens to the victim is irrelevant.

From the public's point of view, however, it matters a great deal whether reasonable mistakes are "whitewashed" as justified and therefore not wrongful or whether they are treated as excuses bearing exclusively on culpability for wrongful conduct.

Distinguishing more clearly between wrongdoing and attribution— between justification and excuse—could make a noticeable difference in the way the public understands verdicts of acquittal. Consider the findings of not guilty in the *Goetz* case or in the state trial of the four Los Angeles police officers who beat up Rodney King. None of these defendants argued that their conduct was justified because the four blacks on the subway or Rodney King was actually attacking them. They claimed, in effect, excuses based on reasonable perceptions of danger. As the situation appeared to them, the argument went, they had reasonable grounds to fear an assault. Yet the findings of not guilty treated them as though their conduct was really justified. It would have been far better—far more comprehensible in the public mind—for the jury to have found first that their conduct was unjustified, that they had violated the rights of the victim, but that they were personally excused. Clarifying the bases for these decisions might mitigate the rage that some people experience when they think of an acquittal as an invitation to others to shoot in the subway or to pull out their police batons at the slightest provocation.

Notes

1. See Maureen McKernan, The Amazing Crime and Trial of Leopold and Loeb (1989).

2. See StGB §216.

3. California Penal Code §26 (children under 14 are not responsible "in the absence of clear proof that at the time of committing the act . . . they knew its wrongfulness").

4. For more on the issue of insanity, see infra text accompanying notes 23–24.

5. California Penal Code §188. Cf. StGB §213 (provocation in mitigation of manslaughter).

6. William Blackstone, Commentaries on the Laws of England, Chap. 8, Book 3 (1765).

7. For thoughts on the distinction between *Recht* and *Gesetz*, see George P. Fletcher, Basic Concepts of Legal Thought 12 (1996).

8. Many offenses, such as those prohibiting homosexuality and incest, have their roots in the Bible. Many writers simply refer to these as "morals offenses." But the morality may simply be the morality of a small subgroup in the society.

9. On the distinction between attempts and completed or consummated offenses, see infra chapter 10.

10. See Exodus 21:37.

11. Larceny Act, 1916, 6 & 7 Geo V, ch. 50, sec. 2931 (Eng.).

12. Id. at §1.

13. For further illumination of the distinction, See H.L.A. Hart, The Concept of Law 124–27 (2d ed. 1994).

14. On the historical development, see infra chapter 8.

15. On the use of deadly force by the police and its relation to self-defense, see With Justice for Some at 55–57.

16. Judith Jarvis Thomson, *Some Ruminations on Rights*, 19 Ariz. L. Rev. 45 (1977).

17. One could just as well use the term "imputation," which Paul Robinson favors in developing an account similar to the one that follows. See Paul Robinson, Criminal Law 279-377 (1997).

18. See MPC § 2.02(2), which describes "purpose" and "knowledge" as "kinds of culpability."

19. See the famous example of the shipwrecked sailors in Regina v. Dudley & Stephens, 14 Q.B.D. 273 (1884). The Court rejected the defense's claim to an excuse, but the Crown accepted the arguments for compassion by commuting the offenders' sentence to six months imprisonment.

20. Immanuel Kant, *The Doctrine of Right* 235, in The Metaphysics of Morals 60 (M. Gregor trans., 1991).

21. On the concepts of "defense" and "confession and avoidance," see chapter 6.

22. See Rethinking Criminal Law at 532–543.

23. I first addressed this problem in an article entitled, *Proportionality and the Psychotic Aggressor: A Vignette in Comparative Criminal Theory*, 8 Israel L. Rev. 367 (1973); see also reflections on this argument, twenty years later, in George P. Fletcher, *The Psychotic Aggressor—A Generation Later*, 27 Israel L. Rev. 227 (1993).

24. Meir Dan-Cohen, *Decision Rules and Conduct Rules: On Acoustic Separation in Criminal Law*, 97 Harv. L. Rev. 625 (1984).

25. See id. at 639–40.

26. See generally A Crime of Self-Defense.

27. See Richard Singer, *Resurgence of Mens Rea II: Honest but Unreasonable Mistake of Fact in Self-Defense*, 28 Boston College L. Rev. 459 (1987).

28. Regina v. Morgan, [1975]2 W.L.R. 923. Andrew Ashworth claims that *Morgan* did not abolish the general rule in England that mistakes of fact must always be reasonable in order to constitute a good defense. See Andrew Ashworth, Principles of Criminal Law 231–32 (2nd ed. 1995). He concedes that the courts seem to be of a different mind.

29. Aristotle, Nichomachean Ethics 1135a–1136a (D. Ross trans., 1925).

30. Kent Greenawalt, *The Perplexing Borders of Justification and Excuse*, 84 Colum. L. Rev. 1897 (1984).

31. Id. at 1908.

32. Id. at 1908–09.

6

Offenses versus
Defenses

While the distinction between wrongdoing and attribution is well understood in Germany and other Continental legal systems, lawyers in the common law tradition are more likely to classify issues by dividing them into the categories of offenses and defenses. Homicide, theft, and rape are offenses. Self-defense, necessity, consent, mistake, and insanity are all defenses. These two modes of classification are at odds with each other. The category of defenses typically includes all claims of justification and excuse, which explains why this distinction was long ignored in the common law tradition. Yet the distinction between offenses and defenses raises an important philosophical boundary that finds application as well in the structure that derives from the distinction between wrongdoing and attribution.

The fundamental idea behind the distinction between offenses and defenses is that some allegations inculpate suspects and others exculpate them. Offenses inculpate, and defenses exculpate. That is why the distinction has procedural implications. Defense counsel should raise "defenses." Causing death appears to inculpate and therefore should be classified as an element of the offense of homicide. Claims of self-defense and insanity appear to exculpate and therefore should be classified as defenses. Offenses and defenses both carry labels. The prosecution charges the offense by name (murder, rape, theft) in the information or indictment. The defense raises one or more defenses (self-defense, insanity) in response.

Whether an issue comes to be thought of as an element of the offense or as a defense depends, in part, on phrasing. If the prosecution alleges nonconsent as an element of battery or rape, or if the defense raises the defense of consent, they are talking about the same thing. Nonconsent and consent are the mirror images of each other. This creates a problem, for how do we know the correct formulation: nonconsent as an element to be alleged by the prosecution, or as consent to be urged by the defense? The problem arises not only with regard to consent. Should self-defense be formulated as a defense, as is the conventional practice, or should the "absence of self-defense" be regarded as an element of every offense to which self-defense might conceivably be a defense?

This is much more than word play. One of the practical questions in criminal trials is: Who should bear the burden of persuasion (by a preponderance of the evidence) on questions like consent, mistake, self-defense, duress, and insanity? When the defendant must bear the burden, we speak of "shifting" the burden. This is a matter on which there is much more controversy than meets the eye.

6.1 Disputes about the Burden of Persuasion

It is commonly said that the prosecution must prove "guilt" beyond a reasonable doubt. But what does the concept of "guilt" encompass? Does it include all issues bearing on liability, or only the elements of the offense? The answer of common law judges was narrow and restrictive: "Guilt" refers to liability according to the elements of the offenses. Matters of defense are somehow outside the purview of "guilt." This is the way judges and theorists commonly and unreflectingly thought about the structure of criminal law in the nineteenth century. And this is the way many judges continue to think about allocating the burden of persuasion on defensive issues such as self-defense and insanity.[1]

True, today on the European Continent, courts are more likely to interpret the concept of guilt broadly to include all substantive issues that bear on liability. When they reach this position, as has been most clearly the case in Germany, the distinction between offense and defense drops out of the vocabulary of criminal lawyers. While German lawyers once spoke of *Einwaende* and *Einreden* ("objections") as the analogue to the common law concept of the "defense," this term is no longer found in the lexicon of criminal lawyers.

In the nineteenth century, courts both in Europe and in common law countries tended to concur that particular issues made up the prosecutor's inculpatory case and other "defensive" issues were to be proven by the defense. The Prussian Criminal Ordinance of 1805 even laid down the general rule: "One having the proof of the act against him is subject to the statutory punishment unless he proves that under the circumstances the act was not an offense."[2] For example, the Prussian High Court held that the defendant in a statutory rape case had to prove that he was mistaken about the age of his sexual partner.[3]

The English commentaries and case law of the eighteenth and nineteenth centuries lacked systematic thinking about the burden of persuasion. Yet in homicide cases, some agreement prevailed about the distinction between inculpatory elements of the offense and exculpatory defenses. The general principle was that any act causing death was sufficient to inculpate the defendant. Matters of justification, excuse, and mitigation were thought of as defenses. The latter claims exculpated the defendant from the incriminating impact of "the fact of killing being first proved."[4] Yet it did not necessarily follow that the defendant should bear the burden of persuasion on exculpatory issues. That inference was left to the work of Foster and Blackstone in the mid-eighteenth century. According to Foster, the prisoner had "satisfactorily" to prove circumstances of "accident, necessity and infirmity."[5] In Blackstone's influential formulation, the defense's case included "circumstances of justification, excuse and alleviation."[6]

Though this consensus prevailed in nineteenth-century jurisprudence, both in common law and Continental jurisdictions, the agreement has given way to local particularities. German courts require the prosecution to disprove all claims bearing on wrongdoing and culpability.[7] Common law courts are sharply divided about whether the defendant should bear the burden on issues such as self-defense and insanity.[8] It is fair to ask why this happened and to expect a convincing account of current trends in the law.

There is a tendency in many quarters to think that procedural institutions can explain the practice of allocating the burden of persuasion to the defense on some issues. Continental writers often invoke the adversary process to explain the penchant of common law judges and scholars to favor a shifting of the burden of persuasion.[9] The assumption seems to be that the adversary process seeks a balance of advantage between two competing parties, prosecution and defense, and therefore encourages a climate of imposing burdens on the defense. But this way of looking at the problem ignores the common attitude that prevailed in Continental "inquisitorial" and in the common law "adversarial" systems in the course of the nineteenth century.[10] The fact is that there is no easy correlation between patterns in allocating the burden of persuasion and a commitment either to an adversary or an inquisitorial system of trial. The Prussian Criminal Ordinance of 1805 contained several provisions imposing the burden of persuasion on the accused and yet the burdens were borne in an essentially inquisitorial trial.[11] The evolution in German law did not occur against the backdrop of significant procedural changes.

My thesis is that the shift in burden-of-persuasion practices has come about as a result of rethinking the nature of criminal guilt and basic propositions that are used to capture the criteria bearing on criminal liability. A willingness to shift the burden of persuasion is characterized by a willingness to state the criteria of offenses in incomplete rules, called in the language of H. L. A. Hart "defeasible" rules of liability.[12] Take the Model Penal Code's definition of criminal homicide as committed by someone who "purposely, knowingly, recklessly, or negligently causes death."[13] There is no hint in this proposition of any of the "defenses" that might defeat the charge of homicide. Defenses, such as self-defense and insanity, defease—in the sense of "defeat"— the proposition that intentionally causing death constitutes criminal homicide.

Defeasing conditions do not deny the proposition that intentionally causing death is homicide. Rather they assume that the actor who has intentionally caused death asserts a totally new argument to circumvent the implications of his or her deed. They do not meet the proposition head-on as one would, say, by denying that the killing was intentional. Rather they go around the rule by asserting a whole new consideration. The terms at common law for this kind of defeasing condition was "confession and avoidance." The defendant confesses the truth of what the plaintiff pleads and nonetheless avoids the implications of his conduct by raising an exception.

The alternative to defeasible rules of criminal liability would be complete or "comprehensive" rules—rules that do not admit of the possibility of confession and avoidance. All challenges must meet the rule head-on by denying one of its elements.

The notion of a "defense" is the product of defeasible rules. A defense concedes the offense and seeks nonetheless to avoid liability. Comprehensive rules do not admit of defenses, for the only way to challenge them is by denying their applicability. For example, if homicide is defined as "intentionally or knowingly causing the death of a human being," the rule is *not* comprehensive. It is defeasible by a showing of self-defense.

Defeasible rules have their appeal. They regulate normal cases. For example, the Ten Commandments provide simple, straightforward rules for the ordinary situation in which one might be tempted to violate the Sabbath, steal, or kill. The commandments say nothing about extraordinary cases, such as whether it is permissible to violate the Sabbath in order to save life. The imperative "remember the Sabbath and keep it holy" is in fact defeased by the necessity to save life. So it is with the rules prohibiting offenses in the special parts of criminal codes. In the run-of-the-mill case, the prosecution need only allege and give proof of the homicide, theft, or burglary. In the extraordinary, exceptional case, the defendant may engage in an end-run around the normal rule by asserting an exception, a defense such as self-defense, duress, or insanity.

Comprehensive rules suppress the distinction between the ordinary and the extraordinary. They state all the criteria that are relevant to the solution of any case that might arise. To move from a defeasible to a comprehensive rule, we need an exhaustive catalogue of possible defenses. The absence of each of these possible defenses must then be stated as an element of the comprehensive rule. A comprehensive rule of criminal homicide would begin like this:

You are liable for murder if (1) you act (2) intentionally (3) to bring about the death of (4) a living human being, and you are not acting in (5) self-defense or while (6) insane. The problem is that it is almost impossible to catalogue all the possible defenses that might justify or excuse the killing. It might be done to effectuate the arrest of a dangerous felon, to carry out a valid death sentence, or under a statute permitting euthanasia.

6.2 From Defeasible to Comprehensive Rules

The general trend of the criminal law, both in Continental and common law jurisdictions, has been from defeasible to comprehensive rules. In other words, more and more issues have undergone a transformation from "defenses" to denials of the elements of the offense. Here are a number of possible factors that have influenced the development.

Formal Reasoning

Sometimes a simple formal argument will lead a court to recognize that the prosecution must disprove a defensive element beyond a reasonable doubt. If the defense can make the claim that a defensive element negates an "element of the crime," it has a solid basis for laying the element to the prosecution's charge. A good example is the 1935 House of Lords decision in *Woolmington v. Director of Public Prosecutions*,[14] in which the trial court had instructed the jury in a homicide case that the defendant had to prove—to "satisfy a jury"[15]—that his gun went off by accident. This instruction made sense against the background of Blackstone's rule that the defense's case included "circumstances of justification, excuse and alleviation."[16] The trial judge was convinced that this rule "has been the law of this country for all time."[17] On the basis of this instruction, the defendant was convicted of murder.

The appeal to the House of Lords led to a reexamination of the time-honored rule requiring the defendant to prove claims of accident. The House of Lords reasoned that the prosecution must prove malice as an element of murder, and malice, it concluded, presupposed that the killing was intentional and unprovoked. If the prosecution had to prove that the killing was intentional, it followed that it had to disprove all claims that were logically inconsistent with an intentional killing. Because an accidental killing would not be intentional, the claim of accident represented the logical negation of the prosecution's burden of proof. It followed that as part of its responsibility to prove an intentional killing beyond a reasonable doubt, the prosecution had to negate and disprove the claim of accident.

The decision in *Woolmington* led to the application of the same mode of formal reasoning in cases of provocation.[18] Because the prosecution had to prove malice beyond a reasonable doubt, it had to disprove provocation, which is logically incompatible with malice. The mode of reasoning in these cases is straightforward. If it is assumed that A (e.g., malice, intention) belongs to the prosecution's case and the defendant asserts not-A (e.g., provocation, accident), then the prosecution must disprove not-A as part of proving A. Of course, observing this mode of formal reasoning does not explain why at different times and places, judges make different assumptions about which issues belong to the prosecution's case. In order to understand the tendency to expand the range of issues charged to the prosecution, we have to consider the other factors at play in this historical evolution.

The Presumption of Innocence

In those cases in which common law courts have been receptive to increasing the number of issues charged to the prosecution, the judges typically underscore the importance of the presumption of innocence. In a leading U.S. Supreme Court case *Davis v. United States*,[19] in which the judges held that federal prosecutors must disprove claims of insanity beyond a reasonable doubt, their opinion exudes praise for the presumption of innocence:

> The plea of not guilty is unlike a special plea in a civil action which, admitting the case averred, seeks to establish substantive grounds of defense by a preponderance of evidence. It is not in confession and avoidance, for it is a plea that controverts the existence of every fact essential to constitute the crime charged. Upon that plea the accused may stand, shielded by the presumption of innocence, until it appears that he is guilty; and his guilt cannot in the very nature of things be regarded as proved, if the jury entertains a reasonable doubt from all the evidence whether he was legally capable of committing the crime.[20]

This insightful language, written in 1895, seems to call into question the very distinction between assertion of the offense and claims of defense in criminal cases. The single plea of "not guilty" controverts every issue bearing on guilt or innocence. And because the defendant is presumed innocent until proven guilty (a presumption that would make no sense in private disputes), there can be no shift in the burden of proof. Also, the plea of "not guilty" challenges every premise of liability, and there are no claims of "confession and avoidance" that need to be raised specially by the defenses. The language of the *Davis* opinion leads to the conclusion that the concepts of "confession and avoidance" as well as "defense" are irrelevant in criminal law.

The Moral Theory of Guilt

The movement from defeasible to derivative rules of liability was driven, in part, by an increasing appreciation of an obvious postulate: The criminal law should punish only the guilty. If the "guilty" were those who could fairly be morally blamed for wrongdoing, then the principle of punishing the guilty, and only the guilty, could generate a unifying perspective on criminal liability. We see the new approach toward guilt suggestively outlined in the paragraph excerpted from the *Davis* opinion. There can be no "guilt" in the moral sense of the term if the defendant is not "legally capable of committing an offense."[21] Similarly, there would be no guilt if any claims of excuse or justification were available.

This new perspective requires that the concept of "guilt" or "culpability" be understood morally rather than descriptively.[22] If "guilt" and "culpability" simply refer to the descriptive *mens rea* or mental state required in the definition of the offense (i.e., intention or knowledge), the argument of the *Davis* opinion is hardly compelling. For this new view of the criminal law to take hold, the notion of "guilt" had to become synonymous with the broader moral meaning of "culpability" or "blameworthiness" for wrongdoing.

It is not surprising, then, that the refinement of the moral theory of culpability coincided in German legal theory history with the progressive shifting of the risk of residual doubt to the prosecution.[23] If all substantive issues, both inculpatory and exculpatory, were threads in the fabric of guilt, then the differences among them appeared less significant. The distinction between whether harm had been done and whether the harm was justified by a claim of self-defense no longer appeared to be an adequate basis for allocating the burden of persuasion. Proceeding from the premise that the prosecutor had to prove the defendant's guilt, late nineteenth-century German courts readily came to the conclusion that the prosecution had to disprove properly raised claims of self-defense and insanity.[24]

The critical factor in the development of a theory of the burden of persuasion unique to the criminal process is the perception of moral guilt as the central, all-encompassing condition of criminal liability. In the same period at the end of the nineteenth century, both German law and Anglo-American law extricated the criminal process from the style of thought rooted in private litigation. This parallel development indicates that the momentum for reform transcended procedural systems as well as particular national policies.

Though the German system carried through the reform, the common law systems have remained ambivalent. The movement to extricate the allocation of the burden of persuasion in criminal cases from the influence of private law resulted in reform is some courts and not in others. In many jurisdictions, the burden on self-defense and provocation was cast on the prosecution,[25] but the burden on insanity and other issues remained on the defense.[26]

In a brief venture into the constitutional analysis of the burden of persuasion, the U.S. Supreme Court appeared initially to elevate the principle of moral guilt from the *Davis* case into a constitutional rule binding on the entire country under the due process clause of the Fourteenth Amendment. In *Mullaney v. Wilbur*, the Court held that in a murder case the prosecution must prove malice and disprove all inconsistent claims, such as provocation, beyond a reasonable doubt.[27] It looked as though the rules of criminal liability in the United States would become definite rules focusing on a moral theory of guilt or culpability.

Two years later, however, the Court relapsed into the style of formal reasoning outlined above that relies heavily on the factors that happen to be articulated in the rule defining liability. In *Patterson v. New York*,[28] five Justices explicitly reinterpreted *Mullaney* to require merely that the state "prove every ingredient in an offense beyond a reasonable doubt."[29] Whether an issue is an ingredient of an offense depends on whether the legislature says that it is, either explicitly or implicitly in its drafting of the offense. The New York code provided a defense of extreme emotional disturbance, a modern version of provocation, but failed to repeat the common law requirement of malice. Therefore, according to the language of the code, extreme emotional disturbance did not formally negate any element of the prosecution case (other than the general requirement of guilt). It followed, in the minds of the Justices, that New York was free of constitutional restraints in shifting the burden of proof to the defendant to prove an "affirmative defense." The Court affirmed their formalist way of thinking in 1987 when it held that there was nothing constitutionally suspect about a state requiring a defendant to prove a claim of self-defense by a preponderance of the evidence.[30] Because self-defense did not negate "an element of the offense," the state could permissibly shift the burden of proof on that issue to the defendant.

6.3 The Necessity of the Distinction Between
Offense and Defense

The presumption of innocence and the moral theory of guilt provide powerful reasons for requiring the prosecution to bear the burden of persuasion on all issues related to innocence and guilt. The better result in the long run would be to ignore the distinction between offense and defense for purposes of shifting the burden of persuasion. But it does not follow that the distinction between offense and defense should disappear from the criminal law. It is a necessary conceptual tool for explaining a number of important stands that we take in common law jurisdictions and which have their counterpart in Continental legal systems.

At minimum, the distinction between "elements of the offense" and "defenses" provides some guidance for common law judges who must decide when they will instruct the jury on particular questions. Jury instructions are prolix as they are; it would only confuse the lay decision makers if judges were obligated to give instructions on all possible defenses, whether they were properly raised in the case or not. The conventional and seemingly correct rule guiding common law judges in this area is that the judge must instruct the jury on all elements of the offense *plus* properly raised defenses. A defense properly raised is one for which the defendant has provided "some evidence" on behalf of the claim.

It turns out, then, that the distinction between elements of the offense and defenses is rooted deeply in the legal mind. It influences Continental as well as common law thinking. Continental lawyers, following the German example, may believe that the rules of liability are all comprehensive rules, but they cannot eliminate the distinction between offenses and defenses, or, as they would express it today, between inculpatory and exculpatory factors bearing on criminal guilt.

In the German lexicon of criminal liability, the inculpatory case is called the *Tatbestand*, and the exculpatory considerations are divided between claims of justification and claims of excuse. As we noted in the last chapter, the claims of justification negate the element of wrongdoing or unlawfulness, and the claims of excuse negate the element of culpability or guilt. The full picture looks like this.

Prosecution's Case	*Challenged By*
Tatbestand (elements of the offense)	Factual denials
Wrongdoing	Defenses of justification
Guilt or culpability	Defenses of excuse

This schema generates different images, depending on how you read it. If you read just the left hand column, you get the impression that German law stands for comprehensive rules that consist of the *Tatbestand* (or Definition of the Offense), wrongdoing, and culpability. I choose the term "Definition" because it captures the idea that in the typical or normal case, realizing the *Tatbestand* implies liability. The Spanish use the suggestive term *Tipo* to capture this idea of typicality (an equivalent but less graphic term would be "elements of the offense"). In the normal case, therefore, those whose actions reveal the Definition of the offense are liable. Only in exceptional cases will an issue of justification or excuse generate a defense.

This tripartite structure expresses the way German textbooks present their system. But in practical terms, wrongdoing consists in no more than absence of claims of justification; and guilt means no more than absence of excuses. Thus, it is possible to read the schema to stand for the common law way of thinking: The inculpatory case is represented by the Definition; the exculpatory case consists of defenses, either of justification or of excuse.

The truth is that both of these readings are correct. For some purposes, such as allocating the burden of persuasion, we should stress the parallel nature of the three pillars of the prosecution case: Definition, Wrongdoing, Guilt. These three categories generate a comprehensive rule and provide a target for all of the defense's exculpatory arguments. At the same time, some aspects of criminal justice require us to consider the distinction between the inculpatory definition of the offense and the exculpatory claims of justification and excuse. We turn now to one of these disputes where the alternative way of thinking becomes critical.

To illustrate with a concrete example, suppose that a physician Alex intends maliciously to inject air into the veins of a patient David. To avoid any possibility of resistance, Alex approaches David and pulls out the needle surreptitiously. Just at that moment David, who is angry at Alex because of the amount of his last medical bill, punches Alex in the nose and knocks him unconscious. The question in this simple scenario is whether David is guilty of a criminal battery for punching Alex. If David had caused him to fall and hit his temple against a sharp object, with fatal consequences, the question would be liability for homicide. In either case, David's only possible defense would be, as he discovered, after the event, that Alex was at that moment trying to kill him. Had he known of Alex's malicious attack, David would have a good claim of self-defense. The problem is whether he should be able to invoke the defense solely on the objective ground that at that moment Alex was engaged in a kind of aggression that would trigger a right of self-defense and David's response would have been appropriate as the defensive use of force.

This is a problem that has engaged serious debate in the literature. A number of years ago Paul Robinson wrote a piece in the *UCLA Law Review* arguing that claims of justification should apply regardless of whether the defendant knows of justifying circumstances or not. His argument is that the norm of justification is purely objective; it does not require a subjective state of mind for its rationale to hold.[31] At the time I wrote a reply explaining it seemed right that virtually all legal systems in the world require a subjective element for the defense of self-defense and necessity. In the example given above, David would be liable for a criminal battery. The objective circumstances of Alex's attack should be irrelevant.[32] Since then, it is fair to say, we have attempted to improve our positions but neither side has come up with a knock-out argument.[33]

For the sake of clarity, let us refer to Robinson's view as the objective theory of justification. A subjective view, which neither of us supports, holds that the determinative factor of justification is what the actor believes. The language of the Model Penal Code § 2.04 supports this totally subjective view: All that matters, apparently, is what the defender "believes." I hold a combined or mixed theory of justification: Both the objective elements and a "justificatory intent" are required.

There is little support in the statutory and case law, either in the United States or abroad, for Robinson's objective theory. But that should not be decisive. If he has the better argument, his view should take as the proper goal of law reform. In popular sentiment, there is some intuitive support for the objective theory, at least in part. The dispute about self-defense in the 1987 trial of Bernhard Goetz gives us a good example. As will be recalled, four young black men surrounded Bernhard Goetz in the subway and one of them asked for five dollars. Goetz pulled out a concealed pistol, shot and wounded all four of them. Tried on charges of battery and attempted murder, Goetz defended on grounds of self-defense. One major point of dispute was whether the four youths really intended to attack Goetz. The press and the public regarded it as relevant that in the pockets of two of the youths, the police later found two screwdrivers. The newspapers even reported, incorrectly, that the screwdrivers were sharpened, better to serve as weapons.[34]

The public as a whole seemed to believe that the possession of the screwdrivers was revealing evidence about the allegedly aggressive intentions of the four youths. But Goetz clearly did not know of the screwdrivers at the time he pulled his gun and began shooting. Therefore, according to New York's subjective theory of self-defense, the presence or absence of the screwdrivers was irrelevant to Goetz's claim of justification. Yet if a justification addresses who is ultimately right or wrong, then the possession of the screwdrivers would seem to be relevant to show that the four youths probably had aggression on their minds. But the question remains whether Goetz is personally justified—after all he is on trial, not the four youths.

But the question of justification is not who is ultimately the more evil party or whether the victims—the four black youths—deserve to be punished. The question is solely whether Goetz or any other defendant should be exempt, under the circumstances, from the ordinary rules prohibiting the use of violence against others. Although trial lawyers often put the victim on trial, this is the nominal purpose of claiming a justification.[35] But the question remains whether a proper theory of justification might lead nonetheless to the same result that objective factors alone are sufficient to generate a valid claim of self-defense or necessity. The lines of argument support the objectivist thesis. One centers on the nature of the distinction between offenses and defenses, the other about the nature of the harm implied by a violation of the norm.

As to the first, it is tempting to deny the distinction between offenses and defenses and treat defenses simply as negative elements of the prohibition. If that were the case, then the objective effect of the victim's aggression would be the same as the objective effect of the victim's already being dead. Either would be sufficient, in itself, to block a conviction for homicide. But this argument ignores the fact that defenses of justification consist of several elements—just as the rules defining the offense include several distinct elements. In order to prevail on a justification, all the elements must be in place. If the prosecution disproves one of the elements, it defeats the defense. This shows that the logic of justification is more complicated than simply tagging on negative elements to the definition of the offense. Claims of justification represent conflicting norms that collide with the prohibition of the offense and under circumstances prevail over the prohibition. For example, the commandment to observe the Sabbath conflicts with the imperative to protect human life, and the latter will typically prevail.

Robinson could respond to this argument: Fine, I agree with everything you have said, but you have not disproved my central claim that where the conduct is objectively justified, there is no relevant social harm. If Alex is engaged in attacking David and David's actions would have been an appropriate response to this attack (had David known about it), then there is no "net social harm" to Alex. Let us see whether this is plausible.

Alex, of course, is bleeding. He is injured by David's punching him. What could Robinson mean when he says that there is no relevant social harm? Could he simply mean that the conduct is justified and if the action is justified, the resulting harm is not really "social harm?" I believe so. It is simply true by definition according to Robinson that if conduct is justified, the injured party cannot properly complain about being "harmed" and therefore there is no "social harm." But if this is true by definition, it is hardly an argument. The claim of "no social harm" is simply Robinson's clarification of what he means by "justified harm."

The notion of harm is closely tied to our conception of norms, and this is how the two arguments come together. Most, though not all, norms of the criminal law are designed to protect specific legal interests—what the Germans call *Rechtsgüter*. The norm against homicide protects life; the norm against larceny protects property and possession; the norm against rape protects sexual autonomy; and the norm against battery protects bodily integrity. Life, property and possession, sexual and bodily integrity—these are all protected legal interests.

The simplest argument against Robinson's position is that it obliterates an important moral distinction between conduct that violates a protected legal interest and conduct that does not. The difference is one between two different kinds of lawful conduct. Justified conduct is "lawful" if it violates a protected legal interest but does so in conformity with a norm of justification. Conduct is also called "lawful" if it fails to infringe against any prohibitory norm at all. Robinson's theory of social harm eliminates this distinction by subjecting Alex's interest in bodily integrity to forfeiture by aggression. Under Robinson's theory, aggressors have no legitimate interest in not being injured or killed.

Let us suppose that this view is correct, that there is no social harm in killing an aggressor. This argument, in itself, could not account for self-defense as a justification. As we shall see in chapter 8, self-defense includes at least two objective factors other than the fact of aggression. The defender must respond with necessary force and the force must also be proportional to the attack. Let us suppose in our hypothetical case, Alex wishes merely to administer an unpleasant gas to David. Not knowing of this impending wrongful invasion of his body, David responds by killing Alex. Now you could say that because Alex is an aggressor, there is no harm. Yet because of the excessive force, the conduct is *not* justified. How does one explain David's becoming liable for homicide if there is no harm in killing an aggressor? The fact is that the logic of justification cannot be reduced to a single factor, such as aggressor, that can be assimilated, as a negative element, into the elements of the offense.

If these arguments were not sufficient to refute Robinson's objective theory of justification, we need only consider a *reductio ad absurdum* of the theory devised in a recent paper by Russell Christopher.[36] Using our example of the physician Alex intending to inject air into the veins of patient David, suppose we apply the objective theory and conclude that David's hitting Alex is justified. Why not also ask the question whether Alex is justified in trying to commit a battery or even a homicide against David? After all, David makes his move to punch Alex as Alex is approaching David with the needle poised. If objective factors justified aggressive and harmful conduct, then it seems that Alex's use of force in repelling David's attack would also be justified. We end up, then, with the infelicitous conclusion that both Alex and David are justified in using force against each other.

But it is ordinarily assumed that justified force is available only against an unlawful attack. And it is ordinarily assumed, further, that if the use of force is justified, it is not unlawful. Herein lies the contradiction. Robinson's analysis leads to the conclusion that both sides are justified and thus neither side is acting unlawfully, but if neither side is acting unlawfully, neither side could be justified.

One way to resolve this contradiction would be to suggest that the actor who began the aggression first should be the one who is seen as unlawful and unjustified. If Alex started moving toward David before David started moving his fist, then Alex would be the aggressor. But what is the argument for this temporal tie-breaker? Why should it matter who first manifests an aggressive intention? Perhaps the test should be who first forms an intention to commit aggression? None of these tests makes any sense in the abstract. The only relevant perspective could be what the defender David knows at the time of striking Alex. Of course, if that is the standard, the proper question would be who first manifests (not merely forms) an aggressive intention. But recall that under the objective standard, David's knowledge and intentions are irrelevant, which leaves us wondering why under the objective approach it should matter who moves first.

The defender of the objective approach might concede all these objections and still feel unconvinced that the defender's knowledge and reasons should matter to the claim of justification. At stake is a theory of justification that concedes the aggressor is harmed but insists that the action is right and lawful. This view of justification requires us to think of the justificatory norm as overriding and defeating (defeasing) the elements of the offense. The justification overrides the offense because it represents a good reason for inflicting the harm that the offense represents. Saving oneself or another from an aggressive attack is a good reason for using force. Intervening to save someone or something endangered by natural forces provides a good reason for the justification of necessity or lesser evils. But good reasons do not exist in the abstract. They must be reasons that those who use force should actually possess. This is about the best case that one can make for the requirement of justificatory intent.

6.4 Can a Statutory Justification be Unlawful?

The distinction between elements of the offense and defense becomes critical in assessing the permissibility of retroactive judicial redefinition of either the elements of the offense or the claims of defense. In most countries of the Western world, the courts may not create new offenses and then apply them to acts committed before the date of their judicial creation. Doing so violates the general prohibition against ex post facto laws, or the more general principle *nulla poena sine lege*.[37] But it is not so clear that courts may not retroactively tamper with claims of defense. First, they may recognize nonstatutory defenses—a practice that both common law and Continental courts engage in.[38] The more serious problem is the opposite one: May courts curtail or disregard statutorily recognized defenses?

The problem is illustrated, dramatically, by the prosecution of the East German border guards for attempting to murder fleeing citizens of the German Democratic Republic (GDR). After the collapse of the GDR in 1989 and the unification of Germany a year later, a German court put the border guards on trial. An informal directive of the National Security Counsel had authorized border guards to shoot all persons trying feloniously to leave the country. The guards rather sensibly appealed to this directive—informally called the *Schiessbefehl* [order to shoot]—to justify the alleged acts of attempted murder, but the courts of unified Germany would not recognize the alleged justification. The directive might have constituted a justification under GDR law, the court conceded, but this directive supposedly violated basic human rights. And if the statute was unjust, the court reasoned, it could not provide a justification for shooting someone with the intent to kill. The court declared the guards guilty of attempted murder.[39] Critics of the decision cried "foul." Disregarding a defense, in effect, creates a new offense: The guards' conduct is retroactively deemed punishable in a united Germany while it would not have been punishable in the GDR.

If there is no basic difference between elements of the offense and claims of justification, then the critics of the German decision have a strong case. If the legislature has exclusive authority to define the "elements of the offense," then it should have the same authority over the negative elements we call "claims of justification." Perhaps there should be an exception for the recognition of new claims of justification that aid the defense, but the principle should apply with full force to inhibit judicial innovations harmful to the defense. Disregarding the border guards' statutory claim of justification clearly hurts the defense.

A less dramatic version of the border guard problem is posed by the question whether courts may simply curtail the scope of existing defenses. The German statutory definition of self-defense appears to admit the possibility of using defensive force greatly disproportionate to the threat of the attack, for example, deadly force to prevent the theft of an apple.[40] We will discuss the rationale for this broad view of self-defense in a later chapter; for the time being, our interest is directed to judicial efforts to curtail this broadly defined defense by imposing a rule of reasonableness.[41] The problem posed by this development is precisely that curtailing a justification implicitly recognizes a new area of criminal liability, namely, the set of cases that would be justified if the statute were strictly applied. My hunch is that German as well as American courts could accept this slight reduction in the scope of statutory justification. Yet the difference between disregarding a little bit of a statutory justification and disregarding the entire justification is merely a matter of degree.

Admittedly, the position of the German courts is bolstered by their having a vivid sense of extrastatutory law—the Right. The GDR justification violates the Right and is therefore disregarded. Common law courts would not use this language, but one would like to think that they might reach the same result by holding a statutory justification unconstitutional. Yet it should be noted that disregarding a justification violates the interests of the criminally accused, and therefore it is not clear who would be in a position to assert a constitutional right to disregard the justification.

We end this chapter with a recognition that working out the distinction between offense and defense remains a complicated task. For some purposes, such as allocating the burden of persuasion, it might seem better to overcome the distinction altogether and treat all issues bearing on guilt under a single common denominator. This is the view implicit in the "comprehensive" rules of liability that have emerged in Continental jurisprudence. For other purposes, such as the necessity of "justificatory intent," the distinction between the offense and claims of justification (defense) proves to be critical. Also, as we have seen, jurisprudential problems arise in denying recognition to defenses that would be taboo, if the denial of recognition were understood as creating a new offense or expanding an existing one. The distinction remains implicit in these numerous areas, even though Continental jurists no longer explicitly recognize the concept of "defense." That the distinction exists and that it has an impact on legal argument all over the world is beyond dispute.

Notes

1. See cases cited *infra* in notes 25, 26, and 28.

2. Prussian Criminal Ordinance §367, discussed in Kussner, *Uber Beweislast und Prasumtionen im preussischen Strafverfahren*, 3 GA 32 (1855). The roots of this ordinance are in the Constitutio Criminalis Carolina of 1532, which also required the accused to prove defensive issues (e.g., §141 self-defense). A. Schotensach, Der Strafprozess der Carolina 78–81 (1904).

3. Judgment of November 4, 1853, [1854] Justiz-Ministerial-Blatt fur die Preussischei im Gesetzgebung 5. The High Court reached the same conclusion on the defense of mistake of fact to a charge of assisting an illegal immigrant. Judgment of November 30, 1853, 2 GA 255 (1854).

4. The phrase is from M. Foster, A Report of some Proceedings of the Commission for the Trial im of the Rebels 55 (1762).

5. Ibid.

6. 4 Blackstone 201.

7. See George P. Fletcher, *Two Kinds of Legal Rules: A Comparative Study of Burden-of-Persuasion Practices in Criminal Cases,* 77 Yale L. J. 880 (1968).

8. See supra note 1.

9. Geyer, Lehrbuch des Strafprozessrechts 710–11 (1880); G. Vidal & J. Magnol, Cours de droit criminel et de science penitentiaire 1035 n. 2 (9th ed. 1949).

10. For more on the difference between inquisitorial and adversarial thinking, see the discussion of the defendant as subject of the proceedings, supra in chapter 3.

11. See Kussner, *Über Beweislast und Präsumtionen im preussischen Strafverfahren,* 3 Goldtdammers Archiv 32–34 (1855).

12. See H.L.A. Hart, *The Ascription of Responsibility and Rights,* 49 Proceedings of the Aristotelian Society 171 (1949).

13. MPC § 210.1.

14. [1935] A.C. 462.

15. Id. at 465.

16. 4 Blackstone 201.

17. Ibid.

18. Mancini v. Director of Public Prosecutions, [1942] A.C. 1 (provocation). The rule was extended to claims of self-defense in Chan Kau v. The Queen, [1955] A.C. 206.

19. 160 U.S. 469 (1895).

20. Id. at 485–86.

21. Id.

22. On the moral theory of guilt, see supra text at 155–158.

23. On the general correlation between German theory and the shift in allocating the burden of persuasion, see Fletcher, supra note 7.

24. Two important cases were the Judgments of November 13, 1885, 7 Rechtsprechung 664; and of October 23, 1890, 21 RGSt. 131. In the first case, the court endorsed the view of the trial judge that both participants in a brawl should be acquitted on the ground of self-defense if it appeared possible that either might have started it. In the second case, the court affirmed an acquittal on the ground of insanity. According to the opinion of the trial judge, there was a "probability" of insanity. Apparently, the prosecution thought that this was not enough for an acquittal; the court held that a "possibility" of insanity was sufficient to acquit.

25. See Martin v. Ohio, 480 U.S.228, 236 (1987) (noting that in all but two states, the burden of disproving self-defense is on the prosecution).

26. This was notably the case in Great Britain and in California. *Woolmington* was extended to self-defense in Regina v. Smith, 173 Eng. Rep. 441 (1837), but the English courts still expect the accused to persuade on the issue of insanity. Regina v. Smith, 6 Crim. App. 19 (1910). Similarly in California, the courts extended the rule of reasonable doubt to self-defense, People v. Toledo, 85 Cal. App. 2d 577, 193 P.2d 953 (1948), but not to insanity, People V. Wolff, 61 Cal. 2d 795, 394 P.2d 959, 40 Cal. Rptr. 271 (1964).

27. Mullaney v. Wilbur, 421 U.S. 684 (1975).

28. Patterson v. New York, 432 U.S. 197 (1977).

29. Id. at 215.

30. Martin v. Ohio, 480 U.S. 228 (1987).

31. Paul Robinson, *A Theory of Justification: Societal Harm as a Prerequisite to Criminal Liability*, 23 UCLA L. Rev. 266 (1975).

32. George P. Fletcher, *The Right Deed for the Wrong Reason: A Reply to Mr. Robinson*, 23 UCLA L. Rev. 293 (1975).

33. See Rethinking Criminal Law at § 7.4; Paul Robinson, *Competing Theories of Justification: Deeds v. Reasons*, in Harm and Culpability (A.P. Simester and A.T.H. Smith eds., 1996).

34. See A Crime of Self-Defense at 3, 26, and 219 note 3.

35. See With Justice for Some, in particular, chapter 4.

36. See Russell Christopher, *Unknowing Justification and the Logical Necessity of the Dadson Principle in Self-Defense*, 15 Oxford Journal of Legal Studies 229 (1995).

37. For an extended discussion of this principle, see chapter 1 at pp. 12–14.

38. On the German side, see the Judgment of the *Reichsgericht*, March 11, 1927, 61 RGSt. 242, which recognized the general extrastatutory defense of necessity.

39. See the decision by the Constitutional Court, 95 BVerfG 96 (1996).

40. StGB § 35 (permitting all necessary force).

41. The doctrinal label is *Rechtsmissbrauch* or *abus de droit*—a doctrine peculiar to Continental legal thinking. For the details, see George P. Fletcher, *The Right and the Reasonable*, 98 Harv. L. Rev. 949 (1985).

7

Intention versus Negligence

There are some situations in life in which people set out to accomplish certain goals and they realize their aims exactly as planned. They set out to go to the library and they arrive at the library. They set out to steal a book and they steal a book. Obviously, the aims are sometimes good, sometimes bad. But very often people get where they want to go. These are case of intentional conduct, of setting one's sights on realizing a particular target, whether the goal be socially desirable (going to the library) or criminal (stealing a book).

In many situations, however, we accomplish both good and bad—not as the object of our intentions but as the unwitting side effects of our conduct. Imagine that someone drops a wallet full of cash, a starving mother then finds it and uses the funds to save the lives of her three children. Losing the wallet was an accident, and good came of it. Or suppose that a pharmacist mislabels a bottle of poison as a nutritional food supplement and then casually leaves a package of the bottles in the back of his store. A street person finds the bottles of poison and after reading the labels, drinks the poison and dies. Mislabeling the bottle was an accident, more or less, but great harm came of it.

The person who dropped his wallet might feel good that his money was applied to a good purpose, but it would be odd for him to claim credit—to expect praise and appreciation from others—for saving the lives of the three children. But the pharmacist who mislabeled the poison might be responsible, both morally and legally, for the death of the person who consumed the poison. This difference should puzzle us. Praise for good deeds seems to presuppose an intention to do good, but blame for harmful deeds need not be attended by an intention to harm.

Granting credit and giving praise require, it seems, a choosing to do good, an investing of oneself in philanthropy.[1] Wrongdoing differs. If the pharmacist could avoid endangering the public by taking appropriate measures, he is required to do so. Of course, there is much work to be done in figuring out what these appropriate measures are. But if he pays too little attention to the measures necessary to protect the public from the poisons in his shop, his causing harm will be labeled *negligent*. And negligently causing harm can provide a basis for criminal liability as well as moral censure.

Since Roman lawyers carved out applications for the terms *dolus* (intention) and *culpa* (fault, negligence), lawyers in the Western legal tradition have relied upon this pair of words to assay both criminal and civil responsibility. Receiving praise for doing good requires a good intention. But it seems that we can be blamed for the harm we bring about either by intention or negligence. All legal cultures in the West recognize the distinction between intentional and negligent wrongdoing, but there is great disagreement about the contours and the implications of these ways of being held responsible.

Probing the contours of intention and negligence poses, as do the themes of other chapters, numerous philosophical and conceptual problems. The first problem is: What exactly are these two things, *dolus* (intention) and *culpa* (negligence)? One could say that they are ways of committing offenses. They are typically described as the internal side of the offense, as forms of culpability, as aspects of *mens rea*. None of these descriptions, as we shall see, offers a precise fit.

Questions abound. It is generally assumed, for example, that intentionally committing a crime is worse than committing it negligently. Intentional homicide is more culpable, more blameworthy, than negligent homicide. The question is why. What is it about intentional conduct that makes it worse? Is it the factor of knowledge, of desire, of commitment, of likelihood of execution? And if *dolus* (intention) is worse than *culpa* (negligence), does it follow that nothing could be worse than *dolus?* Do bad motives, for example, make intentional killing even more heinous?

At the low end of the culpability spectrum, the problem is how to set the minimum threshold of negligence. Is it possible to cause harm without being branded as negligent? Let us return to our example of the street person who drinks poison from the mislabeled bottles. Suppose a zealous prosecutor wishes to go after the people who manufactured the bottles. To make things simple, suppose a glassblower working by herself manufactured the bottles used by the pharmacist. Without her having supplied the bottle, the poison would never have been poured into that particular vessel. Her defense against being held responsible would be that she merely engaged in the socially desirable practice of making and selling bottles; she bore no responsibility for the way the bottles were subsequently used. Accordingly, it would be difficult to criticize or blame her for the consequences of the pharmacist's negligence. Her role in the death of the street person was purely *accidental*—without fault or culpability on her part. Negligence, then, comes into focus as a faultful or blameworthy accident as opposed to an accident free of blame.

We could think of these four possibilities as stations on a continuous track of steadily increasing responsibility. Let us represent that continuum in the following way.

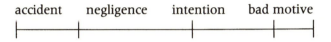

accident   negligence   intention   bad motive

The rest of this chapter explores the criteria for making these distinctions as well as the assumptions behind this ranking of ways of causing harm.

7.1 Accidents and Negligence

In order to understand the proper place of negligence in the criminal law, we have to recall our earlier discussion of the distinction between crimes of harmful consequences and crimes of harmful actions. Accidents are possible only where there is a conceptual gap between the action and the consequence. This is the case with regard to homicide, battery, and arson but not true relative to rape, larceny, and burglary.[2]

The implication for present purposes is that if harm can occur accidentally—and only if it can occur accidentally—can it be the product of negligent risk-taking. The only difference between accidents and negligence is the ability of the actor to avoid the harm by exercising due care, that is, acting reasonably or nonnegligently.

On the basis of these propositions, we can formulate a rather clear statement about the limited place of negligence in the criminal law.

Only crimes of harmful consequences can occur negligently.

This means that as a conceptual matter we cannot have a crime of negligent rape, negligent larceny, or negligent burglary. But we can— if we so choose—punish crimes of negligent homicide, negligent arson, negligent destruction of property, or negligent battery.

It is worth reviewing why crimes of harmful actions cannot occur negligently. The reason is that in light of the logical dependence of harm on the action, there is no causal process that can go awry and produce, for example, a human sexual penetration, a human dispossession of property, or a human breaking in. Try to imagine what an accidental taking of property would look like. Suppose someone accidentally falls off a roof, lands next to a necklace left on the ground, and rolls down the hill with the necklace caught up in his clothing. As soon as he gets up, he notices the necklace and returns the necklace to its owner. If this rolling down the hill constitutes "taking" and "carrying away" the necklace, it would be an accidental taking. But the better view seems to be that this unusual turn of events would be nothing more than an accidental and temporary dislocation of the object. As the terms are ordinarily understood, the notions of sexual penetration, dispossession of objects, and breaking in presuppose a purposeful human action. The hypothesis seems sound: The harms required for certain offenses (rape, larceny, burglary) cannot occur absent a human purpose. This means that they cannot occur accidentally.

This is not to say that mistakes are impossible in the offenses that do not admit of accidental perpetration. It is easy to imagine innocently minded people as mistakenly engaging in intercourse without consent, taking the property of another, or breaking into the home of another. Suppose that absentmindedly you leave the library without having first having checked out the book you were reading. That is a taking by mistake. The most difficult problems in rape cases occur as a result of someone's thinking that his or her partner had consented to intercourse.

The difference between mistakes and accidents turns out to be fundamental in this inquiry. Mistakes can occur in all forms of offense. But accidents can occur, as I have argued, only when there is an independent causal process between the action and the harmful consequence. Causal processes can go awry and produce a result totally different from the actor's expectations. When the unexpected result comes about without any fault on the part of the actor, then it is an accident.

To answer the question, when does an accidental harm become negligent, we should take a look at a legal formulation of negligence. The Model Penal Code's definition is a good place to start:

§ 2.02(2)(d): A person acts negligently with respect to a material element of an offense when he should be aware of a substantial and unjustifiable risk that the material element exists or will result from his conduct. The risk must be of such a nature and degree that the actor's failure to perceive it, considering the nature and purpose of his conduct and the circumstances known to him, involves a gross deviation from the standard of care that a reasonable person would observe in the actor's situation.

The first sentence of this definition enables us to resolve cases we have considered at the boundary between accidents and negligence. To be negligent, the actor's conduct must imply "a substantial and unjustifiable risk" of producing the relevant harm. This standard enables us to dispose rather easily of the liability of the bottle manufacturer in the example posed above. The risk that each bottle produced would be used to transmit poison to an unsuspecting victim was minimal—hardly "substantial." Any time the risk is less than substantial, any resulting harm falls into the category of accidental harm.

If the risk is substantial—say, the risk of collision and injury in driving a car—it might be "justifiable." The justification of risk depends on the balance of its costs and benefits. Its costs are the substantial risk of harm and its benefits are measured by the reasons people have for engaging in the risk. Driving has many benefits, both in the interest of the economy and of the pleasure of drivers and passengers. In the judgment of most people, these benefits outweigh the enormous costs in automobile-related injuries and deaths.

In the American literature, this process of balancing the expected costs and benefits of risk-taking is labeled "the Learned Hand" formula. In a famous torts case,[3] Judge Learned Hand defined negligence as the taking of an unreasonable risk. Unreasonableness was defined as unjustified under the formula: expected costs versus expected benefits. Expected costs are the total harm that might result from the risk as multiplied by the probability that this harm will occur. The same formula applies in calculating probable benefit. If expected benefits outweigh expected costs, the risk is reasonable and justified; if the opposite, the risk is unreasonable and unjustified.

The second sentence of the Model Penal Code (MPC) test represents several innovations in American legal thinking. Note that the formulation presupposes "the actor's failure to perceive" the risk. This is anticipated in the first sentence with the phrase: the actor "should be aware" of the substantial and unjustifiable risk (but is implicitly not aware of the risk). Thus, the MPC stakes a clear distinction between recklessness (MPC § 2.02(2)(c) in which the actor *perceives but ignores* the risk and negligence in which the actor *fails* to be sufficiently attentive to grasp the risks entailed by his conduct. The German literature refers to this distinction as that between two forms of negligence, conscious and unconscious negligence. It is worth noting that not all English-speaking legal systems use the term "reckless" to denote risk-consciousness; the English, for example, use "reckless" to refer to egregious cases of negligence.[4]

The remainder of the second sentence of the MPC definition focuses on the behavior of a "reasonable person . . . in the actor's situation." The basic idea is that a reasonable person would have paid closer attention to the cues of danger under the circumstances. The person who drives a car should notice whether the headlights are on. The person who carries a rifle should notice whether the safety on the trigger is in the proper position. The pharmacist should notice whether the poison has been correctly labeled. Driving, carrying a gun, working with poison—these are risk-breeding acts that should put one on notice. Failure to take heed can engender what the MPC calls in § 2.02(2)(d) "a gross deviation from the standard of care that a reasonable person would observe in the actor's situation."

Some people think there is something suspect about blaming people for this "gross deviation" from the behavior that might be expected of a reasonable person. The MPC obviously concurs that recklessness—with its requirement of a choice to ignore a known risk—is worse than negligence. Also, the model code provides that negligence is sufficient for liability only if so provided by statute. If the relevant statute is silent, the minimally required form of culpability is recklessness—namely, a choice to run a "substantial and unjustifiable risk" that the actor's conduct will realize a material element of the offense in question.

The assumption seems to be that if you know about a risk and decide to run it anyway, your action displays greater contempt for the interests of others than if you never learned of the risk at all. This is the widely shared assumption. But is it always correct? Compare two versions of the prosecution against the Ford Motor Company for locating the gas tank in a vulnerable position in the rear-engined Pinto. In case I, the company simply never bothers to study whether it is safe or dangerous to build their car with gas tanks in front. In case II, the company undertakes a systematic study of the costs and benefits of locating the gas tank in front. It concludes that in light of the number of expected deaths from collision and the costs of locating the gas tank in a safer position, the benefits of keeping the gas tank in its relatively vulnerable position outweigh the costs. The two cases exhibit the difference between sloppiness and indifference, on the one hand, and good faith but slightly callous risk-running, on the other. Sloppiness and indifference are considered mere negligence. But if a judge and jury disagree with the company about the balance of costs and benefits, the company can be charged with having recklessly endangered the lives of millions of people. This, in fact, happened in the prosecution of the Ford Motor Company for having marketed the explosion-prone Pinto.[5] Still, one wonders whether the sloppy and indifferent company is not in fact worse than the company that acts in good faith but comes to the "wrong" decision about the costs and benefits of its risk-taking conduct.

Even if, in general, recklessly causing harm is worse than negligently causing harm, negligent indifference to risk might still be a sufficient basis for criminal liability. Failing to pay attention to dangers implicit in one's conduct is a vice, a fault, a basis for moral criticism. We censor others for this fault when they forget appointments or fail to look where they are going. When written on a grand scale, the fault of risk-indifference should be sufficient to warrant liability for causing harm. Yet, from time to time, theorists argue that negligence is not really fault, not really a proper basis for criminal liability.[6] They say that *mens rea* requires a "mental state" and negligence represents a blank mind—hardly a mental state that could qualify as *mens rea*. Others go beyond this purely formal reasoning and argue that no one can be blameworthy for anything without making a choice. There is nothing blameworthy, they claim, about failing to take note of the danger implicit in one's conduct.

Whatever the reason, it is clear that in the common law tradition, negligence is a suspect basis of liability. The only case of negligently causing harm that is clearly subject to criminal sanctions is negligent homicide. Negligent arson, negligent battery, and negligent destruction of property are all exempt from liability. Some Continental legal systems are more liberal about subjecting negligent harm to liability.[7]

The common law tradition of limiting the scope of negligence seems logical and sensible—if debatable at the margins. Yet the MPC has brought about a major transformation in the scope and applicability of negligence. Any material element of an offense might be brought about—may "result" in the ambiguous language of the Code—either intentionally or negligently. The basic shift is from using negligence to describe a certain set of accidents to using the term to describe, as well, faultful mistakes. If mistakes may be committed negligently, then any offense—not just the restricted list discussed in this chapter—might be committed negligently. As a result, curious terms like "negligent rape" have come into the American legal vocabulary. Rape would be negligent if a man engaged in intercourse with a woman whom he negligently assumed had consented. The negligent mistake about consent renders the entire action negligent. Later we shall consider whether this is a proper way of speaking about mistakes, but for now we must note that in recent years the field of negligence has, under the influence of the Model Penal Code, greatly expanded its potential field of application.

7.2 Negligence: Objective and Subjective

Why is negligence so troubling as a ground of liability? There are some, as suggested above, who do not regard negligence to be a form of *mens rea* or a proper ground for blaming either causing harm or making mistakes. There are others who insist that negligence is an *objective* standard and that, therefore, negligence invariably entails a depersonalized and unjust judgment of responsibility and blame. The negligent are not judged on the basis of what they have actually done but on the extent of their deviation from the mythical standard of the reasonable person. This critique of negligence has become acute in recent years as many feminist scholars have argued that the standard of the reasonable person has a male bias built into it and that, therefore, the proper standard for judging female suspects should be a "reasonable woman" standard.[8]

The terms "objective" and "subjective" get in the way of clarifying this dispute and trying to resolve it. The problem is that the terms mean different things to different people. Sometimes "subjective" is taken to mean: as the suspect personally believes. For example, in a famous nineteenth-century case, *Commonwealth v. Pierce*,[9] the alternative to an external or objective standard of negligence was thought to be one in which the defendant's good faith was controlling. In *Pierce*, the defendant, practicing publicly as a physician, caused the death of a patient by applying kerosene-soaked flannels to her skin. Concluding that the standard of liability was "external," Justice Oliver Wendell Holmes, Jr. wrote that the question was whether the treatment would have been "reckless in a man of [reasonable] prudence."[10] The point of saying that the standard was "external" was to stress that good faith was not a defense and that the defendant might be guilty, even though he thought he was doing the prudent thing. In one sense, then, the conflict between objective and subjective should be restated as between "external" standards and "internal" standards of good faith.

In a modern replay of the problem in *Pierce*, Bernhard Goetz argued, after he had shot four young men who surrounded him in the subway, that the New York statutory standard of "reasonably perceiving" a threat of robbery should be judged by the subjective standard of good faith. Remarkably, the appellate courts[11] and even a law professor agreed with him.[12] When the case finally reached the New York Court of Appeals (the highest court in the state), the judges unanimously decided that the statute implied the standard of the reasonable person and that therefore Goetz's perception both of danger and of the necessity of shooting should be judged according to an external community standard of reasonable behavior.[13]

The beauty of the MPC provision on negligence is that it distinguishes clearly between the external or objective standard of an unreasonable risk and the actor-specific issue of personal responsibility running the risk. In this respect, the structure of the MPC provision traces the distinction we developed in chapter 5 between wrongdoing and personal responsibility. The wrongdoing of negligence consists in running the substantial and unjustifiable risk of causing harm. Responsibility for running the risk is resolved by the inquiry into what a reasonable person would do under the circumstances.

With this structural distinction, however, we have not resolved the question whether the actor-specific issue of responsibility should be understood objectively or subjectively. And once again, the terminology itself breeds confusion. One argument is that the very invocation of the reasonable person entails some "objectification"—an abstract and depersonalized standard that is per se unjust. The implication of this critique is that the just standard is one that is "subjective." The fact is that every standard for responsibility is external or objective—a community standard of responsible behavior. The only coherent basis for blaming someone for engaging in harmful action (e.g., taking a substantial and unjustifiable risk of harm) is to compare the suspect's decision to act with a standard of proper behavior.

Even where the actor "chooses" to engage in the risk, the choice provides an adequate ground for criminal responsibility only if the choice deviates from the expected behavior of a reasonable person. According to the MPC's definition of recklessness, an actor is criminally responsible for choosing to disregard a "substantial and unjustifiable risk," only if the "disregard [of the risk] involves a gross deviation from the standard of conduct that a law-abiding person would observe in the actor's situation."[14] The term "law-abiding person" takes the place of the "reasonable person"; but the principle remains constant: The only way to judge responsibility for reckless and negligent risk-taking is to measure the actor's conduct against community expectations. The choice to disregard the risk is not per se culpable; it is culpable only if it falls short of the community standard of reasonable [law-abiding] behavior.

Since the criterion of "choice" does not eliminate the problem of judging conduct against a community standard, the nagging question remains: How do we distinguish between a just and an unjust standard of negligence? Is it clearly better, more just, to individualize the standard of responsibility to include all the factors that bear on the actor's decision to run the risk? Indeed, should we individualize the standard of judgment to the point that we consider "the infinite varieties of temperament, intellect and education"[15] that lead different people to act differently. In assessing whether someone like Bernhard Goetz reasonably perceived a risk of danger and reasonably reacted to his perception, his prior experience with crime in the subway becomes relevant; if mugged in the past, he would understandably and reasonably perceive the early stages of a possible mugging as threatening.[16] If a small woman is attacked by a large man, these differences in gender and size become relevant in assessing whether her response to the perceived attack is reasonable under the circumstances.[17] My claim here is not that the standard should be "subjective" (dependent on the actor's good faith) but rather individualized in order to achieve a fair standard of judging individual behavior.

Many theorists despair of the possibility of a just standard of negligence because they think that it is impossible to individualize the standard of judgment. If the "reasonable person" is adjusted to the infinite variety of individual differences, the standard for judging would collapse into the object to be judged. We would be forced to embrace the slogan of infinite understanding: *Tout comprendre, c'est tout pardonner*. [If we know everything about the defendant, we must excuse him.] Therefore, if we make the standard of judgment too particular, we have no choice but to excuse or mitigate the crime.

If the reasonable person were defined to be just like the defendant in every respect, he would indeed do exactly what the defendant did under the circumstances. But this excessive individualization rests on a mistake. Objective factors bearing on the decision to act might be relevant, but it would not follow that all the features of the defendant's character would enter into the equation. If the defendant's head injury or impotence is considered in assessing the likely behavior of a reasonable person, it does not follow that "the actor's situation" includes his insensitivity, greed, zeal for adventure, or even his wickedness as a person.

Excessive and mistaken individualization derives from the failure to attend closely to the types of character traits that properly subject wrongdoers to judgments of blame. Suppose that out of a zeal for thrills and adventure, a motorist habitually drives 100 mph. Is she subject to blame for this excessive risk-taking? The answer is yes. The obvious difference between a head injury and a lust for thrills lies in the actor's potential self-control. A head injury is beyond the actor's control, but a lust for thrills is subject to discipline and correction. We properly expect people to control their lust for adventure—so far as it affects the safety of others—precisely as we expect them to control their greed, jealousy, and other vices of character. Those who fail to discipline their vices hardly warrant preferential treatment by having their vices incorporated into the standard by which they are judged—as though the greedy man should be judged by the greedy man standard.

Holding someone to a community standard, therefore, is not necessarily a form of injustice. So long as the defendant is excused on the basis of objective, conduct-influencing factors, such as physical impediments, the standard of responsibility remains attentive to individual capacity. The standard can be properly individualized, be fair and sensitive to differences that matter, and still provide a proper standard of judgment.

7.3 The Structure of Culpable Intentions

A major conceptual divide runs between the culpability of risk-taking (negligent, reckless, and even knowing risk-taking) and the culpability of intentions. The former is manifested exclusively in running a particular objective risk. The peculiarity of intentions is that they can exist independently prior to actions as well as in acting. This is the difference between intending to kill Mike tomorrow and killing Mike intentionally. One can harbor intentions, reflect on them, even recant and change one's intentions before harm is done. None of this is true about risk-taking. Risks exist in the real world, not just in the mind of the actor.

The simple fact that intentions can exist independently of actions inclines one to accept the following picture of intentional crime: First comes the intention—an internal and private experience, and then comes the action—an external realization of the intention. In the transition from the holding of the intention to the action performed intentionally, the phenomenon of intention supposedly stays the same. The internal mental state, formed before the action, accompanies the action and confers upon it its particular quality as a criminal deed.

This picture of criminal action hardly fits the cases of knowing, reckless, or negligent criminality, but as a plausible rendition of intentional crime it is deeply rooted in the literature of criminal theory. It accounts for one of the basic principles of criminal responsibility: the required union of act and intent.[18] If today I have the intent to steal a specific book, and tomorrow I walk away with the book by mistake, I do not steal it. I must have the intent to steal at the very moment that I walk away with the book. Or recall the scene from the film *Nine to Five*: A secretary wishes to kill her boss. While preparing him a cup of coffee she mistakenly (not accidentally!) puts a substance in the coffee that turns out to be poison. She may have a background plan and even an unconscious intention to kill him, but she does not intentionally poison him. What counts is not the preliminary or the background or subconscious intention of the actor, but the adverbial question: Did the actor intentionally deprive the owner of possession of the book or intentionally induce him to drink poison?

This peculiarity of intentional action—that the intention can exist prior to the action—leads to the appendage of *unrealized* intentions as an aggravating factor for many offenses. An unrealized intention to kill distinguishes simple assault from assault with intent to kill. The intent to commit a felony distinguishes the misdemeanor of possessing a handgun without a licence to the aggravated, felony version of the same offense. Common law burglary was perhaps the first offense to employ this technique. Criminal trespass committed by breaking and entering a house becomes burglary when the act of entering is accompanied by an intent to commit a felony inside the house. In all of these cases, the appended intent is unrealized: it is merely a plan that accompanies the primary action of assault, possessing the gun, or entering the house.

For some not very clear reason, many writers and judges in the common law tradition think that there is a difference between *general* intentions and *specific* intentions. General intentions are simply those that accompany the action, as, for example, the intention to rape accompanies the action of raping. Specific intentions are supposedly well defined, as is the intention required for larceny: the intention to deprive the owner permanently of his or her property. This distinction is illusory for in modern criminal law all intentions are well defined.

In some jurisdictions, the distinction between general and specific intent is used to generate a compromise in the treatment of voluntary intoxication as an excuse. The general rule is that intoxication will negate a specific but not a general intent. These terms "general" and "specific" are then interpreted so that a general intent is equivalent to the intention for the base crime and the specific intent is the factor that aggravates the offense. Thus, intoxication would be admissible to mitigate the offense of assault with intent to kill to simple assault. The significant application, however, occurs in homicide cases. The factor of malice, which distinguishes manslaughter from murder, is treated as a specific intent. The implication is that intoxication can reduce a homicide to manslaughter, but it cannot generate a total excuse to the felony.[19]

There are easy and hard cases of intentional conduct. The easy cases are those in which the actor realizes his criminal ambition. Oswald shoots several times at JFK with the intention of killing him. Oswald kills JFK; that is an easy case. The MPC § 2.02(2)(a), which uses the term "purposely" to mean "intentionally," prescribes simply that "a person acts purposely with respect to . . . a result [of his conduct if] it is his conscious object to . . . cause such a result." It was Oswald's conscious object to kill JFK. Nothing could be more straightforward.

But Connally is standing nearby. One shot hits Connally and severely injures him. With respect to Connally, is Oswald liable for recklessly disregarding the risk or, more seriously, for intentionally causing injury? Under the strict definition of intention as having a conscious object to bring about the result, Oswald did not intend to kill Connally. But a long tradition in the common law supports a broader interpretation of intention to include cases of so-called indirect intentions. The indirect intention includes those side effects that are inevitable or at least practically certain of occurrence. The MPC distinguishes in this context between purposely and knowingly causing harm. Purposefulness is limited to cases of having a conscious object to bring about the result. Knowingly causing death includes cases in which the actor is "practically certain" that his action will cause death.[20]

It is difficult to know whether Oswald was "practically certain" that his shooting at JFK would injure Connally or some other bystander. Of course, if JFK were standing behind Connally, then injuring the two would have been the expected consequence of his shooting. The term "practical certainty" is too ambiguous to apply it with much confidence in a borderline case.

You can imagine a spectrum of cases ranging from Connally standing in front of JFK, to Connally's being in the front seat, to his being in the next car, to his watching the parade from a helicopter. As one proceeds along this spectrum, the odds of hitting Connally decline. The knowledge of certainty that can be attributed to Oswald also declines. At a certain point, wounding Connally would no longer be "knowing"; it would have to be qualified as reckless. And as to Connally riding in a helicopter above, hit by a freakish ricochet, the injury would probably not even be negligent; it would qualify as purely accidental.

So far as the declining scale of culpability is based on probability and imputed knowledge of probability, the approach is purely cognitive. An alternative way of thinking about intentional as opposed to negligent conduct is to focus on the actor's internal posture or attitude toward the harm caused. Does Oswald want or desire to injury either JFK or Connally? The German legal tradition places great emphasis on the *Wissen und Wollen* [knowing and wanting] as the basic elements of intentionally causing harm. It is clear that Oswald desires the death of JFK but what about injuring Connally?

The German response to this question is to interpret the category of intention broadly to include cases where the actor does not affirmatively seek to avoid the harmful result. Oswald was presumably perfectly happy to wound or even kill Connally if necessary to kill Kennedy. The German courts would label this a possible case of *dolus eventualis* or "conditional intent" and ask the refined question whether Oswald "had become reconciled" with the side effects to Connally[21] or had taken this harm into account as a cost of attaining one's goal. These rather weak tests would be sufficient to classify Oswald's assault and battery against Connally as intentional. As translated into the language of the MPC, an attitudinal approach analogous to the standard of *dolus eventualis* would lead to a rather more certain classification of Oswald's shooting Connally as "knowingly" causing bodily injury.

An attitudinal theory of intentions and knowledge leads to a wider range of intentional criminality. Interpreting the notions of wanting and desiring in a case like Oswald's shooting Connally can lead to results that a purely probabilistic or cognitive approach would not favor. Yet practical considerations speak in favor of the common law's cognitive approach.[22] It is difficult to know what the actor really wants. It is not the kind of question that a jury can readily answer. Yet the question of wanting or desiring may be very important in answering the question: Why is intentional conduct worse than reckless risk-taking? The answer might well be that in the case of intentional conduct, the actor invests more of her personality in trying to reach the intended result. The investment of self is expressed in the language of desire. The purely cognitive approach to intention may be easier to apply, but it seems to bear little relationship as to why we assume that *dolus* is much worse than *culpa*.

7.4 On Motives

In ordinary life, we assume that motives matter and provide a basis for distinguishing between really bad and not so bad intentional conduct. For example, a good or bad motive might weigh heavily on the evaluation of a crime like homicide. The motive of bringing about an easy death, euthanasia, is thought to make intentional killing less culpable, while a motive of self-interest, say killing for hire or in order to inherit from the victim, makes the killing worse. Racial hatred is thought to be another consideration that aggravates either intentional killing or intentional battery (causing physical harm).[23] In the case of theft, there is a difference in the popular mind between stealing in order to enjoy a better material existence and stealing in order to avoid starvation. The proper question about all these motives is although they count in popular opinion, should they bear, legally, on the degree of deserved punishment.

One school of thought holds that motives should be irrelevant. The critical question is whether one person voluntarily invades the protected sphere of another. It might be worse to bring about this invasion intentionally rather than negligently, but the actor's ultimate reasons for acting have no bearing either on the degree of wrongdoing or the degree of responsibility.[24] This approach seems to hold for property offenses and perhaps other areas, but motives seem to play a critical role in numerous offenses, for example:

1. *The grading of homicide*. The current American approach to murder considers motives such as premeditation, deliberation, and killing-for-profit. German law explicitly distinguishes between murder and manslaughter, in part, on the ground whether the killer "acted out of base motives."[25]

2. *Hate crimes*. It has become common in American state legislation to punish aggravated assaults on the basis of a motive of racial antipathy.[26] The criminal not only hurts the victim but at the same times issues the insult: "I hate the group for which you stand." The Supreme Court has upheld this form of aggravated liability.[27]

3. *Sado-masochistic beatings*. The general rule that consent will justify physical invasion of the body suffers an exception in the case in which the person inflicting the battery has a sadistic purpose and the recipient receives masochistic pleasure for the beating.[28]

4. *Treason*. Common law treason is committed by adhering to the enemy, giving them aid and comfort. If it turns out that your son is an enemy agent, do you commit treason by providing him with room and board? It all depends on your motive in doing so.[29]

These motives fulfill different functions. They aggravate intentional criminal acts (homicide, hate crimes), override defenses (sado-masochistic beatings), and provide the minimal conditions of liability (treason). A single theory to explain all these functions might not be within our reach. At minimum, bad motives are reasons for acting that put the actor in a bad light. The criminal not only violates the protected sphere of the victim but reveals himself to be a person who can and will act for contemptible reasons.

The more one concentrates on intentions and motives in criminal behavior, the more one is inclined to think that the mere content of these "mental states" renders a criminal blameworthy and subject to punishment. It is as though the intent or the motive provides the core of the crime and the subsequent harmful action merely confirms the wicked state of mind.

The view that the intention is the essence of particular crimes and indeed of crime in general provides support for those who think that negligence is somehow an aberrant form of liability. Intention is choice. It is conscious wickedness. Negligent risk-taking does not derive from a conscious choice, and therefore it is not a proper basis for criminal liability. In this concluding section, I wish to call into question this common way of thinking about the difference between intentional and negligent wrongdoing.

7.5 The Distinction Between Intention and Negligence Revisited

Imagine the following variation on the case of Oswald's shooting and killing JFK. A KGB man is standing behind Oswald with a gun pointed to his head. If you do not hit Kennedy, he says, I will kill you as well as your family. Oswald then shoots. How does this additional factor bear upon the analysis of Oswald's criminal liability? Intuitively, it seems as though Oswald should be able to invoke a defense to defeat or mitigate his guilt. But if he shoots to kill, he does so "intentionally"— though under pressure. This might not be so obvious under a standard of intention that stresses desiring and wanting the final result, but it is obvious under the common law and MPC definition of intention and "the conscious choice" to achieve a particular objective. If Oswald acts intentionally regardless of the gun pointed at his head, how he could possibly escape liability for murder?

The answer is that the KGB agent's pointing a gun at Oswald generates a potential *excuse* for his intentionally killing JFK. The excuse is called "duress" and it rests, according to the MPC § 2.09(1), on "a threat to use unlawful force against his person . . . which a person of reasonable firmness in his situation would have been unable to resist." Intentional wrongdoing is subject to be defeated on grounds of justification, such as self-defense and necessity (considered in the next chapter) as well as excuse, such as duress, insanity, involuntary intoxication, and some forms of mistake. These claims of justification and excuse are integrated into the analysis of reckless and negligent risk-taking, but as to intentional wrongdoing, they are considered extrinsically to the finding of intention. As a result, we have two radically different forms of analysis, which I shall diagram here to elicit their structural similarities.

Reckless and Negligent Risk-Taking

First stage: Did the actor run a substantial risk of harm?

Second stage: If so, was the risk *unjustified?* Let us suppose that in the example above Oswald suddenly turned on the KGB agent and grabbed the latter's rifle, causing it discharge in the direction of the crowd below. This would be a justified risk, in view of the necessity of saving JFK's life.

Third stage: If the risk was unjustified, does the choice to run the risk or the failure to perceive it imply a culpable deviation from the standard of the reasonable person in the actor's situation? If grabbing the KGB agent's rifle in the foregoing example was unjustified, did disregarding the risk to the crowd below violate the standard of the reasonable person in the actor's situation? Possible excuses, such as Oswald's emotional attachment to his threatened family, enter into the definition of the actor's situation.

Intentional Wrongdoing

First stage: Did the actor have the conscious object of injuring the victim? If so, the actor inflicts the injury intentionally.

Second stage: If so, was the act of injuring the victim justified, say on grounds of necessity (lesser evils) or self-defense?

Third stage: If the harmful act was unjustified, did the actor have an excuse for inflicting the harm? If the excuse is duress, were the threats directed against the actor of the sort that "a person of reasonable firmness in [the actor's] situation would have been unable to resist"?

Note the striking parallels in the structure of analysis. With regard both to risk-taking and intentional wrongdoing, the second stage is about the issue of justification and the third stage is about possible excuses. Further, if the excuse is duress, then the question of responsibility is resolved by applying a standard of reasonable conduct in the actor's situation. Other excuses also require us to make a judgment about whether the actor could have overcome the factors that distorted his judgment or his ability to act normally under the circumstances.

In the end, there is only one major difference between the analysis of negligence and of intentional wrongdoing. The affirmation that the harmful conduct was negligent comes *after* the findings at stages two and three that there is no adequate justification or excuse for the conduct. The affirmation of intentional conduct comes *before* the inquiry about justification and excuse. But the intentional conduct is culpable and subject to punishment only if, after the inquiry at stages two and three, the intentional act of harming the victim proves to be both unjustified and unexcused. The conclusion after stage three is the same. The conduct is negligent or reckless because it deviates from the expected conduct of a reasonable person under the circumstances. Similarly, intentional conduct is culpable only if the intentional actor deviates from the expected conduct of a reasonable person under the alleged circumstances of excuse.

In neither case does the mere act of choice render the actor culpable. We established this point in analyzing responsibility for recklessness, where we concluded:

> The choice to disregard the risk is not per se culpable; it is culpable only if it falls short of the community standard of reasonable [law-abiding] behavior.

It turns out that the same proposition applies, with a slight change of wording, to the case of someone who intentionally causes harm under duress: "The choice to cause the harm is not per se culpable; it is culpable only if it falls short of the community standard of resisting threats to the same degree as would a person of reasonable firmness."

This is an extremely important finding, for it undermines the widespread belief that choice is the essence of culpable action and because there is no choice in a case of negligence, negligence cannot qualify as a form of *mens rea*. It turns out that both culpable intention and negligence must be judged under a community standard of reasonable behavior under the circumstances. What do we fairly expect of people whose actions might cause harm to others? That they become aware of the risk latent in their conduct? Yes, but only so as can be fairly excepted under the standard of a "reasonable person in the actor's situation." That they resist threats to themselves and to others? Yes, but only so as can be fairly expected under the standard of a "person of reasonable firmness."

You could look at the difference between negligence and recklessness, on the one hand, and intention, on the other, as the difference between a conclusive judgment of culpability and a mere presumption of culpability. In the case of negligence and recklessness, because the possible claims of justification and excuse are built into the respective definitions, a finding of negligence or recklessness proves to be conclusive on the question of culpability or blameworthiness. In the case of intentional conduct, however, the finding of an intentional injury is merely presumptive of culpability and criminal liability. The presumption can be defeated by a good claim of justification or excuse.

This chapter began with the stark contrast between intention and negligence. We find, in conclusion, that this distinction is oversimplified. There are important conceptual differences between causing harm intentionally and causing harm negligently. Intentions exist prior to action; indifference to risk comes into being with the risk itself. Yet the culpability of intentional conduct bears a structural resemblance to the culpability of negligent risk-taking. Both judgments of culpability require an assessment of justification and excuse. The only difference is that intentions are analyzed prior to a consideration of these "defenses" while the criteria of justification and excuse are included in the definition of reckless and negligent risk-taking. This is one of those conceptual distinctions in the law that probably has a greater impact on the pattern of our thinking than it deserves.

Notes

1. There is an interesting exception for accidental discoveries. If a scientist stumbles upon a great discovery while trying to do something totally different, the discovery is hers—it is attributable to her actions. For further discussion of this exception, see George P. Fletcher, Basic Concepts of Legal Thought 97–98 (1996).

2. See the earlier discussion in chapter 4 at pp. 60–62.

3. See T.J. Hooper, 60 F.2d 737 (2d Cir. 1932).

4. See Caldwell, [1982] A.C. 341, which rejects the assumption that recklessness presupposes consciousness.

5. See E.R. Shipp, Can a Corporation Commit Murder? The New York Times, May 19, 1985, Sec. 4, P. 2.

6. See, most notably, Glanville Williams, Textbook of Criminal Law 90–91 (2d ed. 1983); Jerome Hall, *Negligent Behavior Should Be Excluded from Penal Liability*, 63 Colum. L. Rev. 632 (1963).

7. See StGB §309 (negligent arson), §163 (negligent perjury).

8. For an excellent and nuanced study of women as criminal offenders, see Anne Coughlin, *Excusing Women*, 82 Cal. L. Rev. 1 (1994).

9. 138 Mass. 165 (1884).

10. Id. at 176. Note that Holmes is not using the term "reckless" in the sense stipulated in MPC sec. 2.02(c).

11. For a discussion of these cases, see A Crime of Self-Defense at 47–50.

12. See Richard Singer in the New York Law Journal, February 18, 1986, p.1.

13. See People v. Goetz, 68 N.Y. 96, 497 N.E.2d 41 (1986).

14. MPC §2.02(c).

15. Holmes wrote that the law should pay no heed to "the infinite varieties of temperament, intellect and education which make the internal character of a given act so different." O.W. Holmes, Jr., The Common Law 108 (1881).

16. See A Crime of Self-Defense at 205–07.

17. See State v. Wanrow, 559 P.2d 548 (Wash. 1977).

18. See, e.g., California Penal Code §20; Williams, supra note 6, at 154–58.

19. For an example of confusion in this area, see the decision by the Canadian Supreme Court in R. v. Daviault, [1994] 3 S.C.R. 63 (S.C.C.) (intoxication negates specific intent).

20. MPC §2.02(2)(b).

21. This is a liberal translation of the German phrase: *sich mit der Rechtsgutverletzung abfinden.* On this and other formulae for defining *dolus eventualis,* see Cramer in Schönke-Schröder, §15, notes 68–79.

22. In the common law as well, some writers favored an approach that considers elements of desiring and wanting. See Holmes, supra note 15, at 53 ("the wish" for specified consequences is an essential aspect of intention); J. Salmond, Jurisprudence 393 (7th ed. 1924).

23. For a critical view of the popular trend, see Anthony Dillof, *Punishing Bias: An Examination of the Theoretical Foundations of Bias Crime Statutes,* 91 Northwestern L. Rev. 1015 (1997).

24. On these critical concepts in the theory of deserved punishment, see chapter 3 above.

25. StGB §211(2).

26. See Dillof, supra note 23, at 1016.

27. Wisconsin v. Mitchell, 113 S.Ct. 2194 (1993).

28. See Regina v. Brown, [1993] 2 All E.R. 75, 84 (H.L.) (rejecting human rights argument against punishing sado-masochism).

29. See United States v. Haupt, 330 U.S. 631 (1947).

8

Self-Defense versus
Necessity

As we noted in the analysis of intentional and negligent criminality, claims of justification and excuse pervade the criminal law. The definition of intentional wrongdoing enables us to see the criteria of justification and excuse in bold relief, for these issue are considered on their footing, as "defenses" to crime. This conclusion of chapter 7 provides a bridge to the topic we now consider: claims of self-defense and necessity, both as claims of excuse and of justification.

These two ideas—self-defense and necessity—are leitmotifs for charting the history of criminal responsibility in its various stages of development. Both ideas emerge relatively early as excusing conditions and, in the course of history, generate claims of justification that function either as the supplement or as the replacement of their original excusing functions.

8.1 *Se Defendendo* and Necessity as Excuses

Excuses express compassion. The assumption is that there are situations in life in which people have no choice but to engage in harmful and unjust actions. Their back is to the wall. They must steal or kill in order to survive. They or their children are starving and therefore they must grab the nearest loaf of bread. They are stranded at sea. They must dislodge someone else from the only available plank in order to survive. But these actions are unjust for they entail attacks on innocent people—or at least on people who are not wrongful aggressors themselves.

From roughly the thirteenth to the sixteenth century, the only form of self-defense recognized at common law was *se defendendo*, which came into consideration whenever a fight broke out and one party retreated as far as he could go before resorting to defensive force. If he then killed the aggressor, *se defendendo* had the effect of saving the defendant from execution, but it left intact the other stigmatizing effects of the criminal law. The defendant forfeited his goods as expiation of his having taken human life. The murder weapon was also forfeited to the crown as a deodand, a tainted object. Killing *se defendendo* was called excusable homicide, for though the wrong of homicide had occurred, the circumstances generated a personal excuse that saved the manslayer from execution.

The defense of *se defendendo* springs more from compassion for the predicament of the trapped defender than from a passion for justice or the dictates of reason. If we would all act the same way if caught in the same circumstances, we can hardly condemn and execute the manslayer who had no reasonable alternative.

As discussed, Immanuel Kant responded to the same criteria of compassion when he recognized the excuse of necessity in the famous case of a shipwrecked sailor who, under the pressure of circumstance, "shoves another, whose life is equally in danger, off a plank on which he has saved himself."[1] Though the life-saving act of the shipwrecked sailor is wrong, the actor enjoys a subjective or personal immunity from punishment. Thus, the life-threatening situation comes into relief as a basis for excusing conduct in the same way that the circumstances of killing excuse the deed in a case of *se defendendo*. Both acts occur under overwhelming pressure. In neither case does the need reflect negatively on the character of the offender. The circumstances block any possible inference from the deed to the nature of the person who committed the deed. In the end, we can fault the act of killing an innocent person, but we cannot blame the person caught in a maelstrom of circumstance.

Se defendendo was an early form of self-defense, and necessity was an analogous excuse that was rooted in the instinct of survival. Though at their outset these excuses were similar in their structure and function, their subsequent evolution differs sharply. In 1532 Parliament recognized that self-defense could be a justification in specific cases;[2] the consequence was that the person who used deadly force would be totally acquitted. There was no longer a forfeiture of property to signify the unlawful and wrongful nature of the killing. *Se defendendo* coexisted with the newly recognized justification well into the nineteenth century, but it gradually fell into desuetude.

Se defendendo could have provided the framework for the recognition of a claim of necessity comparable to Kant's theory of necessity as a personal excuse. But that expansion, which could have been easily justified, never occurred in the common law. The weakness of the common law to cope with situations comparable to that of Kant's hypothetical shipwrecked sailor became obvious when at the end of the nineteenth century, the English courts confronted a case of problematic conduct committed under the urgent necessity of an actual shipwreck on the high seas. After prolonged deprivation of food and water, two sailors on a raft, Dudley and Stephens, decided to kill and cannibalize an ailing cabin boy named Parker. They, as well as a third shipmate, survived and were subsequently charged with murder.

The Queens Bench confronted the challenge of finding a basis in the common law either to justify or to excuse homicide in extremis.[3] Neither option received serious consideration. There seemed to be no possibility of justifying the intentional killing of an innocent person. And though an excuse seemed to be plausible, the English court never perceived the analogy between *se defendendo* and the killing committed by Dudley and Stephens under circumstances of comparable necessity. Nor did it see that there might be an analogy between the recognized defense of duress, based on threats from a human being, and the threat of imminent death faced by Dudley and Stephens. Though the Court lacked compassion for the urgency of the situation, the Queen heeded the widespread understanding at the time that no one could plausibly blame the shipwrecked sailors for seeking to survive, even by unjust means. The Crown commuted the Court's sentence of death to six months' imprisonment.[4]

German law evolved differently. Kant's discussion of the plank case influenced the drafting of the first pan-German Criminal Code in 1871. A clearly stated provision on personal necessity, § 54, became a cornerstone of the Bismarckian Reich's national jurisprudence. The provision covers threats both that derive from natural forces and those issued by human agents. Though the 1871 code was ambiguous about whether particular defenses were claims of excuse or justification, the theoretical literature began to treat necessity precisely as Kant opined: as a factor that denied not the wrongfulness but only the personal culpability of the necessitated act.

On the basis of this provision in their code, German scholars could not quite comprehend the decision of the Queen's Bench in *Dudley & Stephens*. It seemed obvious that the shipwrecked sailors should have been excused for their admittedly wrongful act. By the end of the nineteenth century, then, Anglo-American and German law had taken different turns on the relevance of necessity as an excuse.

8.2 Self-Defense as a Justification

The Western notion of self-defense as a justification originates, if not earlier, in the biblical passage authorizing a homeowner to kill a burglar breaking into his private sphere. Exodus 22:1 provides, according to many translations, that no blood be shed for the thief slain while breaking in. Another interpretation of the Hebrew text *(lo damim lo)* is that the homeowner should bear no blood guilt for the slain thief, the implication being that this was a justified and lawful slaying.

As the justificatory nature of self-defense emerged in Western legal thought, the principle of justification took on two different forms. One form rested on the supreme importance of each person's life. The core case of self-defense was repelling aggression in order to save one's own life.[5] These origins are reflected in the denomination used in the Model Penal Code (MPC): "Use of Force in Self-Protection" (MPC § 3.04). From this core case, the defense gradually expanded in two directions— first, toward lesser interests such as physical and sexual integrity and even property;[6] and second, toward the protection of third persons whose equivalent interests are threatened, example, MPC § 3.05: "Use of Force for the Protection of Other Persons." At common law, for example, the use of force to protect third parties was limited to people closely related to or otherwise under the protection of the actor. After a long process of development, the defense of others now enjoys contours parallel to the defense of self.

German legal culture took a different line of development. At a relatively early stage, the notion of self-defense expanded to include all rights that might be subject to attack. Thus, the term to describe the defense was not "self" defense but "necessary defense" *(Notwehr)*. In Latin legal cultures, the analogous term is "legitimate defense" *(legitima defensa)*. The centerpiece of the defense is not life or safety as protectible interests but rather the legal sphere of the individual as defined by the range of personal rights. The defense has a distinctly libertarian grounding. The freedom and the autonomy of the individual are absolutes that require defense by the use of force to repel incursions and encroachments.

The problem in Continental European, particularly in German legal, culture has not been how to expand but rather how to curtail the range of protected rights. This has been hotly disputed, as we shall see, with regard to the use of deadly force to protect interests in property.

Despite these differences in line of development, most legal systems today share legislation that focuses on four characteristics of self-defense or necessary defense. These four characteristics are the issues of imminence, necessity, proportionality, and an intention to repel the attack. Let us take a close look as these four general requirements and their variations.[7]

The requirement of *imminence* means that the time for the use of force will brook no delay. The defender cannot wait any longer. This requirement distinguishes self-defense from the illegal use of force in two temporally related ways. A preemptive strike against a feared aggressor is illegal force used too soon; and retaliation against a successful aggressor is illegal force used too late. Legitimate self-defense must be neither too soon nor too late.

In the case of a preemptive strike, the defender calculates that the enemy is planning an attack or surely is likely to attack in the future, and therefore it is wiser to strike first than to wait until the actual aggression. Preemptive strikes are illegal in international law as they are illegal internally in every legal system of the world. They are illegal because they are not based on a visible manifestation of aggression; they are grounded in a prediction of how the feared enemy is likely to behave in the future.

In cases of interpersonal as well as international violence, the outbreak might be neither defensive nor preemptive. It could be simply a passionate retaliation for past wrongs suffered by the person resorting to violence. Retaliatory acts seek to even the score—to inflict harm because harm has been suffered in the past.

Retaliation, as opposed to defense, is a common problem in cases arising from wife battering and domestic violence. The injured wife waits for the first possibility of striking against a distracted or unarmed husband.[8] The aggressor may even be asleep when the response comes. Retaliation is the standard case of "taking the law into one's own hands." There is no way, under the law, to justify killing a wife batterer or a rapist as retaliation or revenge, however much sympathy there may be for the wife or rape victim wreaking retaliation. Private citizens cannot function as judge and jury toward each other. They have no authority to pass judgment and to punish each other for past wrongs.

In fact, those who defend battered women who strike back rarely admit that their purpose is retaliation for a past wrong. The argument typically is that the actor feared a recurrence of the past violence, thus the focus shifts from past to future violence, from retaliation to an argument of defending against an imminent attack. This is the standard maneuver in battered-wife cases. In view of her prior abuse, the wife arguably has reason to fear renewed violence. Killing a battering husband while he is asleep then comes into focus as an arguably legitimate defensive response rather than an illegitimate act of vengeance for past wrongs.

There has been some dispute lately about the imminence requirement. The MPC § 3.04 ambiguously substituted a test of immediately necessary, namely, whether the defender "believes that such force is immediately necessary for the purpose of protecting himself." The requirement of immediacy should run parallel to the standard of imminence. If the feared aggressor is sleeping or still looking around for a weapon, it is hard to qualify the action as "immediately" necessary. Nonetheless, there are many voices in the literature favoring a loosening of the imminence or immediacy requirement in order, primarily, to alleviate the conditions of battered women who kill.[9]

The *necessity* of the defensive response is in fact a distinct requirement. Think of the situation of Bernhard Goetz in a New York subway, surrounded by four young "street toughs" demanding money. Goetz shot at all four, causing permanent injury to one, Darrell Cabey. Were these shots necessary under the circumstances? Was there an effective response less drastic than firing at the four feared assailants? Would it not have been enough merely to show the gun in its holster? Or to draw and point the weapon without firing?

The uneven grind of the accelerating train made Goetz's footing uncertain. During his initial exchange he rose to his feet and was standing in close quarters with his feared assailants. Showing the gun in the holster or drawing it would have risked one of the four young men taking the gun away and shooting him. Gauging necessity under the circumstances turns, in the end, on an elusive prediction of what would have happened if Goetz had tried this or that maneuver short of shooting. There is no objective way of knowing for sure what indeed was necessary under the circumstances.

The requirement of *proportionality* adds a problem beyond the necessity of the defensive response. To understand the distinction between proportionality and necessity, think about the ratio between the means of resistance and the gravity of the attack. Necessity speaks to the question whether some less costly means of defense, such as merely showing the gun or firing a warning shot into the air, might be sufficient to ward off the attack. The requirement of proportionality addresses the ratio of interest threatened both on the side of the aggressor and of the defender. The harm done in disabling the aggressor must not be excessive or disproportionate relative to the harm threatened and likely to result from the attack.

Some examples will illuminate the distinction. Suppose that a liquor store owner has no means of preventing a thief from escaping with a few bottles of scotch except to shoot him. Most people would recoil from the notion that protecting property justifies shooting and risking the death of escaping thieves. It is better from a social or collective point of view to suffer the theft of a few bottles of liquor than to inflict serious physical harm on a fellow human being. The principle of proportionality holds, in effect, that the aggressor remains a human being, even when he threatens the rights of another, and therefore the interests of the aggressor must also be relevant in drawing the limits of defensive force.

It is not simply that property rights must sometimes give way to our concern for the lives and well-being even of aggressors. Suppose that the only way for a woman to avoid being touched by a man harassing her is to respond with deadly force—by, say, cutting him with a razor blade. May she engage in this act necessary for her defense rather than suffer the personal indignity of being touched? It is not so clear. Of course, if she were threatened with rape, she could use every necessary means at her disposal to protect herself. No legal system in the Western world would expect a woman to endure a rape if her only means of defense required that she risk the death of her aggressor.

Proportionality in self-defense requires a balancing of competing interests, the interests of the defender and those of the aggressor. As the innocent party in the fray, a woman defending against rape has interests that weigh more than those of the aggressor. She may kill to ward off a threat to her sexual autonomy, but she has no license to take life in order to avoid every minor interference with her body. If the only way she can avoid being touched is to kill, that response seems clearly to be excessive relative to the interests at stake. Even if our thumb is on the scale in favor of the defender, there comes a point at which the aggressor's basic human interests will outweigh those of an innocent victim, thumb and all. There is obviously no way to determine the breaking point, even theoretically. At a certain point our sensibilities are triggered, our compassion for the human being behind the mask of the evil aggressor is engaged, and we have to say "Stop! That's enough."

The common law tradition has had a much easier time with the problem of proportionality than has the German legal system. For English lawyers, the question was always: Which interests justify the use of deadly force? They had little trouble concluding that petty interests in property would be insufficient to justify taking the life of the aggressor. Blackstone captured this sentiment when he formulated the test: No act "may be prevented by death unless the same, if committed, would also be punished by death."[10] Since petty theft was not punished capitally, the defender could not use deadly force to protect minor interests in property.

German lawyers backed themselves into a conceptual trap by positing that anyone whose rights are threatened may use deadly force to assert and defend his legal sphere. John Locke concurred that one should not yield an inch to an aggressor.[11] The idea of law requires the use of force to defend threatened rights. Kant conceded that as a matter of "ethics" one might let the petty thief get away rather than kill him,[12] but the law should not require people to surrender their rights, however minor, to aggressors.

To modify this extreme position on the sanctity of rights, German criminal lawyers have brought to bear the civil law doctrine of "abuse of rights." Conceding that in principle the property owner had a right to kill the escaping petty thief, the owner would still commit a crime if he exercised his right in an abusive way. This may seem like a self-contradictory way of thinking, but it seems necessary both to recognize the absolute right of self defense as provided in the German Criminal

Code § 32 and apply the principle of proportionality in recognition of the aggressor's humanity.

The preceding three characteristics of self-defense—imminence, necessity, and proportionality—speak to the objective characteristics of the attack and the defense in response. In addition, according to the consensus among Western legal systems, the defender must know about the attack and act with the *intention* of repelling it. Why should someone invoking deadly force receive the benefit of a justification if he acted maliciously, without fear of attack? Surprisingly, some leading scholars think that in a case of criminal homicide, the accused should be able to invoke self-defense, even if he does not know about the attack.[13] Their argument is that if you cannot be guilty of homicide by killing someone who is already dead (no matter what your intent), you should not be guilty of homicide by killing an aggressor (no matter what your intent). No harm, no crime. And there is arguably no harm in killing an aggressor.

Yet there is an important moral difference between pumping lead into a dead body and killing an aggressor in self-defense. We can comfortably say that there is no harm in the former case (except perhaps interference with a dead body), but injuring or killing a human being remains a harm, even if the harm is inflicted in self-defense. If they are victims of self-defense (unlike dead bodies that are not harmed), the least the law can demand is that the defender inflict harm only when he has a good reason to act. If he does not know that he is being attacked, he cannot have a good reason for killing another human being.

The danger in modern legislation is employing, in simplified statutory language, the requirement of *intended* self-defense as the solvent for dissolving the objective requirements of imminence and necessity into the defender's perceptions of these features of the situation. According to the MPC, for example, "the use of force . . . is justifiable when the actor *believes* that such force is immediately necessary for the purpose of protecting himself against the use of unlawful force. . . ."

The only fact that need be established is the actor's belief in the immediate necessity of using force. If Goetz believed that he had to shoot to defend himself, then he had a good claim of self-defense (if his belief was unreasonable or he was negligent in his belief, he would lose the defense if charged with an offense committed negligently, MPC § 3.09(2)). The upshot of this subjectification of self-defense is the elimination of the difference between real self-defense and reasonably mistaken self-defense.[14]

Continental European lawyers are very clear about the difference between real self-defense and mistaken or putative self-defense. The principles of self-defense address a conflict in the real world, a conflict between an aggressor and an innocent person. When the criteria of the defense are reduced to the actor's belief, in the style of the MPC, then the real conflict is transformed into a problem of good faith or reasonable belief in using force.

8.3 Necessity or Lesser Evils as a Justification

The general idea behind necessity as a justification in criminal cases is that it is lawful and right to violate a nominal criminal prohibition in order to save another legal interest that is at risk. It is correct, for example, to take your neighbor's car, if there are no alternative means available, in order to get your seriously ill child to the emergency room. It is socially desirable to blow up a privately owned house in order to prevent the spread of a raging fire. It is correct, as well, to abort a fetus at the early stages of gestation in order to save the life of the woman carrying the fetus. The critical difference between self-defense and necessity is that necessity legitimates an invasion against the interests of a totally innocent party (the neighbor whose car is taken or house is blown up, the fetus aborted).

Violence in self-defense is always directed against an aggressor and for that reason, proportionately more force is permitted in self-defense than in cases of necessity. For example, everyone agrees that a woman threatened with rape may kill the sexual aggressor. But it would be difficult to justify, under principles of necessity and balancing evils, a greater harm to the threatening rapist than the female is likely to suffer. Using numbers to make the point, let us suppose that the rape represents a harm of 50 and high probability of death stands for a harm of 70 to the aggressor. This disparity would be permissible under the principle of proportionality demanded in cases of self-defense, but it would not be acceptable under the criteria of necessity as a justification.

The remarkable feature of necessity as a justification is its relatively recent vintage. If you look back to the criminal codes of the nineteenth century, you will not find a single one that recognizes the general principle that it is lawful and right to violate a criminal prohibition in order to ward off an imminent risk of even greater harm. For codes revised in this century, necessity has become a standard feature of the criminal law. This is true not only in Germany[15] and the United States,[16] but in the countries of the former Soviet Union.[17] Why does necessity emerge as a latecomer to criminal justice while self-defense is deeply rooted in the history of legitimate violence?

The answer is revealing. Self-defense is grounded in the principle of individual rights and individual survival. The foundation of necessity is not the individual perspective but the collective point of view. Individual actors, acting in necessity, are supposed to think about the costs and benefits of their conduct for the society as a whole. It is good for the society to blow up a house to prevent the spread of a fire, and that neutral Archimedean view of the action justifies the intrusion against an innocent, nonaggressive party.

The remarkable fact about Western legal systems converging on necessity as a justification is that there are at least two distinct philosophical foundations for the claim. The German system came to recognize the claim of lesser evils by way of judicial recognition of transcendental norms in the legal system. Lawyers in the Anglo-American tradition have argued for the same theory as an offshoot of positivist and utilitarian theories of law. The point of the ensuing discussion is to trace how these divergent traditions have converged on a single defense with comparable contours.

Though the German Criminal Code of 1871 failed to recognize necessity as a justification, the BGB, or Civil Code, which came into force in 1900, identifies two distinct grounds for the justified invasion of property interests. Both of these applied in criminal as well as civil cases. BGB § 228 provides that destroying or damaging "the object of another in order to avert an imminent risk to himself or another" is not wrongful. The actor is liable for damages only if he faultfully brought about the risk. This situation is exemplified by the facts in *Cross v. State*,[18] in which a rancher shot and killed marauding moose in order to prevent them from destroying his crops.[19]

BGB § 904 requires owners of property to tolerate intrusions "if the intrusion is necessary to avert an imminent risk and the harm avoided is disproportionately large relative to the harm that accrues to the owner of the object." Under the latter provision, the owner is always entitled to collect damages. This situation is illustrated by two leading tort cases, *Ploof v. Putnam*[20] and *Vincent v. Lake Erie Trans. Co.*[21] In the former case, a ship captain sought to take refuge from a storm by mooring his ship to another's dock. The dock owner refused to permit the mooring and the ship was destroyed in the storm. The court held that the dock owner was obligated to tolerate the intrusion under the circumstances and therefore was liable for damages to the ship. The *Vincent* case supplements this principle by holding that if the dock owner does tolerate the intrusion and suffers damages to the dock, he can collect damages from the ship owner taking refuge from the storm. Both of these rules are incorporated in the German Civil Code §§ 904, 906.

These were the only justificatory provisions recognized in the early twentieth century.[22] If the interest invaded was something other than property, neither of these provisions from the BGB would apply. The recurrent problem in the early decades of the century was abortion to save the life of the mother. The injury to the fetus was not an injury to property and therefore fell outside the justificatory provisions of the civil code. If the physician was unrelated to the mother, the Criminal Code provision on necessity as an excuse (§ 54) could not prevent a conviction of the physician for illegal abortion. Thus, it was in abortion cases that the German courts faced the greatest pressure to expand the range of justificatory claims.

The decisive case broadening the range of justificatory grounds came to the German Supreme Court in 1927.[23] A German physician ordered an abortion after he diagnosed a serious risk of suicide if the distraught mother were required to carry an apparently illegitimate child to term. The case had been tried twice, and both times the trial courts had acquitted the physician as well as the mother. Yet the German system does not permit nullification of the law at the trial level, for the prosecution is empowered to appeal an acquittal. In the second round, the prosecutor only appealed the acquittal against the physician who had authorized the abortion.

It was fairly clear that under the statutory law of the time, the physician was guilty. The relevant provision of the code, § 218(3), proscribed "the killing of the fetus." There was no reference to an exemption or possibility of justification in cases of danger to the life of the mother, nor was there any modifying word in the statutory proscription, such as "maliciously" or "unlawfully," that might have lent itself to interpretation on behalf of the defendant. He killed the fetus and there was no recognized claim of justification or excuse. By the letter of the statutory law, he was patently guilty.

The narrow point of this dramatic decision was the recognition of a new theory of justification: the abortion would be justified if, after conscientious weighing of the competing interests, the doctor properly concluded that the interests of the mother outweighed those of the fetus.[24] To grasp the Court's reasoning, we have to recall the commitment of the German legal culture to a notion of Law as Right, a set of principles justifiable on their intrinsic rectitude.

If the Law as principle is understood as going beyond the enacted, positive law, then the conduct that violates the Law—the act of wrongdoing—must also be seen as bearing negative moral condemnation. The indispensability of wrongdoing and of "wrongful" conduct in criminal prosecutions provided the pillar for the German Supreme Court's erecting a new theory of extrastatutory justification. As the Court wrote in 1927: "The concept of an offense requires both that the alleged conduct conform to the definition of the offense and that it be wrongful (*rechtswidrig*)."[25] The judges in the abortion case interpreted the requirement of wrongfulness to permit the judicial recognition of a new claim of justification, based on the balancing of competing interests and the favoring of the lesser evil. Thus, the social principle of minimizing costs to society entered into the German concept of Right. Acting in the name of greater good (lesser evil) was socially justified conduct. Aborting the fetus to save the life of the mother was deemed, therefore, to be justified. The general principle recognized in this precedent shaped the course of German law for nearly half a century.[26] When the new Criminal Code was enacted in 1975, the judicially developed justification of extrastatutory necessity finally found legislative grounding.

Section 34 of the new code restates and refines the applicable law:

> Whoever engages in action in order to thwart an imminent risk, to himself or another, to Life, Limb, Liberty, Honor, Property or other Legally protected Interest, acts not wrongfully, provided that in comparing the two conflicting interests, the interest protected substantially outweighs the interest invaded. This provision applies only so far as the action is an appropriate means to thwart the risk.

This provision provides a useful perspective on the evolution of the common law. After the nearly fatal setback to the principle of necessity in the *Dudley & Stephens* case, the social principle of serving the greater good eventually prevailed, at least in American law. The MPC struck an innovative position by adopting the following language:

> § 3.02. Justification Generally: Choice of Evils.
>
> (1) Conduct which the actor believes to be necessary to avoid a harm or evil to himself or to another is justifiable, provided that:
>
>> (a) the harm or evil sought to be avoided by such conduct is greater than that sought to be prevented by the law defining the offense charged; and
>>
>> (b) neither the Code nor other law defining the offense provides exceptions or defenses dealing with the specific situation involved; and
>>
>> (c) a legislative purpose to exclude the justification claimed does not otherwise plainly appear.

The general outlines of the German and MPC provision are similar, but there are important differences.

First, the MPC does not recognize the necessity of an imminent risk of harm. This is a peculiar omission. It would be far-fetched to recognize the claim of necessity when there is no pressing need to act. Imagine that a group of homeless people decide to camp out in your living room. They think it is "necessary" to do so to avoid the risks of sleeping outside in the dead of winter. That surely cannot be enough, even if it is the case that objectively speaking, the danger to the homeless outweighs the loss to you of giving up your living room.

As the code has been adapted by the courts and several state legislatures,[27] the requirement of imminent risk has asserted itself. In *Kroncke v. United States*,[28] the defendant sought to justify the stealing of draft cards on the ground that interfering with the Selective Service would shorten the war in Vietnam and thus save endangered human lives. The Court of Appeals rejected the defense and asserted a version of the requirement of imminent risk. The defense of necessity applies, the judges reasoned, only if the action was undertaken to avoid a "direct and immediate peril."[29] A more tolerant view of the defense would be incompatible with the basic obligation in a democracy to resort to legitimate political means as the way to further the common good.

Second, unlike the German code, the MPC defers to the legislature's intent to regulate specific areas of possible criminal behavior. If legislated language appears "to exclude the justification claimed," then the legislative will prevails. Implicitly, the defense of necessity is grounded not in a high principle of law but rather in legislative delegation. Because the legislature cannot foresee all variations of conflicted situations, it allows the courts to act in its place in working out the details of the social interest. Of course, if the legislature has the confidence that it can exhaustively regulate a high-profile field such as abortion, then its judgment preempts judicial power in the field.

Third, the MPC describes the defense of necessity as "justification generally." This is a peculiar use of language, which suggests that the drafters of the MPC regarded the principle of balancing conflicting interests to be the single universal ground of justification. This interpretation is supported by § 3.01, which describes "justification" as an "affirmative defense," using the term "justification" not as a category of diverse defenses but as a single defense with different instantiations, such as self-defense, defense of others, defense of property, and the like. Favoring the greater interest, then, becomes the foundation of all justificatory claims.

This position, adopted almost casually in the MPC, represents a revolution in judicial thinking. The principle of necessity as a justification enters the law in the twentieth century and seems immediately to conquer and displace the distinct rationale of necessary defense. Recall that self-defense or necessary defense is grounded in the supremacy of individual rights; necessity speaks in the idiom of the collective interest in minimizing harm. To ignore this radical disparity in perspective is to trivialize the ideas that have shaped the history of criminal law.[30]

To summarize, the evolution of German law is based on the recognition of the collective interest in minimizing harm as a higher transpositive principle of law. The American doctrine of necessity, as manifested in the MPC, is both positivist and utilitarian. It is positivist so far as it recognizes judicial rulings on necessity as surrogate legislation; it is utilitarian for it prescribes the balancing of interests as the correct mode of rendering these quasi-legislative decisions. The end result in concrete cases might be the same, but the rationale for getting there rests on different philosophical premises.

8.4 Conflicts Between Self-Defense and Necessity

So far as they both function as claims of justification, self-defense and necessity collide in their sphere of application. Self-defense offers the advantage of permitting a greater use of force against aggressors than is admissible under the strict balancing of interests under the principle of necessity. In view of this advantage, the contours of self-defense come under pressure. Theorists are constantly tempted to nudge cases from the realm of necessity into the domain of self-defense. For example, a moving (but not acting) human body or a growing fetus is not properly labeled an aggressor, but many people are tempted to fudge in these cases so that the case is considered one of self-defense and killing becomes a permissible option.[31] This kind of ambivalence about abortion is evident in Jewish law, which originally held in the Talmud that a fetus threatening the welfare of the pregnant woman is not an aggressor *(rodef)*[32] but later, in Maimonides, supported the view that abortion is justified as akin to defending against an aggressor.[33]

A major arena of conflict between the two defenses is the case of faultless aggression, typified by the problem of being trapped in an elevator with an obviously psychotic aggressor. If you have no other way of saving your life, you may certainly kill the psychotic aggressor without risking conviction for murder. The problem is whether the appropriate ground of defense is an excuse of either self-defense or necessity or a justification of either self-defense or necessity. It is easy to solve the case as a matter of excuse, but this fails to account for our intuition that if a third party stranger had to choose between you and the aggressor, he would be right and proper in favoring you, the innocent victim facing death, over the aggressor endangering your life. An excuse of necessity would be limited to parties who stand in a closer relationship with you.

So far as common law scholars have addressed this problem, they have argued in the language of necessity without ever being very clear whether they think of necessity as an excuse or a justification.[34] The interesting question is whether one can *justify* killing the psychotic aggressor under a theory of balancing the conflicting interests? We would have to find that the interest protected was greater (and substantially greater under the German code) than the probable consequences to the assailant. Yet the most that can be gained from the use of deadly force to repel the attack is the saving of one's life. If it is life against life, it is hard to see why we should say that it is right and proper for one person to live and the other to die.

The fact is that in the case of the psychotic aggressor, we are inclined to favor an acquittal, even if the loss to the aggressor is greater than the gain to the defendant. Indeed, for all the defending party knows is that there is only a possibility of death if he does not resist.

To fend off this possibility, he chooses the highly probable death of the aggressor. When probability factors are included in assessing the competing interests, it is clear the defendant engages in conduct with a higher expected loss (near certain death) than expected gain (a probability of death). Would it make any difference if the defendant were threatened with loss of limb, rape, or castration? One would think not.

The commentators who have looked at the problem as one of necessity may well have thought that the life of the insane aggressor is worth less than the life of the defendant who is standing his ground. One finds analogies between psychotic aggressors and attacks by wild animals.[35] If one thinks of the psychotic aggressor as subhuman, one might be able to justify the defensive killing as an act preserving the greater value. This is an intriguing if startling approach, but one that is apparently inadequate. Among its other defects it fails to account for the case of temporary psychosis. If the aggressor is a brilliant but temporarily deranged scientist, it would seem rather odd to say that his life is worth less than that of his victim, who for all we know might be a social pariah.[36]

The better way to solve the problem of the psychotic aggressor is to recognize that the aggression against which self-defense is directed must be wrongful but not necessarily culpable aggression. This requirement, explicit in the German code and the MPC, also provides that the actor must believe in the necessity of repelling "unlawful force." In a later convoluted provision of the MPC, § 3.11, the drafters indicate that they regard the aggression of a psychotic as "unlawful." The argument for legitimating the use of force against wrongful but not culpable aggression is that an unjustified breach of the legal order encroaches upon the freedom and the autonomy of another person. The primacy of individual rights, then, leads to the view that everyone in the society should be able to intervene to defend and restore the legal order. The only way to do this, arguably, is to repel the attack—whatever the cost. If there is a justification for the intrusion, then, of course, it is no longer wrongful or unlawful.

This way of analyzing the problem of the psychotic aggressor admittedly has a classic ring to it. This is the traditional Kantian and Lockian way of thinking about the sanctity of individual freedom. The aggressor is the enemy, whether he is culpable or not. The classic view of self-defense has extreme consequences. It was difficult, for example, to qualify the degree of permissible force by the principle of proportionality.[37] After all, if freedom is the absolute, then there should be nothing wrong with shooting a thief escaping with a petty bounty.[38] Defending the rights of the free, it was thought, demands no less.

The tendency in German theory today is to recognize the humanity of the aggressor, both with regard to the issue of proportionality ("abuse of rights") and the relevance of the aggressor's culpability. If the aggressor is not culpable, the demands of proportionality restrict the scope of permissible self-defense.[39] Linking the culpability of the aggressor with the permissible degree of defensive force seems, however, to confuse the institutions of punishment and of self-defense. The question of the aggressor's personal desert intrudes upon the analysis of the measures the potential victim may use to defend his rights. If the wrongful nature of the attack, whether by a psychotic or a culpable actor, proves to be a less-compelling rationale for self-defense, then necessity might indeed be the better way to justify the use of force against a psychotic aggressor.

The future boundary between self-defense and necessity will depend in large part on how important the distinct rationales of the two defenses remain in our legal consciousness. The collective, utilitarian argument for balancing competing interest is well grounded in modern legal thought, and therefore we can assume that the defense of necessity will remain a powerful argument. Whether self-defense flourishes as a theoretically distinct defense depends largely on the political future of libertarian thinking.

Notes

1. See discussion and citation *supra* ch.5 at note 20.
2. 24 Henry VIII, c. 5 (1532).
3. 14 Q.B.D. 273 (1884).
4. Id. at 288.
5. The biblical example is interpreted to rest as well on the protection of the homeowner's life. The Talmudic interpretation of this provision is that even if the thief intended merely to steal, the homeowner would resist the taking of his property, which would cause the thief to threaten the life of the homeowner. Babylonian Talmud, Tractate Sanhedrin 72a.
6. Note that under MPC § 3.06, the defense of property is considered a separate defense.
7. The characteristics described here are common to Western systems of criminal justice. For a totally different approach to the legitimacy of defensive force, see the Talmudic materials discussed in George P. Fletcher, *Talmudic Reflections on Self-Defense*, in Crime, Punishment, and Deterrence: An American Jewish Exploration 61 (David Gordis ed., 1991); id., *Defensive Force as an Act of Rescue*, 7(2) Social Philosophy and Policy 170 (1990).
8. See, e.g., People v. Torres, 128 Misc.2d 129 (1985), recognizing the admissibility of expert testimony on the "battered wife" syndrome.
9. On the dangers of loosening the imminence requirement, see the analysis of the Menendez brothers case in With Justice For Some at 137, 141–47.
10. Blackstone 181.
11. John Locke, Treatise of Civil Government 14 (Sherman ed., 1937).
12. Immanuel Kant, The Metaphysics of Morals 60 (M. Gregor trans., 1991).
13. See Glanville Williams, Textbook of Criminal Law 504 (2d ed., 1983)

("The law would be oppressive if it said: it is true that you took this action because you felt it in your bones that you were in peril, and it is true that you were right, but you cannot now assign reasonable grounds for your belief, so you were only right by a fluke and will be convicted.");2 P. Robinson, Defenses to Crime 12–29 (1984).

14. On the proper treatment of mistaken self-defense, see chapter 9 infra.

15. StGB § 34.

16. MPC § 3.02.

17. See former Soviet Criminal Code (RSFSR) § 14; see also the contemporary Russian Criminal Code § 39.

18. Cross v. State, 370 P.2d 371 (Wyo. 1962).

19. Note that BGB § 228, which imposes a limit on the permissible harm, parallels the rule of proportionality in a self-defense case. The drafters of the BGB obviously thought of the person using force as acting in a situation comparable to self-defense. This form of necessity is usually called "defensive necessity."

20. 81 Vt. 471, 71 A. 188 (1908).

21. 109 Minn. 456, 124 N.W. 221 (1910).

22. The common law recognized the justified damage to property necessity as an early stage of development. See Mouse's Case, 66 Eng. Rep. 1341 (K.B. 1609).

23. Judgment of March 11, 1927, 61 RGSt. 242.

24. The requirement of "conscientious weighing" became explicit in the Judgment of April 20, 1928, 62 RGSt. 137, 138 (the issue was importing illegal goods into the Ruhr district).

25. 61 RGSt. at 247.

26. During the Nazi period, leading authors still endorsed the principle of extrastatutory necessity based on the 1927 abortion decision. See Hans Welzel, Der Allgemeine Teil des deutschen Strafrechts in seinen Grundzuegen 63–64 (1943).

27. E.g., Del. Code tit. 11, § 463 ("to avoid an imminent . . . injury which is about to occur . . ."); Colo. Rev. Stat. § 18-1-702 (same language as Delaware); Ky. Rev. Stat. § 503.030 ("imminent . . . injury").

28. 459 F.2d 697 (8th Cir. 1972).

29. Id. at 701.

30. The MPC is, in fact, self-contradictory on this point. It is clear that the drafters perceived necessity as fundamentally different from self-defense, for the former requires an *actual* balance of advantage to justify a nominal legal infringement, see MPC § 3.02(1)(a); self-defense is justified if the actor merely *believes* in the immediate necessity of using force, see § 3.04(1).

31. See Robert Nozick, Anarchy, State and Utopia 34–35 (1974); Judith J. Thomson, *Self-Defense*, 20 Phil. & Pub. Aff. 283, 287–89 (1991).

32. Babylonian Talmud, Tractate Sanhedrin 72.

33. R. Moshe ben Maimon, Mishneh Torah [Code of Maimonides, Book XI, tr. V, ch. 1, @ 9 (ed. & trans. Hyman Klein 1954).

34. Jerome Hall, General Principles of Criminal Law 436, note 85 (2d ed. 1960); Glanville Williams, Criminal Law: The General Part 733 (2d ed. 1961).

35. Most strikingly in Bouzat & Pinatel, Traité de Droit Pénal et de Cri-

minologie 362 (1970); cf. J. Hall, *supra* note 34, at 436, note 85 (analogy to natural force).

36. The same point was made by Loeffler, *Unrecht & Notwehr*, 21 Zeitschrift fur die gesamte Strafrechtswissenschaft 537, 541 note 7 (1901), who criticizes those "who regard it as modern to depreciate the life of the insane."

37. See the discussion above accompanying notes 11–12.

38. See "Proportionality and the Psychotic Aggressor," *supra* note 23, at 367, 379–81.

39. T. Lenckner in Schönke/Schröder, § 32, note 52.

9

Relevant versus Irrelevant Mistakes

Mistakes express dissonance. Something looks one way to the actor and another way to the society at large. The society insists that it has the correct view—that the criminal result actually occurred, the victim was really hurt. The suspected offender claims that he saw things differently, that he did not perceive reality the way other people do. The way it looked to him, he was doing nothing wrong, or at least nothing as serious as appears to have occurred. It might appear to others that a suspect shoots and injures a police officer, but as the shooter sees the situation, any of the following might be true:

1. He might be engaged in target practice and think that he is shooting at a cardboard display of a police officer.

2. He might think the officer is a private security guard when he in fact is a federal officer.

3. He might think that the officer is a civilian who is attacking him and that he must respond in self-defense.

4. He might think that the officer is corrupt and that it is his duty to arrest the officer and to take him into custody by first disabling him.

All of these mistaken thoughts might be running through the actor's head as he is shooting at what appears to him as the form of an officer in blue. Some of these thoughts—particularly the thought that he is shooting at a cardboard dummy of an officer—might make him seem morally innocent of the charge of injuring and therefore committing battery or attempted murder against the officer. Other thoughts, such as his belief that the officer is corrupt and that it is his duty to shoot him, seems more problematic. Why is it, one wonders, that some of these thoughts might constitute mistakes that are relevant to the actor's criminal culpability and others are thought to be irrelevant? Let us begin by considering two types of mistakes that are often considered to be irrelevant to criminal liability.

9.1. Irrelevant Mistakes

In order to convict a defendant of crime, the prosecution must establish that the crime occurred in a state or territory over which the court has competence to adjudicate criminal liability.[1] To convict someone for an offense under California law, a California prosecutor must prove, absent unusual circumstances, that the crime occurred in California. Suppose that the shooting of the police officer occurs in California, but the actor thinks that she and the officer are both on the Nevada side of Lake Tahoe? Is this a relevant mistake? Unfortunately not. What counts is where the act occurs, not the actor's impression about where she happens to be.

Suppose that an employee in an embassy thinks that by virtue of his job, he should enjoy diplomatic immunity for his offenses. He engages in drunk driving. In fact, employees of his rank do not have immunity. Is this mistake relevant? Fortunately not. Again, the question is whether in fact the actor has immunity not whether he thinks so.

The irrelevance of these mistakes presses us to formulate a view about why mistakes should ever be relevant. Why is a mistake about location different from a mistake about whether the object aimed at is a living human being or a cardboard dummy? As Aristotle formulated his view about mistakes as excuses, a relevant mistake negates the voluntariness of the actor's choice to engage in the act. He does not voluntarily kill a human being if he did not know that it was a human being that he targeted. And the background assumption is that he cannot be held responsible, be blamed, for an act that he did not voluntarily commit.[2]

As applied to our hypothetical cases, the question is refined: When does involuntariness of the action undermine the actor's responsibility for what he does? The mistake about location (California as opposed to Nevada) would have no bearing either on the actor's decision to act or on the wrong that she has committed. Battery and attempted murder are just as wrong whether they are committed in one state or another. The mistake about diplomatic immunity bears a slightly different analysis. Drunk driving is just as wrong whether committed by a diplomat or an ordinary citizen, but in this case the actor's mistake does bear on his motivation for flouting the law. He might say that if he had known of his status and his exposure to arrest, he would certainly not have violated the rules of safe driving.

This case of drunk driving by someone who thinks he enjoys diplomatic immunity should remind the reader of the problem considered in chapter 1: How do we draw the line between substance and procedure? If the mistake is about a substantive issue—such as whether the perceived target is a cardboard dummy or a living human being—there is no doubt that the mistake bears on that for which the actor may be properly held responsible. But if the mistake is about a procedural issue—such as the competence of the court or a diplomat's immunity from prosecution—then the mistake seems to have little bearing on the wrong committed or on the actor's responsibility.

In the preceding discussion two tests emerged for marking the distinction between substance and procedure in assessing the relevance of mistakes. One test is whether the mistake bears on an issue that related to the wrong committed; the other is whether the actor would have chosen to commit the deed, had he known of the true state of affairs. Under the first test, both actors, mistaken about geography and about diplomatic immunity, appear to have made mistakes extrinsic to the factors bearing on the wrongs they have committed. But under the second test (would you have done it had you known?), the drunk driver mistaken about his immunity might have a good defense.

The better test, I believe, is the first one. The claim of the drunk driver is morally no more persuasive than that of a concentration camp murderer who claimed that he was mistaken about the statute of limitations applicable to murder. These are mistakes by wrongdoers who invoke procedural devices to secure themselves against prosecution for admitted wrongdoing.

We can conclude, then, that the right approach is to inquire whether the action as perceived by the actor is less wrong than the action actually committed. If so, then the mistake is relevant to the assessment of responsibility and criminal liability. The German Criminal Code contains an illustrative provision that prescribes a special procedural impediment to theft offenses committed within the family.[3] These offenses are subject to prosecution only if the victim files a complaint. One could argue that the status of the victim as a member of the family makes the offense less egregious, but the better view seems to be that though the theft is equally wrong, the family should try to solve the problem on its own terms before resorting to the processes of criminal justice. Therefore, if the suspect thinks that the goods are owned by someone in the family, but they are in fact owned by someone outside the family, that mistake does not bear on the gravity of the wrong in stealing.[4]

The academic analysis of this German provision is sensible, but an actual American case illustrates the way in which the pursuit of the correct result can get highjacked by political considerations. Recall the second hypothetical listed above: the actor thinks that his intended victim "is a private security guard when he in fact is a federal officer." Suppose that assault of a federal officer is an aggravated offense punished in the federal courts. Does the status of the officer bear on the degree of wrongdoing or just on the question whether the federal courts have jurisdiction? This problem came before the Supreme Court in *United States v. Feola.*[5] The defendants conspired to assault some persons who, unbeknownst to them, were federal undercover agents. The preliminary question, prior to the analysis of the conspiracy charge, was whether the intended offense, namely, assaulting a federal officer, was affected by the conspirator's ignorance of the officer's identity. Justices Stewart and Douglas argued that there was no doubt that the offense was in the nature of an aggravated assault; therefore, a mistake about the aggravating circumstances should be relevant in assessing the actor's culpability.[6] Yet the majority of the Court, in an opinion written by Justice Blackmun, reasoned that the "federal element" was jurisdictional, analogous to the requirement for federal theft statutes that the stolen goods have entered interstate commerce.[7]

Blackmun seems to concede the relevance of the mistake to the wrongdoing of shooting a federal agent, but inconsistently concludes the mistake should be irrelevant. Because Congress intended to protect federal police functions, this goal would arguably be compromised by permitting mistakes to undercut the actor's culpability. The thrust of this argument is not that the status of the officer is extrinsic to the question of culpability, but that other "policy" values should lead to disregarding considerations bearing on the actor's responsibility. This rhetorical strategy illustrates the way in which courts can easily depart from the pursuit of justice for the sake of immediate political goals.

The confusion between the principled and the politically motivated "irrelevance" of mistakes occurs all the time, particularly in American courts torn by the conflict between the pursuit of justice and the necessity of politics. A good example is the trial of Mike Tyson, the renowned boxer, who was accused in July 1991 of raping Desiree Washington, a social date who came to his hotel room in Indianapolis. Tyson claimed that she had consented. She said that she had said, "no." The trial became a cause celebre for feminists who insisted, properly, that a woman who voluntarily goes to a man's hotel room late at night does not thereby consent to sexual relations. Nonetheless it was possible that Tyson *believed* that she had consented;[8] in other words, if she had not consented, that at least he was mistaken about whether she wanted to have sex with him. Yet the political importance of sending the message "no means no" to men who take women's sexual favors for granted overwhelmed arguments in favor of considering Tyson's alleged mistake as relevant to his responsibility for having forced sex on an unwilling partner.

Sending a message to the public and doing justice in the particular case represent distinct and conflicting goals of criminal trials.[9] The former speaks to the future; the latter pursues the truth about a unique event that has already occurred. Jury verdicts must mediate between these conflicting objectives. They can inform the public that "no means no" but also consider whether as a personal matter the defendant is excused or responsible for the wrongful act of sexual imposition.

If a woman has in fact not consented, she has suffered wrongful sexual aggression; the invasion called "rape" has occurred. But it does not follow that the particular defendant, the man standing in the dock, need be held responsible for the rape. If he was insane at the time of the deed, he will not be held accountable. And so too, it should be the law that if he acted under an honest and reasonable mistake about consent, he will not be held liable.

Contrary to this sensible view about the relevance of Tyson's mistake, the trial court refused to instruct the jury on the issue. The jury had no option to acquit, even if they believed that Mike had an "honest and reasonable belief" that Desiree had consented to have sex with him. Amazingly, the Indiana appellate court affirmed the trial court's decision not to give the jury an instruction on the criteria for assessing Tyson's mistake. Many courts decide the issue of mistake in this way, particularly in cases of statutory rape where the actor is reasonably mistaken about the age of the girl.[10] They all engage in a tragic error. Recognizing the relevance of mistake—of the defendant's "honest and reasonable belief"—provides a splendid means of reconciling the conflicting trial objectives of upholding a rule ("no means no") and doing justice in the particular case.

The term "strict liability" in the criminal law should be understood as the practice of disregarding a mistake or accident where as a matter of principle the mistake or accident should be relevant to the defendant's responsibility for bringing about a criminal harm. In other words, if the mistake ought to be *relevant* but is treated as *irrelevant*, then liability is strict. It makes sense to say, that on the issue of mistaken consent, the Indiana court imposed strict liability on Mike Tyson. It would not be correct, however, to describe liability as strict as to the issue of mistaken geography or mistaken diplomatic immunity, for these mistakes do not pass the first test of relevance in principle.

The maxim that ignorance of the law is no excuse is so well entrenched in many legal systems that one is not likely to think of this form of mistake as a factor bearing on culpability and responsibility. As a result, the practice of disregarding mistakes of law may not initially appear to be a form of strict liability. In *Hopkins v. State*,[11] the court held a clergyman liable for the statutory offense of posting signs soliciting couples for marriage, even though he had been advised by the state attorney general that the particular signs did not violate the statute. There is no denying that in a case of this sort, the court imposes liability regardless of the actor's culpability in violating the statute. Of course, to make this point we have to use the term "culpability" in the moral sense, meaning fairly subject to blame for violating the statute. If the term "culpability" simply meant "having the intent required for violation of the statute," there is no doubt that Hopkins acted culpably. Yet, reducing culpability to a question of intent does not eliminate the problem whether it is just to convict someone who acts in reliance on apparently competent legal advice.

It is hard to see a criminal conviction as fair and just when the "offender" did everything in his power to determine whether conduct such as posting signs advertising marriage service is legal in the jurisdiction. Accordingly, the 1975 German Criminal Code recognizes in § 17:

> If the actor does not perceive at the time of engaging in a criminal act that he is committing a wrong (*Unrecht*), he is not culpable, provided that the mistake was unavoidable. If the actor could have avoided the mistake, the penalty may be reduced.[12]

The Model Penal Code (MPC) has also recognized a defense for relying on official advice that turns out to be mistaken. Section 2.04(3) of the Code provides:

> A belief that conduct does not legally constitute an offense is a defense to a prosecution for that offense based upon such conduct when:
>
> (a) the statute or other enactment defining the offense is not known to the actor and has not been published or otherwise reasonably made available prior to the conduct alleged; or
>
> (b) he acts in reasonable reliance upon an official statement of the law, afterward determined to be invalid or erroneous, contained in (i) a statute or other enactment; (ii) a judicial decision, opinion or judgment; (iii) an administrative order or grant of permission; or (iv) an official interpretation of the public officer or body charged by law with responsibility for the interpretation, administration or enforcement of the law defining the offense.

The differences between these two provisions on mistake of law illustrate the structural gulf between the German and American style of solving problems of criminal responsibility. The German provision is general and bespeaks a principle, namely, that if you are unavoidably mistaken about the legality of your conduct, you cannot be properly blamed for your wrongful act. The American proposal—and we should remember that the MPC is merely a recommendation for law reform—is a specific and detailed response to obvious cases of injustice like *Hopkins*. There the defendant reasonably relied on "an official interpretation" of the law by an officer, namely, the attorney general of the state, charged with rendering interpretations for guidance of the public. Hopkins would therefore gain the "defense" recommended by the MPC, but note that the MPC does not give us a hint why, in principle, reasonable reliance on official interpretations of the law should bar a criminal conviction. The drafters do not imply that disregarding mistakes of law is a form of strict liability or otherwise violates basic principles of justice. As a result, the drafters themselves had no qualms about shifting the burden of proof on the new defense (MPC § 2.04(4)).[13]

The dominant view toward mistakes of law remains captive to the outmoded dogma that everyone should know what the law is. Ignorance is supposedly no excuse. In the early stages of the criminal law, when the range of offenses was limited to violent aggression and obviously immoral conduct, it was plausible to assume that everyone knew the law. If someone did not realize that rape or homicide was wrong, one might properly expect a proof of mental illness in order to make out a believable claim. In a time when criminal statutes are filled with technical economic offenses, even the most well-informed business people can run afoul of the law.

The practice of disregarding mistakes of law derives, in large measure, from the kinds of political considerations that lead the U.S. Supreme Court in the *Feola* case to impose strict liability with regard to the status of the victim as a federal officer. There are always political and utilitarian considerations that speak against recognizing excuses. The courts are afraid of those who might feign ignorance of the law. They think that by convicting the morally innocent they can stimulate others to become better informed of their legal obligations. Some writers even make the erroneous conceptual argument that if we recognize mistake of law as a defense, we will allow everyone to decide what in fact the law is.[14] But, of course, recognizing an excuse of mistake of law does not render the conduct lawful; it merely provides an excuse—a denial of culpability—for engaging in wrongful, unlawful conduct.

It should be apparent by now that it is difficult to maintain a principled approach to the problem of mistake. This difficulty is evident in the drafting of the Model Penal Code. As we have seen, the code takes a nonprincipled approach to mistake of law, and further, the drafters abandon the problem of mistake of fact to legislators who must decide the "culpability" level for each element of every offense. Once the legislature has specified which of the four possible mental states—purpose, knowledge, recklessness, or negligence—should go with the material element of every offense, the problem of mistake dissolves. The mistake is conceptualized as simply the negation of a required mental state. Thus, MPC § 2.04(1) provides:

> Ignorance or mistake as to a matter of fact or law is a defense if: (a) the ignorance or mistake negatives the purpose, knowledge, belief, recklessness or negligence required to establish a material element of the offense.[15]

This approach to the problem of mistake is flawed for two basic reasons. First, it is unrealistic to expect legislators to solve problems that are theoretical and philosophical in nature. Determining the difference between relevant and irrelevant mistakes is, at bottom, a philosophical problem—not one that legislators can solve simply as an act of will. Furthermore, by treating as equivalent all mistakes bearing on any "material element" of any offense, the MPC ignores the structural significance of different kinds of "material elements." The Code defines "material elements" in effect to include all substantive as opposed to procedural elements.[16] The drafters totally overlooked the significance of the kind of element to which the mistake relates. As we shall see, it makes an extraordinary difference whether a mistake pertains to an element of the definition, an element of a justification, or an element of an excusing condition.

Thus, we shall consider the problem of the relevance and irrelevance of mistakes in the context of six categories—the three basic levels of liability, each bifurcated between mistakes about factual issues and about evaluative questions that implicate legal principles. The following schema presents the variety of issues ignored in the Model Penal Code's approach:

Mistakes about Material Elements

	fact	law
definition	1	2
justification	3	4
excuse	5	6

9.2 Mistakes about Factual Elements of the Definition
(Type One)

The mistakes represented by square one are the easiest to analyze. There is a general agreement here and abroad that a mistake about one of these core elements of the offense will negate the intent required for intentional commission of the offense. This is how one would expect a legal culture to react to the mistake about whether the target aimed at is a person or a cardboard dummy. The Germans achieve this result by prescribing in §16 of their code that a mistake about an element of the Definition precludes a finding of intentional commission of the offense. Common law jurists approach this problem by finding, in the relevant statute or case law, an authoritative definition of the required intent. Once the intent is given, the result follows deductively: the mistake either negates the intent or it does not. If the intent for murder is defined as the intent to kill another human being, then a mistaken belief that the intended target is a cardboard dummy will negate the intent and block prosecution for intentional homicide.

A corollary to this deductive matching of mistakes against the required intention leaves open the possibility of liability for negligence. If the mistake is the kind for which the actor could be found at fault, then it is possible to hold him or her liable for negligently bringing about the element of the offense. This becomes relevant, of course, only if the offense is one, like homicide, that admits of negligent commission. Note this approach to liability for negligent mistakes implies that certain kinds of unreasonable and faultful mistakes cut in two directions. One edge—the element of mistake—eliminates liability for intentional conduct; the other edge—the element of fault—establishes liability for negligence.[17]

9.3 Mistakes about Legal Aspects of the Definition
(Type Two)

The elements of the Definition often contain references to mixed questions of law and fact. Bigamy is defined as going through a marriage ceremony while already married. The element of "being already married" belongs presumably to the Definition of the Offense. Suppose the person going through the marriage is mistaken about whether a divorce received in the Dominican Republic is valid. He thinks he is single but in fact he is still married. Under the German approach, all mistakes about elements of the Definition preclude a finding of intentionally committing the offense. The mistake about being divorced is a mistake about the Definition, and therefore by acting in good faith the second-time groom does not intentionally commit bigamy.[18] And significantly, even if he is very negligent about the offense, he is not guilty, for bigamy is not an offense that can be committed negligently.

I know of no case in the common law tradition that holds that any mistake, however unreasonable, about the validity of a prior divorce will negate the intention required for bigamy. The leading cases recognizing the relevance of the mistake hold that the mistake must be reasonable.[19] Apparently the intent required for bigamy does not include the state of being married at the time of the second ceremony. The argument for recognizing the mistake, but only if free from fault, is not obvious.[20] It just seems unjust to convict someone of bigamy when he or she believed in good faith that the marriage was a legitimate option.

The common law courts rely heavily on the logic of negating intent and therefore have an easy time of cases where the authoritative intent includes the focal point of the mistake. A good example is a mistake about the ownership of an object taken and carried away. From the standpoint of the owner, the taking looks like larceny, but if the taker thinks the object is abandoned, then he does not take with the larcenous intent to take an object belonging to another. *Morissette v. United States*[21] makes the point well. The defendant was convicted under a federal statute[22] for taking bomb casings from government land. Though he claimed to have believed the casings were abandoned, the trial court read the statute merely to require an intent to take the casings from federal land.[23] Given this construction of the required intent, the trial court correctly found that the defendant's mistake did not negate the intent required for the offense.

The U.S. Supreme Court unanimously reversed the conviction. Justice Jackson's opinion for the Court interpreted the federal statute against the background of common law larceny and concluded that larceny required an intention to take from "the owner." Note that the problem for the Court was how it should construe the intent required for the offense and it opted for the traditional definition. German law would reach the same result about taking *eine fremde bewegliche Sache* [a movable object belonging to another] under the Code's definition of larceny in § 242.[24]

For German jurists, the problem is not so much a matter of interpreting the statute as it is construing the wrongdoing of larceny. If the actor thinks that he is taking abandoned objects, he has no sense of engaging in wrongdoing. But compare this with a case in which a husband and wife jointly own a car. In the midst of a marital dispute, the husband takes the car with the intent of holding on to it permanently. He acts surreptitiously because he does not want his wife to try to stop him, but he also believes that what he is doing is at most a tort and not a crime. He interprets the phrase "belonging to another" to mean "be-

longing entirely to another." Since he is half-owner of the car, he assumes that he cannot be guilty of larceny.

It turns out that the surreptitious husband is right about the common law meaning of "objects belonging to another"[25] but wrong about
the German interpretation of the same phrase. If the events occurred
in Germany, the conduct of the surreptitious husband would realize
the objective elements of larceny; his only defense would be a mistake
about the meaning of an object "belonging to another." German theorists properly balk at treating this mistake as equivalent to a mistake
about whether the object is abandoned as in *Morissette*. The defendant
in the latter case had no reason to act secretively, for he thought that
he was engaged in a perfectly legal even beneficial activity of scaveng-
ing unused bomb casings. But the surreptitious husband thinks that he
had better not get caught; he has a sense for the wrong that he is
committing, even if he thinks that it is technically legal.[26]

German theory has confronted an engaging problem about how to
classify the mistake of the surreptitious husband. It could be classified
either as mistaken statutory interpretation *(Subsumtionsirrtum)* or as a
mistake about the norm prohibiting larceny *(Verbotsirrtum)*. The different legal implications of these two forms of mistake are striking. If the
actor is simply mistaken about the interpretation of the statute and the
classification of his conduct under the law, then his mistake is totally
irrelevant. But if his mistake pertains to the prohibitory norm, then he
has the possibility of securing an excuse under § 17 if his mistake was
unavoidable, or a discretionary reduction in sentence if the mistake was
sincere but avoidable. In other words, it is tactically advantageous to
argue under German law that the mistake was one of law (about the
prohibitory norm) rather than one about the classification of conduct
under the statute. This distinction may be defensible in principle,[27] but
it is easy to conclude that it is too subtle for practically minded judges.

9.4 Mistakes about Factual Elements of Justification (Type Three)

Claims of justification rest both on norms that permit the nominal commission of offenses and the perception of facts that support the application of the norm. The simplest justification is consent, for which the
norm is simply whether the intended "victim" wants or desires the
defendant's conduct to occur. Slightly more complicated is self-defense
which requires three objective elements: (1) an actual attack, (2) a
minimally necessary response, and (2) and a relationship of "proportionality" between the threatened interest and the harm done.[28]

A factual mistake about one of these elements or the elements of
another justification resembles a factual mistake about elements of the

Definition. And some theorists and codes—those that hold that the only relevant difference is between mistakes of fact and mistakes of law—would treat them as identical.[29] In fact, the way we should treat factual mistakes of this sort has confounded both courts and theorists. The German code contains no legislated solution for the problem. It falls in the gap between § 16 (mistakes about the definition) and § 17 (mistakes of law). The problem of putative justification—a claim of justification based on good faith misperception of the facts—poses, therefore, a serious philosophical challenge.

One reason that the problem is so difficult is that we have no consensus about the impact of the mistake of putative justification on the actor's responsibility. A mistake about an element of the Definition itself becomes relevant because it negates the required intention and therefore negates the Definition of the offense. If the Definition is not satisfied, there can be no liability. But why is a mistake of type three—about a factual element of the justification—even relevant at all? Why should the actor get the benefit of his misperceptions? In fact, there are four ways of thinking about this problem that have emerged in the case law and supportive literature.

Putative Justification Negates the Required Intent

This is a surprisingly influential position that has gained considerable support in English, Canadian, and German law. No case better illustrates the logic and the illogic of this view than a series of kinky English House of Lords decisions of the mid-1970s. These are cases in which the defendant informs his drinking buddies that his wife, waiting patiently at home, enjoys forcible intercourse. She may resist and fight back, but in fact she wants to be taken violently. They come home together from the bar and the husband's friends accept his invitation to force intercourse on the crying and tormented wife. In the leading case, the husband named Morgan and his mates were all convicted in the trial court of rape. The codefendants complained on appeal that they honestly believed that the wife, despite her tears, was consenting.[30] The House of Lords came to the startling conclusion that, in principle, the deceived mates had a good defense of good faith mistake.

The judges reasoned that the defendant would not have the intent to engage in nonconsensual intercourse if he believed, however unreasonably, that Morgan's wife had consented. But there was nothing either in the statutory definition of rape or the traditional view of rape that requires this definition of the required intention.[31]

Women were naturally outraged by the decision. A group of male judges decide that in principle if a kinky sailor believes that a woman, despite her screams, "wants it that way," then he goes free. More disturbing than the decision by the House of Lords is the apparent support it received in many quarters of the academic profession. Shortly after the decision, two leading English professors of criminal law wrote into the *London Times* to express support for the decision.[32] The Canadians have followed the *Morgan* precedent. Though English legislation has corrected the specific problem of putative consent in rape cases, the English courts have applied the same principle to mistake about the factual elements of self-defense—for example, if the defendant believes that he is being attacked when he is not.[33]

German lawyers come to the same conclusion as the *Morgan* decision but with their own (unconvincing) reasoning. The dominant position in the case law and literature is to assume analogical application of § 16 to mistakes about the factual elements of a justification.[34] It would follow that in these cases the mistake negates the required intention. The only theoretical support for this position, so far as I can tell, is that the actor's mind is pure. As one leading writer Claus Roxin claims: "What he wants to do is legally unobjectionable—not only according to his subjective perception but according to the objective view of the legislator."[35]

The supporters of this view are quick to point out that if the defendant has made an unreasonable mistake, he can be held liable for the negligent commission of the offense. This solution works neither for rape nor for attempted homicide, both of which presuppose an intentional commission of the offense. Thus, in *Morgan* the implication of the prevailing view in England and in Germany is that the actor goes free. The obvious injustice of this way of thinking about mistaken or putative consent should be enough to convince sensible observers that there is something fishy in the theory that supports the principle.

The fallacy of the English and German position is that they underappreciate the intentional invasion of the victim's protected interests. In *Morgan* you have a victim who feels, properly, that she has been raped. In a case of homicide based on a mistaken perception of an attack, you have an innocent victim killed as a result of the defendant's mistake. In all of these cases of putative justification, the defendant intends to violate the victim's protected interest. In *Morgan* the kinky sailors wanted to impose intercourse by force; in a case of homicide, the defendant intends to kill—even if in mistaken self-defense. It is simply wrong to ignore this intentional invasion and treat a mistaken justification as a factor that negates the intention required for the offense.

Strict Liability: The Mistake is Deemed Irrelevant

Overreaction leads to bad law. There is no doubt that the analysis in *Morgan* is deeply flawed. But it is wrong to overreact to this indulgent treatment of mistaken rapists and conclude that mistakes about the victim's consent are irrelevant. This is what the Indiana courts did in the *Tyson* case.[36] They might have thought they were making a statement about the importance of victims' rights in rape cases. But a rule that expresses too much sympathy for victims is just as politically suspect as one that goes too far in the direction of supporting the interests of defendants.[37]

Putative Justification Is Itself a Justification

The Model Penal Code has taken the unusual position that putative self-defense should be treated just like actual self-defense. If the actor *believes* that he or she is being attacked or that the use of force is "immediately necessary" to repel the attack, then the use of force is justified. In the end, then, there is no difference between facts as they are and facts as they are merely *believed* to be. The MPC is not entirely consistent in collapsing the distinction between actual justification and putative justification, for in the case of necessity as justification the code demands that "the harm or evil sought to be avoided by such conduct is [really] greater than that sought to be prevented by the law defining the offense charged." It is not enough that the actor believes that the action serves the greater interest. As for consent, which the MPC does not treat as a justification, the belief in consent is clearly not equivalent to consent. The consent actually "precludes the infliction of the harm or evil sought to be prevented by the law defining the offense."[38]

It is hard to know what to make out of the MPC's proposition that putative self-defense is equivalent to real self-defense. In practical terms, the outcome is the same as that reached under the dominant English and German views that a mistake about the conditions of justification negates the required intent, but that an unreasonable mistake could generate liability for negligent or reckless commission of the offense.[39] Yet there seems as well to be some theoretical pretension in the MPC's collapsing putative self-defense into real self-defense. There was some authority at common law for the view that if the putative aggressor's conduct actually appeared to be an attack, then self-defense was justified in response.[40] But the MPC takes this view much further and holds that any misconception of the defender should have the same justificatory effect as if the facts were as he believed them to be. This is a curious and not very plausible view.

Understanding the MPC on putative self-defense in a homicide case, for example, requires a comparison of two provisions located in different parts of Article III. Section 3.04 provides that any "belief" in the elements of justification is sufficient to justify the action; the later provision § 3.09(2) provides an exception for negligent and reckless beliefs. To simplify this structure, many legislative reforms relying on the MPC—New York being a leading example—simply combined these provisions and prescribed that the defender must "reasonably believe" in the factual conditions for self-defense. This simplification unwittingly generated a sensible compromise between the extremes of recognizing all mistakes as negating intent and disregarding all mistakes in order to protect the interests of victims.

Reasonable Mistake as an Excuse

The correct view in cases of putative justification should tread the mean between the two extremes. Only reasonable mistakes should be relevant, and they should constitute excuses for behavior that is in fact unjustifiable and therefore wrongful. The best way to see this point is to ask the simple question in the facts of the *Morgan* case: Does the woman subject to attack have the right to defend herself? It seems to be self-evident that she has the right to defend herself against men who mistakenly believe, either reasonably or unreasonably, that she has consented to intercourse. A woman cannot lose her right to bodily integrity just because a man is mistaken about her wishes. But how can the sexual aggression against her be unjustified and wrongful if the aggressor acts under a mistake that negates his intention and therefore negates the Definition of the offense? The only way to recognize the mistake consistently with the aggression being wrongful is to treat the mistake as an excuse.

The same would be true about innocent bystanders who are falsely taken to be aggressors. Consider the facts in the *Goetz* case.[41] Four young black men surround Bernhard Goetz on the New York subway. He believes in good faith that they intend to assault and rob him. Goetz opens fire on all four. If Goetz is mistaken about their intentions or he is mistaken about the necessity of shooting in response, then surely they have a right to defend themselves against Goetz. Again, victims of mistaken aggression can hardly lose their rights just because someone like Bernhard Goetz makes a mistake, even a reasonable mistake. The implications should be the same as in the rape cases: The only way to recognize the mistake consistently with the aggression being wrongful is to treat the mistake as an excuse.[42]

If mistakes about the conditions of justification are treated as excuses negating culpability, then it follows that only nonculpable mistakes can qualify as grounds for exculpation. An unreasonable or faultful mistake is itself culpable and therefore it cannot negate the actor's culpability. New York's adaptation of the MPC inadvertently hit upon this solution by requiring that a person using force in self-defense must reasonably believe in the factual conditions of self-defense.[43]

For some time, the law of New York was unclear whether to construe this provision so that a subjective good faith belief in the conditions of self-defense would be sufficient. The lower courts decided in favor of this subjective view. But on appeal prior to trial in the *Goetz* case, the highest court in New York, the Court of Appeals, unanimously decided that the proper standard is one that measures the good faith of the defendant against a community standard of reasonable behavior. This was, I believe, the correct decision.

9.5 Mistakes about the Norms of Justification (Type Four)

Of all six categories of mistake under discussion, mistakes about the scope of a justification are most clearly and appropriately classified as mistakes of law and subject therefore, in Germany, to the rule of avoidability under §17 and to be treated as irrelevant under English and American law. This adverse classification for the defendant would presumably include all of the following mistakes:

1. The belief that consent was a valid defense in a homicide case.

2. A mistaken balancing of competing interests in a case of necessity.

3. A mistaken judgment about proportionality in a case of self-defense.

The last two mistakes are matters on which we should have considerable sympathy for criminal defendants. To say that an actor is mistaken in balancing interests or in assessing proportionality means merely that the actor disagrees with the court's judgment. These are matters on which reasonable people could clearly disagree, and yet the court's judgment is taken to be law and the defendant is expected to know the law. This rather harsh situation flows, it seems, from the quality of justificatory claims as exceptional privileges for violating protected interests.

One accommodation in the interests of criminal defendants is to treat a good faith but unreasonable mistake of law as a ground for mitigating punishment. This is the position taken in the second sentence of German Code §17: "If the mistake was avoidable, then the penalty *may* be reduced [according to the appropriate rules]." The reduction of the penalty is discretionary. It is not at all clear that if the defendant is subject to a fantasy about the necessity of saving the world by killing an innocent person, the appropriate response is to mitigate the penalty.[44]

9.6 Mistakes about the Factual Elements of Excuses (Type Five)

The category of excuses includes, as I have argued:

(A) excuses bearing on the physical voluntariness of choice:
    1. insanity

2. involuntary intoxication
3. duress and personal necessity

(B) excuses based on mistake:
4. mistake of law
5. reasonable mistake about the factual basis of justification[45]
6. reasonable failure to perceive the running of a substantial and unjustified risk.[46]

The conceptual differences between these claims of excuse and of justificatory claims, such as self-defense and necessity, come most clearly to light when we consider the problem of mistakes with regard to the first category of excuses. To focus on mistakes of this type, let us consider a case of duress based on a mistaken fear. Suppose that the defendant receives a note informing her that a local gang has installed a bomb in her house and threatens to blow it up unless she points a gun at a bank teller and demands the contents of her cash drawer. The defendant carries out the order and turns the money over to the gang. When put on trial for bank robbery, the defendant claims an excuse of duress—recognized in principle both in American and German law.[47] It turns out that the gang was just bluffing; they did not plant the bomb. This means that the defendant was mistaken about whether the danger was real. How should we approach the problem of the defendant's mistake?

The MPC formulation on duress, § 2.09(1) requires that the defendant have been "coerced . . . [by] a threat to use unlawful force against his person or the person of another, which a person of reasonable firmness in his situation would have been unable to resist." A threat to blow up a house is not a threat to use unlawful force against "the person of another," unless the gang threatened to detonate the bomb when her family is at home. Let us add that provision and retain the element of bluff: there is no fact, no danger of bombing. One might well conclude that under the MPC, the mistaken belief that the threat is real is irrelevant. All that counts is whether the defendant feels coerced, and that might happen even if he is mistaken about the facts.

But now suppose that the belief is unreasonable. The threatener says, "Look the bomb is already there, hidden in your basement." The defendant goes home and searches the basement in vain for a bomb.[48] It is not entirely reasonable at that point to feel coerced by the threat. But if the bomb really were in position to explode, the threat would be intimidating and arguably "a person of reasonable firmness" would not have been able to resist it. But the reasonableness of the mistaken belief in the danger differs from the reasonableness of submitting to the threat. Interpreting a provision of this sort, however, a court might well lump them together and reject the claim of duress if it is based on an unreasonable mistake.

The German code has a special clause on mistakes of this sort. In order to be relevant, the defendant's mistaken belief must have been unavoidable—that is, without fault on his part.[49] But this provision is located in a general provision on necessity and duress that emphasizes "an imminent, otherwise unavoidable risk" of harm rather than whether the actor feels coerced. To apply this risk-oriented provision properly, it makes sense to inquire whether the danger is real or mistakenly perceived.

The most important feature of mistakes in this category, however, is that no one would contend that the mistake negates either the wrongdoing or the intent required for the offense—say, for bank robbery. This is the essential difference between mistakes about the conditions of justification, where many are tempted to say the mistake does negate the required intent, and mistakes about the conditions of excuses. The latter mistakes function entirely as excuses themselves, and therefore it makes sense to integrate their analysis into the overall question whether the defendant is culpable or blameworthy for engaging in a wrongful violation of the law.

9.7 Mistakes about Excusing Norms (Type Six)

In considering now whether the principle of mistakes of law can apply to excusing conditions, we ask, in effect, whether one kind of excuse can apply to another. Can one be excused for misunderstanding the scope of an excusing condition? Suppose that in the preceding hypothetical, the threat was merely to blow up the house during the day when no one was there. The actor feels nonetheless coerced to engage in the robbery. When she makes her argument in court, she is rebuffed. Whether in an MPC jurisdiction or in Germany, the prosecutor could point out that the applicable provision on duress does not apply to a threat to property.

Now suppose further that her mistake is reasonable and unavoidable. Could she claim a mistake of law about the scope of her excusing condition? Suppose she was convinced that threats to property would excuse her if she "felt coerced" to submit to them. She came to her conclusion by relying on a legal decision or some other "official statement of the law." Under the MPC she would have to argue that she acted in "reasonable reliance" on this mistaken view of the law and that therefore her mistake falls under the rule of § 3.04(3). She believed that her conduct did not "legally constitute an offense" and therefore, in principle, the MPC's excuse of mistake of law should apply to her mistakes about the scope of duress.

Not so with the German provision of mistake of law, §17, which requires that mistake be about wrongdoing. The drafters implicitly ruled out the possibility of extending the excuse to mistakes about norms, such as excusing conditions, that arise only after a finding of wrongdoing. The German drafters had an insight into an important theoretical point about the nature of excuses.

The best way to see this theoretical point is to understand the difference between conduct rules and decision rules.[50] Conduct rules are addressed to citizens and advise them how to guide their conduct according to law. Decision rules are directed exclusively to judges and provide guidance for judging those who violate conduct rules. Conduct rules include all matters bearing on wrongdoing, including elements of the Definition and claims of justification. Decision rules include the rules of evidence and, most important, all claims of excuse. The important implication is that excuses are not meant to be rules of law to guide the conduct of citizens. They are not norms that should lead one to say, "Ah, yes, if I surrender to this threat, I will be excused." It is for judges and juries—not for those who act in the world—to decide whether a particular act of wrongdoing is excused.

Our hypothetical figure who surrenders to threats to blow up her house may think her conduct is excused, but what she thinks is irrelevant. It is not her business to decide whether her conduct is "coerced" under the law. Whether she is excused lies in the judgment of the court that is the addressee of excuses as decision rules.

The same point holds clearly for insanity. Should we take seriously the judgment of a person at the borderline of sanity who thinks to himself, "It is clear that I qualify under the legal test of insanity (e.g., I cannot conform my conduct to law) and therefore I will be excused if I violate the law." The answer is no. The test of insanity, as a decision rule, is for the court to apply. The same is true about whether a mistake is reasonable or unavoidable. If someone says, "I guess my mistake is unavoidable and therefore my conduct is O.K.," that very act of reflection reveals that in fact the mistake was, to that extent, properly treated as avoidable.

In brief, excuses are not acts executed in reliance on legal norms. And because reliance on legal norms has no bearing on excuse, a mistake of the scope of the legal norm is irrelevant.

9.8 Summary of Mistakes: Relevant and Irrelevant

It is worth recalling that the Model Penal Code failed to understand the radical differences among the various kinds of mistakes that it groups together under the heading of mistakes that negate the mental state for "a material element of the offense."[51] In fact, there are six different kinds of mistake, each one requiring nuance differentiation from the others. To review the six categories:

Type One: Mistake about the Facts of the Definition, e.g., the actor thinks that he is shooting at a cardboard dummy that is in fact a human being. Everyone seems to agree that type 1 mistakes negate the intent required for commission of the offense, but if the defendant is negligent with regard to the relevant element, he or she may be guilty of negligently committing the offense.

Type Two: Mistakes about Norms of the Definition, e.g., a mistake about whether property held in joint ownership with a spouse is property "belonging to another" under the rule defining theft. These are mistakes about whether particular factual situations fall within a prohibition of the criminal law. They are not, strictly speaking, mistakes about the interpretation of the norm and therefore do not qualify as mistakes of law. They are irrelevant to liability.

Type Three: Mistakes about the Factual Basis of Justification, e.g., Bernhard Goetz believes unreasonably that someone who smiles at him is about to attack him. This is the most controversial category. My view is that these mistakes should be treated as excuses, effective only if reasonable.

Type Four: Mistakes about the Norms of Justification, e.g., the actor thinks that consent is a defense in homicide cases. These are pure mistakes of law, for which the better rule would be to excuse all reasonable, unavoidable mistakes. If the mistake is unreasonable, it is not clear that the defendant should get the benefit of his good faith views.

Type Five: Mistakes about the Factual Basis of Excuses, e.g., the actor thinks he is in great danger when he is not. These mistakes should be relevant only so far as they permit the conclusion that the defendant's wrongdoing was, all things considered, not blameworthy.

Type Six: Mistakes about the Norms Governing Excuses, e.g., the actor thinks he is entitled to rely on the advice of his lawyer about what it is legal for him to do. These mistakes should be irrelevant.

It is appropriate to end the chapter with a judgment that certain kinds of mistakes are irrelevant. Yet these are difficult and subtle matters and there is room to argue that good faith reliance on a lawyer's advice should indeed be relevant. The issues raised in this chapter are among the most difficult in the theory of the criminal law. Readers are invited to make their own contribution to the problem.

Notes

1. Alternatively, the court might claim competence by virtue of the suspect's or the victim's nationality. See StGB §7. Germany also claims jurisidiction

on the basis of an injury to German interests (§5) and universal jurisdiction for certain offenses of universal concern (§6).

2. Aristotle, Nichomachean Ethics 1135a–1137a.

3. StGB §247. Cf. Code Penal §380 (exempting specified familial thefts from penal but not civil liability).

4. A. Eser in Schönke/Schröder, § 247, note 13.

5. 420 U.S. 671 (1975).

6. Id. at 696.

7. Id. at 672. See United States v. Crimmins, 123 F.2d 271 (2d Cir. 1941).

8. There were other indicia of consent, such as Washington's insistence that Tyson use a condom and her choosing to be in the upper position during sexual relations. On the analysis of these and other factual considerations, see With Justice for Some at 114–15, 117, 120–31.

9. This conflict came to the fore again in the criminal acquittal of O.J. Simpson, motivated, in part by Johnnie Cochran's impassioned plea to send a message to the L.A. Police Department. See id. at 266–69.

10. The *locus classicus* is Regina v. Prince, L.R. 2 Cr. Cas. Res. 154 (1875). One case going to the right way is People v. Hernandez, 61 Cal. 2d 529, 393 P.2d 673, 39 Cal. Rptr. 361 (1964).

11. 193 Md. 489, 69 A.2d 456 (1950).

12. The penalty should be reduced according to StGB § 49(1), which provides a schedule for reducing the statutory minimum, e.g., from one year to three months.

13. On the complicated reception of MPC § 2.04(3) in the states, see 1 American Law Institute, Model Penal Code and Its Commentaries § 2.04(3) at 268–280 (1985).

14. See Jerome Hall, General Principles of Criminal Law 383 (2d ed. 1960).

15. Part (b) of this section recognizes "ignorance or mistake as to a matter of fact or law [as] a defense if (b) the law provides that the state of mind established by such ignorance or mistake constitutes a defense." This is obviously redundant.

16. MPC § 1.13(10): "Material element of an offense" means an element that does not relate exclusively to the statute of limitations, jurisdiction, venue or to any other matter similarly unconnected with (i) the harm or evil, incident to conduct, sought to be prevented by the law defining the offense, or (ii) the existence of a justification or excuse for such conduct.

17. Note my criticism of extending the concept of negligence to cover mistakes as well as accidents in chapter 7 supra.

18. T. Lenckner in Schönke/Schröder, § 171, note 6.

19. Regina v. Tolson, 23 Q.B.D. 168 (1889); People v. Vogel, 46 Cal. 2d 798, 299 P.2d 850 (1956).

20. In *Tolson*, id., the defendant married a second time after her husband had been absent for seven years. A proviso in the statute on bigamy provided an exemption from liability where the spouse had been continuously absent for seven years. Shortly after the wedding, the defendant's spouse reappeared. The jury found that she was reasonably mistaken about the death of her husband. The Queen's Bench voted 9–5 that she should not have been convicted. In one of several opinions for reversal, Wills, J., reasoned that for a crime under

English law there must be "an intention to do something wrong." In *Vogel,* id. the defendant was allegedly mistaken about whether his first wife had divorced him. The Court concluded that bigamy required a "wrongful intent," which, in Traynor, J.'s opinion for the Court, meant that he was not guilty if he had "a bona fide and reasonable belief that facts existed that left him free to remarry." 299 P.2d at 852.

21. 342 U.S. 246 (1952).

22. 18 U.S.C. §641.

23. 342 U.S. at 249.

24. Eser in Schönke/Schröder § 242, note 12.

25. Rethinking Criminal Law at 25.

26. Claus Roxin, I Strafrecht: Allgemeiner Teil, 407–417 (2d ed. 1994).

27. In principle, the distinction is between a mistake about wrongdoing (§ 17) as opposed to a mistake about the application of positive law *(Subsumtionsirrtum).* Ironically, so far as the official interpretation of positive law might be arbitrary, the mistake about the classification of conduct under the law has a better claim to lenient treatment.

28. For more on self-defense and necessity as claims of justification, see chapter 8 supra.

29. For example, some common law writers have adopted the principle that the defendant should be judged on the facts "as the defendant believes them to be." The leading voice for this subjectivist view is Glanville Williams, Textbook of Criminal Law 135–38 (2d ed. 1983).

30. Director of Pub. Prosecutions v. Morgan, 1976 A.C. 182, 2 All E.R. 347, [1975] 2 W.L.R. 913 (H.L.). See also the later case, Regina v. Cogan, 2 All E.R. 1059, [1975] 3 W.L.R. 316 (C.A.). The possibility of convicting on the basis of reckless indifference to consent is grounded in the Sexual Offenses (Amedment) Act §1 (1976).

31. For earlier criticism, see Rethinking Criminal Law at 699–707.

32. The London Times, May 7, 1975 (J.C. Smith), May 8, 1975 (Glanville Williams).

33. Beckford v. Regina, [1987] 3 All E.R. 425 (conviction reversed because judge incorrectly instructed the jury that the belief in the facts supporting self-defense had to be reasonable).

34. Cramer in Schönke/Schröder, §16, notes 16–18 (discussing various ways in which the principle of §16 lends itself to expansion to cover putative justification).

35. Roxin, supra note 26, at 507.

36. See discussion above at notes 8–10.

37. For a detailed look at the problem of victims' rights in rape cases, see With Justice for Some at 107–131.

38. MPC §2.11(1). Note that MPC §2.11(2)(c) recognizes the possibility that consent might constitute a justification under article III of the Code, but nothing in article III explains how this might be possible.

39. MPC §3.09(2).

40. 1 Hawkins, Pleas of the Crown 110 (1716).

41. The case is explored in detail in A Crime of Self-Defense.

42. German writers seem not to care too much about this point. They are willing to interpret the concept of "wrongful" attack differently from the con-

cept of "wrongfulness" as used in defining offenses. See Roxin, supra note 26, at 538–39; T. Lenckner in Schönke/Schröder, §32, comment.

43. New York Penal Law §35.15. Admittedly, the New York statute treats the reasonably mistaken defense as justified, while I claim here that it is more sensible to see the mistake as an excuse.

44. This is the situation that occurred in the German "King Cat" case, discussed infra at 316–318.

45. See the argument above at notes 41–43 about why reasonable mistakes of type three should be treated as excuses.

46. See the discussion of negligence in chapter 7 supra. Note also that there is an analogous excuse in cases of recklessness, behaving as would a reasonable person in choosing to take a substantial and unjustified risk.

47. MPC §2.09; StGB §35.

48. Note that under StGB §35, this time delay would presumably undercut the excuse. Duress applies only in response to imminent risks.

49. StGB §35(2). If the mistake was avoidable, the penalty must be reduced.

50. See Meir Dan-Cohen, *Decision Rules and Conduct Rules: On Acoustic Separation in Criminal Law*, 97 Harv. L. Rev. 625 (1984).

51. MPC §2.04(1).

10

Attempts versus Completed Offenses

Murder, theft, rape, arson, robbery, and the other hard-core felonies leave damage in their wake. The decedent is killed; the property taken; the body violated. Crime consists in an attack against a tangible human interest. The crime succeeds when the goods of life, limb, property, and freedom fall hostage to hostile intentions.

At the core of the criminal law, then, there lies a victim. One function of criminal proceedings is to address the victim's sense of having suffered unjustly. The victim demands justice—both in seeing the criminal brought to account and even in seeing the offender suffer as the victim has suffered. But retribution is not the only function of punishment. Crimes also threaten the public interest in security. Accordingly, the state takes charge of prosecuting criminals. But the pursuit of justice in response to a crime eventually gives rise to a more basic question: Would it not make sense to intervene and prevent harm before it occurs? If the would-be offender is about to kill or rape, why not stop him at that point and convict him of the crime? Thus was born the idea of attempted crime.

The concept of attempting derives from the completed offense. The primary difference is that the harm—the death, the beating, the loss of property, the sexual penetration—is absent. But when the harm is absent, it is not clear how much the actor must do in order to be guilty of an attempt. In Western jurisprudence the first recorded effort to define a criminal attempt appears in the French Penal Code of 1810.

The drafters took the issue to be so important that in § 2 of the code they defined the threshold of attempting in a phrase *le commencement d'execution* that would later become a staple of Western thinking. At the point that the execution began, but not before that, the actor became criminally liable. This phrase was carried over in the Prussian Code of 1851, § 31, and then in the German Criminal Code of 1871, § 43. An analogous standard found its way into the nineteenth-century English case law.[1] Modified forms of this formula are still common in European legislation.[2]

Of course, it is by no means easy to know when the execution has begun. Does bringing a ladder to the scene of an intended burglary commence the execution? Or sterilizing instruments with the intent to perform an abortion? Or burning down a house with the intent to defraud an insurance company? Whether or not the French formula is easy to apply, it does represent an effort to link the act of attempting with the definition of the substantive offense. This was a way to vest the act of attempting with substantive content and thereby avoid the dangers of an elastic norm applied to any conduct the judges dislike.

Yet this link with the completed offenses could not hold. The same reasoning that led to the recognition of attempts as a distinct offense led, in time, to setting the threshold of liability at ever earlier stages of consummation. If there was no reason to wait until the harm occurred, there was no reason to wait until the harm was "about" to occur. Better to catch the potential offender before she has a chance to get too close to a successful crime. Most Western legal systems agreed at least that there should be a difference, in principle, between preparation and attempts. Mere preparation was not punishable.[3] But the Communist legal systems, a view carried forward in current Russian law, rejected even this restriction.[4] And the Model Penal Code (MPC) pushed back the threshold of attempting so far (any "substantial step" toward commission of the crime) that virtually any act—with the requisite intent—will be enough.[5] Some state statutes justified arrest and conviction, in effect, for any act in furtherance of a criminal design.[6] The drive to protect the public from harm results in liability at ever earlier stages of realizing criminal designs.

10.1 The Search for the Primary Offense

Historically, the attempt derives from the completed offense. But once attempts came to be recognized as a staple of nineteenth-century criminal prosecutions, theorists began to wonder whether with regard to at least some crimes, the attempt might indeed be the more basic offense. In cases of bringing about harmful consequences—homicide, arson, destruction of property—the actor might do everything in his power to bring about the harmful result without succeeding. He might shoot to kill and hit the wall. She might throw a fire bomb with the intent of burning down a house and the bomb turns out to be a dud. He might swing an axe at his enemy and miss. This element of accident in cases of harmful consequences makes one wonder whether the attempt should be regarded as the basic offense and the completed homicide, arson, or battery merely an adventitious aftereffect of attempting with intent.

Our ordinary sensibilities tell us that, of course, it is worse to kill than to shoot and miss. The successful killer deserves a greater penalty than the unsuccessful attempter. At least that is what the woman on the street—or the man in the Clapham bus, as the English say—thinks. In law as in basketball, the rule usually is: No harm, no foul. No one with ordinary sensibilities would advocate the death penalty for someone who merely tried to kill. And yet many of the leading theorists of criminal law, at least in the English-speaking world, hold the view that the consummation of an intended offense is merely a matter of chance and therefore not a proper basis for aggravating the penalty designated for the attempt.[7]

The basic argument for this position begins with the sensible premise that punishment should be imposed on the basis of blameworthiness or culpability. There follows a more controversial point: The only fair basis for culpability is the actions under one's control—that is, what can one be sure of bringing about with the extensions of one's body. This includes basic actions such as speaking, pulling the trigger of a gun, putting poison in coffee, planting a bomb. It does not include the consequences of these actions that depend on intervening forces of nature. It follows, according to the logic of this argument, that these consequences should not be charged to the account of the culpable actor. This is the reasoning that leads so many thoughtful writers to support the view that the attempt—which is supposedly within the control of the actor—should be the primary offense. The basis for punishment should, therefore, be the attempt and not its fortuitous aftereffects.

The more traditional way of thinking about crime and responsibility starts with the bringing about of harm and inquires: Who is responsible for this wrong and to what extent? The attempter merely approaches the harm, merely creates a risk of the harm, and therefore should be held liable for a lesser degree of wrongdoing. A lesser degree of wrongdoing implies mitigated punishment.[8]

The search for the primary or basic offense implies, then, two different concepts of crime. The culpability-centered theory focuses exclusively on the actor who has formulated a criminal intent and has started to act upon it. Whether there is an actual victim, whether the action disturbs the peace, is irrelevant. What counts is the potential of the attempt to bring about harm, if it is not halted in its progression toward execution. The evil of the attempt lies primarily in its defiance of the legal norms designed to protect the interests of others.

The harm-centered conception of crime focuses on the victim. The evil of the offense lies in killing, raping, burning, destroying, maiming, threatening—in general, in bringing about harm to a concrete individual. When there is no actual but only a potential victim, there is by definition a lesser wrong.

It is true that those who merely attempt but do not cause harm have lesser grounds for remorse and guilt.[9] In *Crime and Punishment* Raskolnikov is properly haunted by the thought of having killed an old lady to take her money. If he tried to kill her and failed, it would be curiously neurotic for him to suffer the same pangs of guilt. Recognizing the role of remorse testifies to the close connection between wrongdoing and victimhood. That there is an actual victim—an irreversible harm to another human being—produces a human response that differs radically from the sense of impropriety that comes simply from violating a norm of the legal system.

Those who argue that the attempt is the primary offense, and the completed offense merely a contingent aftereffect, should hold the view that caused harm is generally irrelevant to culpability. It would follow that negligently and recklessly creating risks of serious harm should constitute crimes in themselves. The MPC in fact endorses a crime of reckless endangerment that has found its way into many state criminal codes.[10] The crime typically covers dangerous actions such as Bernhard Goetz's shooting in a crowded subway car. Attempts are always linked to specific offenses—murder, arson, battery, rape, but the crime of reckless endangerment stands on its own. You cannot be guilty both of attempted battery and battery, for the former derives from the latter. Yet you can be liable for both the independent offenses of reckless endangerment and a completed crime of violence, such as battery or homicide. Bernhard Goetz was charged (though later acquitted) on counts of reckless endangerment and battery as well as attempted murder.[11]

Some legal systems have tried to expand the definition of criminal attempts in order to cover the typical action of reckless endangerment: shooting into a crowded room but without a specific intent to injure anyone and in fact not injuring anyone. In a 1968 case in Scotland, the defendant was charged and convicted of attempted murder after having fired several shots into a room with four people in it, including his estranged mistress. The high court in Scotland rejected the defendant's claim that attempted murder required an intention to kill.[12] German jurisprudence would insist upon an intention to kill in this context, but the courts would apply the standard of "conditional intent" or *dolus eventualis* to include cases of endangering others, in which the actor is "indifferent" to whether he kills someone or not.[13]

American law takes a stricter line on attempted offenses.[14] The MPC requires that the actor "purposely engage in conduct which would constitute the crime if the attendant circumstances were as he believes them to be."[15] Suppose, for example, that rape is defined so that the offender is guilty if he engages in intercourse having made a negligent mistake about whether the women has consented.[16] The would-be offender believes, mistakenly, that his date consents and he engages her in a sexual embrace. She rebuffs him. Is he guilty of attempted rape? If "the attendant circumstances were as he believes them to be," a completed act of intercourse would have been a crime, and therefore the rebuffed lover does not have the "conscious object" to engage in unlawful intercourse. He is not guilty of attempted rape.[17]

The theoretical discussion on the intention that should be required for an attempted offense is surprisingly weak. Whether the problem is solved legislatively or judicially, the law should be grounded in a stronger rationale either for expanding or restricting the required intent. There seem to be two possible lines of argument. One begins with the recognition that the concept of "attempting" functions both as the name of the offense and as a conceptual guide for interpreting what the offense is. That is, to be guilty of an attempt one should engage in an attempt—as that term is understood in ordinary English. To engage in an attempt, one must really try to bring about the prohibited harm. One does not *try* to kill, rape, burn, destroy, and maim simply by virtue of these harms occurring as the side effects of one's conduct. One attempts to accomplish these criminal ends only when that is the conscious object of one's action.

A distinct but related argument is that only a direct intention to kill is "essentially murderous."[18] Only a full commitment of the personality to achieving the criminal end should provide a surrogate for actually bringing about that end.

A strict requirement of intention in cases of attempts reinforces the idea that the attempt is an exceptional form of liability. Because it is the derivative rather than the primary offense, because its contours are invariably vague, the attempt finds its precision in the subjective intent requirement.

Yet the principle represented by the invention of the criminal attempt has become well established as a model for defining other offenses that fall short of causing harm. The entire field of inchoate offenses derives from the idea that it is better for the state to intervene before actual harm occurs. The leading cases of inchoate liability in the early stages of harmful conduct are conspiracy—nothing more than an agreement to commit the offense—and possession offenses. Conspiracy offenses represent a transplant into the common law of crimes from private law and have proved to be a critical tool in the prosecution of organized crime. Most European legal systems still do not recognize a general crime of banding together to commit an offense.

Possession offenses are a spin-off from the law of attempts, acquiring the tools of criminal activity being a typical stage in the progression from the onset of a criminal plan to its harmful realization. The most common forms of prohibited possession are drugs and weapons, but the possession of other tools of crime are also prohibited—everything from counterfeit plates to burglary tools. The crime is the possession itself and the typical subjective requirement of knowledge that the prohibited goods are in one's possession.

The major difficulty with the offenses of possession is that they sweep too wide. They encompass cases where there is no potential social harm. People can possess burglary tools without an intention to use them. Unlike drugs and guns, burglary tools are not likely to be dangerous if they fall into the wrong hands. For this reason, courts have responded very skeptically toward statutory provisions that prohibit tools appearing to have primarily a criminal use.[19]

Negligent and reckless wrongdoing have generated their own brand of inchoate liability. Drunk driving—and traffic violations in general—are punishable because they generate a risk of harm. The harm is realized not in the particular case but over the long run of cases.

Thinking of the attempt as the basic offense supports the general trend toward punishing inchoate offenses such as possession of drugs and reckless driving. The trend toward intervention before harm actually occurs supports the view that these offenses are becoming the more basic instruments of criminal justice in the courts today. Yet the structural features of attempts reveals that they are not in fact primary but rather derivative of the completed offense.

10.2 The Structure of Attempts: Impossibility

Punishing attempts generates a window on some of the most basic issues of criminal responsibility. We have already mentioned the problem of legality in defining the threshold of attempting. There is no precise line for distinguishing between nonpunishable preparation and punishable attempt. All we know is that an attempt is some act in furtherance of a criminal intent that falls short of completion. The heart of the offense is in fact the intention—not the action.

Yet the traditional concept of legality attaches to harmful actions not just to criminal intentions. In the nineteenth century, jurists adhered more firmly to the view that an attempt must come close to a harmful action. Oliver Wendell Holmes, Jr., captured this view when he listed the following as relevant variables in assessing whether preparation has passed the threshold of criminal attempt: "the nearness of the danger, the greatness of the harm, and the degree of apprehension felt."[20] But how dangerous must the act be in order to warrant criminalization? There obviously can be no precise answer to that question, yet the emphasis on danger brings home the importance of thinking of attempts as relational events, signaling the eruption of a real threat to the victim.

In this century, a subtle shift has occurred in the danger perceived in criminal attempts. For many who favor earlier stages of liability, the question is not whether the *act* is dangerous to a specific potential victim, but whether the *actor* is dangerous to the society as a whole. As those who worked on the Model Penal Code expressed their philosophy of criminalization: "The basic premise here is that the actor's mind is the best proving ground of his dangerousness."[21] The shift from act to mind, then, coincides with a shift from focusing on the threats posed by dangerous actions to the danger posed by dangerous people.

Nowhere is this shift more evident than in cases where the actor intends to do harm, but the actions she undertakes in fact pose no concrete threat. She points a gun that unbeknownst to her is unloaded. He tries to steal from an empty purse. She buys white powder that she thinks is heroin. These are so-called impossible or, in German parlance, "inapt" attempts. In one sense, however, all attempts are impossible. If his aim had been better and had the intended victim not been moving, the would-be killer would have succeeded. What people mean when they talk about impossible attempts is that some specific factual barrier prevents consummation of the offense: the gun is unloaded, the pocket is empty, the powder is just powder. If these single circumstances were changed appropriately, the criminal result would have been assured.

All legal systems seem to agree that impossible attempts are punishable if the behavior itself produces apprehension or generates apprehension in the mind of an ideal observer. For example, if someone shoots into the bed where her intended victim usually sleeps, the courts readily impose liability for attempted murder.[22] It also follows that pulling the trigger on an adventitiously unloaded gun with the intent to kill should be a proper basis for liability. Though nineteenth-century courts were reluctant to convict in these cases, the empty pocket cases would seem to follow the same pattern.[23] Sticking one's hand into someone else's purse bespeaks larceny. It is behavior that paradigmatically threatens the possessions of others.[24] That there happens to be nothing worth stealing does not negate the manifest danger signaled by the action.

The target of controversy in the theory of attempts is not these cases of manifest danger but rather the range of cases where the action itself is totally innocent on its face. These are the cases typified by purchasing talcum powder (thinking that it is heroin), putting sugar in an enemy's coffee (thinking that it is cyanide), or administering a harmless substance to a pregnant woman (thinking that it is an abortifacient). If these innocuous actions are criminal, it is only because the actor entertains certain thoughts: he wants to engage in an action that would clearly be criminal if the facts were as he believed them to be.

In the nineteenth and early twentieth centuries, many courts sensed that there was something amiss about convicting in these situations of innocuous conduct. A French court held in 1859 that administering an innocuous abortifacient was not an attempted abortion.[25] An English court came to the same conclusion a half century later.[26] One American court acquitted in a case of allegedly attempting to kill with a nonpoisonous substance.[27] But generally, American courts were inclined to convict in cases where the defendant used too little poison to have a fatal effect.[28]

The high court (Reichsgericht) of the newly unified German states signaled the modern trend by convicting in all cases, innocuous action or not, in which the defendant intended to commit an offense and acted on the basis of the intent. In the first year of their published decisions, 1880, the judges were willing to convict of attempted abortion in a case of using an innocuous substance with the intent to commit abortion[29] or attempted infanticide in a case of trying to kill a child who was already dead.[30] Remarkably, the courts took the line that a bad intention was sufficient for liability, even though the academic literature consistently opposed liability for innocuous conduct.[31]

The emphasis on intention as the core of the crime anticipated a central feature of Nationalist Socialist criminal law, namely, emphasizing the offender's attitude (*Gesinnung*) as the essence of criminality. After 1933, German academics caved into the Party line and gave up their effort to refine the objective or external side of attempt liability. After the war, the subjective theory of attempts remained dominant. As expressed in the new criminal code, enacted in 1975, the way the actor perceives the world takes the place of the world as it is. The act of attempting must be judged by the actor's "conception of the act." This means that if the actor assumes that the powder he buys is heroin or that the stuff he puts in the coffee is poison, his conduct is judged according to those facts. That there is no actual danger to anyone in these actions—and no manifestation of danger to unnerve the community—becomes irrelevant.

One might be tempted to treat this postwar position of German law as a simple continuation of the National Socialist theory of *Gesinnungsstrafrecht* (attitude-based criminal law). This would prove embarrassing for American lawyers, for in the 1950s the leading U.S. thinkers came to the same conclusion that in cases of impossible attempts liability should be judged "under the circumstances as [the actor] believes them to be."[32] The MPC goes even further than the 1975 German code, for the American model code penalizes every act or omission that the actor thinks is "a substantial step" toward the commission of the offense. The German law requires at least that the attempter conceives of his action, in the language of the traditional European formula, as the "beginning of the execution of the crime."[33]

The contemporary justification for focusing on the internal attitude of the actor is that acting on the intention to cause harm to others represents a rejection of the legal order. By deciding to commit a crime and acting on the decision, the individual pits himself against the community. In the pragmatic language of the drafters of the MPC, the person who reveals his hostility toward the rights of others becomes too dangerous to tolerate. The purpose of the criminal law should be to protect the rights of orderly citizens by moving swiftly against those who reveal themselves as enemies of the legal order. The frame of mind that underlies expansive attempt liability resembles, therefore, the us-against-them social policy that has led to the use of life sentences against third-time offenders.[34]

The policy dubbed "three strikes and you're out" reveals how far Americans are willing to go to isolate and confine those who are thought to be dangerous. By like token, the approach toward attempt liability under the MPC goes to extremes that are difficult to take seriously. Suppose that a lifeguard advises a swimmer that in view of the rough sea she should not swim out past the breaking waves; he is miffed when she refuses to heed the advice. It appears, then, that she is drowning. In anger he decides not to do anything to rescue her. After about ten minutes of watching her seemingly struggle, he changes his mind and throws her a line. She breaks out laughing for in fact she was only pretending to be in distress. It is rather hard to believe, but under the rule of the MPC as applied to these circumstances, the lifeguard would be guilty of attempted murder. He omits to act when he is duty bound to do so, and under the "circumstances as he believes them to be," he engages in a substantial step toward abandoning the swimmer to her drowning in the rough seas. There would be no liability under the German rule because even under the lifeguard's "conception of the act," he was not beginning the execution of criminal homicide.[35]

The expansive approach to attempt liability under the MPC would not be thinkable if the drafters were not implicitly relying on prosecutorial discretion to sort out the serious from the trivial cases. But what should prosecutors look for among the vast range of cases where individuals make themselves liable for attempts under the MPC? Presumably by using seat-of-the-pants judgments to determine who is dangerous and a real threat to the social order. Whether our life guard is a threat of this sort depends, one would think, on many factors about his biography that are not expressed in his encounter with the swimmer who dismissed his advice.

The drafters of the MPC have no qualms about directing the criminal law away from dangerous acts and toward dangerous actors.[36] It does not occur to them that this shift betokens a radical departure from a basic principle of liberal jurisprudence, namely, that criminal law and punishment should attach to actions as abstracted from the personal histories and propensities of those who engage in them. People make themselves subject to punishment because of what they do, not by virtue of their inherent potential to do harm. Again, one sees in the MPC the same mentality at work that led, some thirty years later, to many states adopting draconian principles of sentencing ("three strikes and you're out") to rid themselves of people perceived to be dangerous.

In summary, two anti-liberal principles convince many jurists that they should punish innocuous attempts—namely, attempts that are perfectly innocent and nonthreatening on their face. The first is the principle of gearing the criminal law to an attitude of hostility toward the norms of the legal system. The second is changing the focus of the criminal law from acts to actors. These two are linked by the inference: people who display an attitude of hostility toward the norms of the system show themselves to be dangerous and therefore should be subject to imprisonment to protect the interests of others.

In legal systems as we know them, however, no one carries these anti-liberal principles to their logical conclusion. For example, a resolute concern about the twin issues of hostility to the legal order and personal dangerousness would lead to liability in two areas where everyone seems opposed. First, those who try by superstitious means, say by black magic or witchcraft, satisfy these two desiderata. Yet the consensus of Western legal systems is that there should be no liability, regardless of the wickedness or firmness of intent, for sticking pins in a doll or chanting an incantation to banish one's enemy to the nether world.[37] Of course, some people argue, without proof, that those who use superstitious, ineffective means will not resort to methods proven to be more effective under scientific criteria of causation. The real reason for exempting black magic attempts from liability is that these superstitious techniques amuse rather than disturb the average person. In extremis, then, the traditional principle reasserts itself: The conduct must appear dangerous and disturbing to the community as a whole.[38]

The same extreme concern about dangerous hostility to the legal order should lead to the punishability of those who think that they are committing offenses when they are not. Suppose that someone lies to a police officer under the mistaken assumption that she is thereby committing a crime. Or suppose that someone has intercourse with a woman under the mistaken assumption that the age of consent is 18 when she is 17—over the de facto minimum of 16. The general view of Western legal systems is that no liability attaches in these cases. The offense, it is said, is not legally possible or it is an "illusionary offense" *(Wahndelikt)*. What this means, I suppose, is that conduct is not a threat to an interest that law has defined as legally protected.[39]

The exemption for legally impossible attempts is hardly convincing. These are cases in which the actor has displayed hostility toward the legal order and for that reason is as dangerous as someone who for strictly factual reasons could not commit perjury or statutory rape. Suppose that in the would-be perjury case the mistake is not about the context in which perjury is possible but about the supposed falsity of the testimony. Or in the putative statutory rape case, suppose that the mistake is not about the minimum age of consent but about the age of the girl (he thinks she is 15 when in fact she is 17). These cases are equally impossible but they would be called "factual" rather than cases of legal impossibility. Those who would punish according to subjective criteria would impose liability in these cases. Serious people must smile at the fragility of these distinctions. As critical a question as criminal liability for an attempted offense should not turn on distinctions that hardly convey a material difference.[40]

These two examples demonstrate that the basic philosophical tensions in the law of attempts have yet to find a proper resolution. The tendency in many countries of the West is toward penalizing more and more conduct according to the actor's perception of the relevant events. Yet this tendency stops short of imposing liability in these cases—superstitious and legally imaginary attempts—where the logic of the subjective approach would point toward criminal responsibility. Further evidence of the philosophically open quality of these questions lies in the resistance of several major jurisdictions to the subjectivist bias now dominant in German and American law.[41]

10.3 The Structure of Attempts: Abandonment

The peculiar quality of attempts as uncompleted crimes is revealed by the possibility of the offender's voluntarily abandoning the criminal plan before anyone is hurt. All modern codes recognize an exemption from liability for these changes of heart that they would not grant to offenders who, say, steal or embezzle money, and then change their mind and wish to return the funds with interest.

The code provisions recognizing this possibility focus on two problems: First, what is the necessary motivations for the abandonment? And further, at what stage of committing the offense is abandonment still possible? The new French code, carrying forward the original provision of 1810, defines an attempt as an action that fails as "a result of circumstances independent of the actor's will."[42] Implicitly, if the attempt fails for reasons that solely depend on the actor's will, then there is no liability for the attempt. The modern trend has been to state the requirement of "voluntary abandonment" affirmatively.[43] The MPC requires a "complete and voluntary renunciation" of criminal purpose,[44] and then goes on to list certain circumstances that imply that the renunciation is *not* voluntary. These include circumstances: (1) that increase the probability of apprehension and (2) that make the realization of the crime more difficult. Other circumstances are mentioned, such as postponing the crime to a later time, that merely make the renunciation incomplete.

Voluntariness provides the key both to understanding the concept of culpability for committing crimes and for applying the concept of abandonment. Excuses, such as insanity and personal necessity, negate the voluntariness of conduct and accordingly, preclude a finding of blameworthy (culpable) wrongdoing. The conditions for negating the voluntariness of abandoned attempts have the opposite effect of excuses. These conditions inculpate rather than exculpate. Unfortunately, these voluntariness-negating criteria carry no single designation in the literature. For the sake of convenience, let us call them "attempt-affirming grounds." These inculpatory, voluntariness-negating grounds are of great theoretical interest: they pose the same question of responsibility as do excusing conditions but in the transposed context of overcoming rather than generating a defense to liability.

The attempt-affirming grounds fall into three plausible categories: (1) the impact of third parties, (2) the impact of the potential victim, and (3) physical disincentives to completing the crime. Generally, so far as the intervention of a third party provides the incentive to abandon the attempt, the action is not regarded as voluntary. If a police officer or a stranger suddenly appears on the scene, the would-be criminal might well desist and flee the scene. This is hardly sufficient to counteract an attempted offense already committed. The Wisconsin code captures this attempt-affirming ground by stipulating that abandonment is effective only if the attempt would have succeeded "except for the intervention of another person or some other extraneous factor."[45]

The protestations of the potential victim have a nuanced effect on the liability of the would-be criminal who desists. An intriguing 1955 German case held that dissuasion by the victim does not necessarily negate the voluntariness of the abandonment. The defendant accosted a young woman whom he had not previously known, threw her to the ground, and tried to kiss her. Instead of resisting physically, the victim induced the defendant to desist with the promise that she would later engage in voluntary intercourse with him. They both stood up and at that moment the girl saw two evening strollers to whom she called for help. At trial the defendant was convicted of attempted rape, his defense of abandonment being rejected on the ground that it was not "voluntary."[46]

The German Supreme Court reversed the conviction in a carefully reasoned opinion that stressed the defendant's precise motives for desisting, prior to seeing two passers-by (if he had stopped because of them, his actions would clearly not have been voluntary). The key question for the German court is whether in considering the victim's promise of sex at a later time the potential rapist remained "master of his decision." If so, then the abandonment was voluntary.

The distinction underlying the German court's reasoning is that the victim's persuasion differs fundamentally from the third category of cases, namely, dissuasion by circumstances. For example, if the victim had been menstruating and the would-be rapist therefore lost interest, his decision would appear to be stimulated by the circumstances rather than the persuasive impact of the victim's promises.[47] This is admittedly a very subtle distinction. How would one classify a case in which the victim frightened off the defendant by telling him that she was infected by the AIDS virus? My hunch is that this would fall on the attempt-affirming side of the line, but one might be forgiven for thinking that this distinction is too fine-grained for the practical administration of justice. American courts would probably impose attempt liability in all of these cases.[48]

In theft and burglary cases, would-be offenders are often dissuaded either by the physical difficulty of the task or the unexpectedly unappealing quality of the intended booty. If the problem is physical difficulty, the law is clear in the United States and in Germany: no abandonment. But suppose that a mugger finds that his victim has only five dollars in his wallet. He gives back the wallet and says, "Forget it. You need the money more than I do." Is that an effective abandonment? A German case holds that the dissuasion of an unattractive bounty fails to negate liability for attempted robbery.[49]

In the end it is difficult to make sense of all these fine distinctions without paying heed to the rationale for recognizing the defense of abandonment. The theories fall into two categories. One line of instrumental reasoning, apparently favored by the drafters to the Model Penal Code, stresses the incentive effects of the defense: It is good to offer the attempter a reason for not carrying through with the offense. No one knows, of course, whether this incentive actually influences people more than the inherent advantage of avoiding detection by abstaining from causing harm. A related argument, considered but rejected in the German literature, treats the exemption from punishment as a reward for reversing the effort to commit an offense. The drawback of this argument is that it proves too much: it does not explain why the same reward should not accrue to someone who seeks to reverse the effects of theft offenses by returning the dishonestly acquired property.

The better reason for recognizing the defense of abandonment is that it is conceptually connected to the attempt itself. The effort to desist and to check the consequences of the attempt shows that the "criminal intent was not as firm as would have been required for the execution of the offense."[50] Though this rationale makes sense, it does not adequately explain the nuanced decisions of the courts. In particular, it does not explain why American thinking tends to demand a total renunciation of the criminal purpose[51] while German law is content with a standard that stresses whether the attempter is the "master of his decision."[52] In the end, unfortunately, we must conclude that the factors influencing the contours of abandonment represent a mixture of conceptual and political considerations.

Notes

1. Regina v. Eagleton, 6 Cox Crim. Cas. 559 (1855) ("acts immediately connected with [the commission of the offense]").

2. StGB §22 (A person attempts an offense if *according to his conception of the fact* he commences the realization of the Definition of the offense (*zur Verwirklichung des Tatbestands ansetzt*)). Código Penal § 16(1) (principio a la ejecutión del delito).

3. E.g., English Criminal Attempts Act, 1981, §1(1) (attempt requires "an act which is more than merely preparatory to the commission of the offense").

4. Russian Criminal Code §§30(1)&(2) (preparation punishable only in the case of "serious" and "very serious" offense).

5. MPC §5.01(1)(c). The MPC was so concerned about the tradition of limiting liability to acts close to commission that it included a catalogue of preparatory acts that "shall not be held to constitute a substantial step." See MPC §5.01(2).

6. See, e.g., Illinois Criminal Code §8–4(a); Oregon Statutes §161.405.

7. See Sanford Kadish, *Foreword: The Criminal Law and the Luck of the Draw*, 84 J. Crim. L. & Crim. 679 (1994); Joel Feinberg, *Equal Punishment for Failed Attempts: Some Bad but Instructive Arguments Against It*, 37 Ariz. L. Rev. 117 (1995). The Model Penal Code §5.05(1) provides that except for the most serious felonies the attempt should be treated as a "crime of the most serious grade and degree" as the most serious crime attempted.

8. Anthony Duff in Scotland has become one of the leading voices for the "objective" harm-oriented theory of attempts in the English-speaking world. See R. A. Duff, Criminal Attempts 348–389 (1996). See also Lawrence Crocker, *Justice in Criminal Liability: Decriminalizing Harmless Attempts*, 52 Ohio St. L. Rev. 1057 (1992). See also Rethinking at 139–146.

9. See Rethinking Criminal Law at 482–483; R. A. Duff, Intention, Agency, and Criminal Liability 338–341 (1990).

10. MPC §211.2 (a misdemeanor, limited to recklessly causing "danger of death or serious bodily harm").

11. See A Crime of Self-Defense at 6, note 11.

12. See Cawthorne's case, [1968] Justiciary Court 32 (Scotland).

13. P. Cramer in Schönke/Schröder, §15, note 84. See the more thorough discussion above at 122–123.

14. See, e.g., Thacker v. Commonwealth, 134 Va. 767, 114 S.E. 504 (1922) (intent to kill necessary for attempted murder, but not for murder); United States v. Short, 4 U.S.C.M.A. 437, 16 C.M.R. 11 (1954) (Brosman, J., dissenting) (arguing that an unreasonable mistake as to victim's consent would not be a defense to consummated rape, but should be a defense to the inchoate offense of assault with intent to rape).

15. MPC §5.01(1)(a).

16. This is the approach that I advocate in criticism of the *Morgan* decision. See pp. 159–163 supra.

17. Whether under these facts he would be guilty of the complete crime of battery would depend on whether his mistake excluded the intent required for battery. See chapter 9 supra.

18. See Dutt, supra note 9, at 204 (1990).

19. Benton v. United States, 232 F.2d 341 (D.C.Cir. 1956) (statute prohibiting tools that "reasonably may be employed in the commission of any crime" declared unconstitutional); Judgement of Landgericht in Heidelberg, October 2, 1958, 1959 NJW 1932 (lower German court refused to apply provision of 1871 Criminal Code prohibiting the possession of burglary tools).

20. Holmes, The Common Law 68 (1881); cf. Commonwealth v. Kennedy, 170 Mass. 18, 48 N.E. 770 (1897).

21. Wechsler, Jones & Korn, *The Treatment of Inchoate Crimes in the Model Penal Code of the American Law Institute: Attempts, Solicitation and Conspiracy*, 61 Colum. L. Rev. 571, 579 (1961). Cf. MPC §5.01, comment at 32 (Tent. Draft No. 10, 1960).

22. State v. Mitchell, 170 Mo. 633, 71 S.W. 175 (1902). Judgment of April 12, 1877, Recueil Sirey 1877.I.329 (French Cour de Cassation).

23. A Prussian court held that it was not criminal to break into a room for the purpose of stealing if it turned out that the goods sought were not there, Judgment of the Prussian High Court, February 22, 1854, 1854 GA 548. Ten years later an English court held that it was not criminal to stick one's hand into an empty pocket with an undisputed intent to steal. Regina v. Collins, 169 Eng. Rep. 1477 (Crim. App. 1864), but a French court came to the opposite conclusion Judgment of November 4, 1876, Recueil Sirey 1877. I. 48. *Collins* was overruled in Regina v. Ring, 17 Cox Crim. Cas. 491 (C.C.R. 1982). And the German view today also favors conviction. See text at notes 32–33 infra.

24. For more on the theory and relevance of manifest criminality, see Rethinking Criminal Law at 146–157.

25. Judgment of January 6, 1859, Recueil Sirey 1859, I. 362.]

26. Regina v. Osborn, 84 J. P. 63 (1920).

27. State v. Clarissa, 11 Ala. 57 (1847)(slave (!) used "Jamestown weed" in an attempt to kill her master; no evidence that the weed was harmful).

28. Commonwealth v. Kennedy, 170 Mass. 18, 48 N.E. 770 (1897); State v. Glover, 27 S. C. 602, 4 S. E. 564 (1888).

29. Judgment of May 24, 1880, 1 RGSt. 439

30. Judgment of June 10, 1880, 1 RGSt. 451.

31. For example, Andreas Thomsen notes that from the very beginning of its jurisprudence, the Reichsgericht favored the subjective theory of attempts but that nonetheless the "hegemonic theory" [*herrschende Lehre*] favored von Liszt's view that absolutely impossible attempts (those not "concretely dangerous") should be exempt from punishment. See Andreas Thomsen, Das Deutsche Strafrecht 81–82 (1906).

32. MPC §5.01(1)(c).

33. See text at notes 1–2 supra.

34. See, e.g., Cal. Penal Code §1170.12 (West. Supp. 1997) (the list of felonies triggering the statute number over 500 and include marijuana possession and petty theft).

35. German theorists have no difficulty extending their subjective theory of liability to impossible attempts by omissions. See Hans Heinrich Jescheck and Thomas Weigend, Lehrbuch des deutschen Strafrechts 638–39 (5th ed. 1996).

36. See text accompanying note 21 supra.

37. W. LaFave & A. Scott, Jr., Criminal Law 517 (2d ed. 1986). Judgment of June 21, 1900, 33 RGSt. 321; Eser in Schönke/Schröder, §23, note 13, at 297; People v. Ellmore, 128 Ill. App. 312, 261 N.E.2d 736 (1970) (dictum). But cf. MPC §5.01, comment at 38 (Tent. Draft No. 10, 1960), §5.05(2) (permitting discretionary punishment).

38. This standard is admittedly ambiguous. The "community as a whole" is expressed in the observations of a hypothetical person who represents the general traits of the time and place.

39. According to the MPC, if the act is "inherently unlikely to result" in the commission of a crime, liability should be resolved by a judicial inquiry into whether the actor "presents a public danger." MPC §5.05(2). By its terms, the provision appears to cover both cases of superstitious attempts and legal impossibility. But the commentary to the code concedes that cases of legal impossibility should be exempt from all liability—regardless of whether the actor poses a "public danger." MPC §5.01, comment at 31 (Tent. Draft No. 10, 1960). For the policy of German law, see Judgment of July 1, 1959, 13 BGHSt. 235 (actor mistakenly assumed that specific ration cards were covered by the law of forgery; held, no liability for attempt).

40. For my own approach to these problems, see the theory of manifest criminality as developed in Rethinking Criminal Law at 146–157.

41. This, so far as I know, is the situation in Italy and Japan.

42. Code Penal §2 ("si [la tentative] n'a ete suspendue ou si elle n'a manqué son effet que par des circonstances independantes de la volonte de son auteur . . ."). The first part of this provision defines an attempt as "manifested by a commencement of the execution." It seems that provision of failed attempts applies to any stage of commission, even prior to the "commencement of the execution."

43. StGB §224(1).

44. MPC §5.01(4), second part.

45. Wis. Stat. Ann. §939.32(2).

46. Judgment of April 14, 1955, 7 BGHSt. 296.

47. See Judgment of October 5, 1965, 20 BGHSt. 279 (victim found to be

menstruating and defendant loses interest; held not to be a voluntary abandonment).

48. See, e.g., People v. Crary, 265 Cal. All. 2d 534, 71 Cal. Rptr. 4578 (1968); People v. Staples, 6 Cal. App. 3d 61, 85 Cal. Rptr. 589 (1970). But cf. People v. Graham, 176 App. Div. 38, 162 N.Y.S. 334 (1916) (defendant spilled gasoline on bed and then told his son, "I won't do it; God has stayed my hand"; no liability for attempted arson.)

49. See Judgment of February 20, 1953, 4 BGHSt. 56; A. Eser in Schönke/Schröder, §24, note 48.

50. Judgment of February 28, 1956, 9 BGHSt. 48, 52.

51. See Model Penal Code and Commentaries, Part I (2) §5.01, at 358–360 (1985) (stressing the connection between the issue of renunciation and the question of the suspect's dangerousness).

52. See discussion at 183 supra.

11

Perpetration versus Complicity

When a single offender acts alone, he or she is the sole perpetrator or principal. Problems arise when other people get involved. The degree of participation of others varies from a minimal contribution (giving advice, supplying tools or transportation) to taking charge and executing the commission of the crime. Those who counsel, assist, advise, or solicit are called accessories. They are *complicitous* in the acts of the perpetrator.

The paradigm of the accessory is the person who drives the car to the scene of the crime where, as planned, the perpetrator enters a home or a store to commit a serious felony. The question, then, is whether the driver, who remains in the car, becomes complicitous in the felony committed by another.

How one person can become complicitous in the acts of another is by no means obvious. Some ancient legal systems rejected the idea altogether. Jewish law held to the maxim: "In matters of crime no one can represent another."[1] The thinking that would lead to this view would be something like this: Crime entails contamination of the criminal. The only way that contamination can occur is by "hands-on" commission of the offense. Advising, counseling, assisting, or even commanding—these things may be wrong because they facilitate crime, but they do not pollute or contaminate the accessory. At first blush, it appears that this idea survives in the German doctrine of *eigenhaendige Delikte* [crimes that must be committed by one's own hand]. Examples are: incest, perjury, abuse of office. In all of these a personal attribute or status (blood relative, witness, officeholder) is essential to the wrong committed. But, in fact, it is possible to solicit these offenses or to be an accessory in assisting the deed.[2]

Whatever the position in ancient legal systems, the idea of complicity in the actions of another has become a standard part of modern moral thought. We no longer think solely in terms of individuals acting solely on their own account but of groups of people interacting in order to produce a crime of shared responsibility. This is particularly true today in light of the attention paid currently to crimes committed by large bodies of people acting in implicit cooperation—governments, corporations, criminal organizations. When criminality attaches to groups, several questions arise that fall into two main headings:

1. Are only individuals liable for the crime? If so, how should we allocate responsibility among the different participants in the scheme?

2. Should we hold the entire group as a group (government, corporation, criminal organization) liable for the crime?

For the time being, we will concentrate on the question of allocating responsibility among individual actors. But the question of holding groups liable qua groups has become acute in modern criminological thinking, and at the end of this chapter we shall turn to that fundamental problem.

As for holding individual actors responsible, it would make sense to hold each liable according to his or her contribution to the crime. This would follow the analysis we used for measuring responsibility for attempts—each actor accountable according to the degree of danger represented by his or her own action. But as there is debate about whether attempters should be punished less severely than those who complete offenses, legal systems divide on the question whether they should punish accessories less severely than perpetrators. American and French law support the equivalent treatment of all parties, while German and Russian law incline to the view that accessories should be punished less severely.

Thus, there are two fundamentally different approaches to complicity. Some jurisdictions favor the "equivalence" theory, which holds that all accessories should be punished like perpetrators. This is well stated in the California Criminal Code: all those "concerned in the commission of a crime . . . [including those who] aid and abet in its commission . . ."[3] are to be held as principals. Generally, we can take American as well as other common law jurisdictions as representative of the "equivalence" theory. Then there are those jurisdictions, represented chiefly by Germany, that hold to the view that perpetrators and accessories each should be punished according to his or her relative contribution to the crime. The German code provides, for example, that the punishment for accessories must be mitigated according to the same criteria that apply in cases of attempts.[4] When this effort at differentiation is undertaken, numerous problems of line-drawing confront lawyers and judges. One of these is how we should distinguish between two kinds of accessories, those who aid in the offense, and those who conceive of the offense and solicit its commission. It is clear that the latter mode of participation (instigation or *Anstiftung*) is far more serious than merely assisting, or aiding-and-abetting someone else who initiates the crime.

Though American lawyers may say as a formal matter that they believe in the equivalence of all modes of participation, they do not mean it with regard to the distinction between instigation and aiding-and-abetting. This is evident in the current American debate about assisted suicide. In early 1997, the U.S. Supreme Court considered whether terminally ill patients had a constitutional right to have physicians assist them in terminating their lives.[5] Libertarians may feel strongly about the importance of exempting physicians and others from criminal sanctions for assisting in suicide, but no one argues that physicians should have the right to induce, instigate, or "drive" others to commit suicide.[6] It clearly makes a difference whether the initiative comes from the patient or from the person who provides assistance.

Also, at the level of sentencing, it is hard to believe that juries and judges would not pay attention to the difference between the person who pulled the trigger and his assistant who drove the car to the scene of the intended murder. Regardless of the formal commitment to the "equivalence" theory, American law retains the apparatus of the common law that distinguishes among principals in the first, instigators, and aiders-and-abettors. This implies that judges, for the purposes of sentencing, can readily perceive and gauge relative degrees of participation in the crime.[7]

11.1 The Formal Equivalence of Perpetrators and Accomplices

This may be the area of the law where at least the formal and theoretical differences between American and German thinking are most dramatic. American lawyers justify their commitment to the "equivalence" theory by invoking the doctrine of "vicarious liability." This doctrine implies that one can be responsible for the actions of another as though they were one's own actions. The guiding maxim is: *qui facit per alium facit per se* [he who acts through another acts through himself]. The accomplice is the metaphysical alter ego of the perpetrator. And thus the actions of the perpetrators are transferred, magically, to the accomplice.

This approach to criminal liability represents the application of a private law doctrine that has its most sensible application in contract law. You could not develop a sophisticated body of commercial law without imagining that agents make contracts in the name of their principals, who then acquire rights and become liable as though it were their own contract.[8] The entire body of corporate law presupposes that corporations can become liable for the debts and acquire the claims of those who represent the corporations in dealings with others.

German legal thinking resolutely rejects the application of this private law doctrine in criminal cases. Its guiding principle is that everyone should be held accountable and punished according to their own actions.[9] The notions therefore of "vicarious" or "imputed" liability—doctrines by which individuals are held liable for actions that they do *not* commit—should be anathema to the criminal law.

One could say that as a general matter, Americans are a bit easy about the conceptual differences between private law and criminal law. There is some evidence for this view. Americans recognize "punitive damages" in tort cases[10] and "strict liability"—liability with proof of fault or culpability—in criminal cases.[11] It would seem obvious to German thinkers that punitive damages should be limited to criminal cases, and that strict liability might be appropriate in tort disputes (e.g., liability for ultrahazardous activities) but not in criminal cases that supposedly postulate individual punishment according to individual culpability.

Further evidence for the fluid line between private and criminal law in American thinking—and one that has a bearing on the theory of complicity—comes to light in the American use of the doctrine of conspiracy. The idea of conspiracy emerges in English legal history in the early fourteenth century as statutory intervention, without criminal consequences, against the bringing of false charges.[12] Punishable conspiracies to commit fraud became the first common law adaptation of the statute to criminal liability. Eventually, with only these sources to support him, the scholar Hawkins declared in 1716 that "all confederacies whatsoever wrongfully to prejudice a third person are highly criminal at common law."[13] This is how the idea entered the common law and became a favored weapon in the prosecutorial arsenal.

The modern doctrine of conspiracy renders criminal any agreement between two or more persons to commit a crime.[14] The idea that an organization itself is criminal could have led to punishment of the conspiracy as an entity in itself, but in fact it led to the creation of a separate crime defined by *participating* in a conspiracy.[15]

In every case, therefore, in which two or more individuals agree to carry out a crime, the conspirators are guilty both of the substantive crime they commit and of the additional crime of conspiracy. Even if only one party actually carries out the crime, they are equally guilty of conspiracy. It need not follow from this equality of liability under the criteria of conspiracy that multiple actors would also be equally guilty of the substantive offensive, regardless of how much they contributed to the final result.

To illustrate, both driver D and intending robber R would be liable for a conspiracy to commit robbery. Their liability for conspiracy would attach as soon as they made the agreement and, as required in some places, one of the parties engaged in an "overt act" in furtherance of the conspiracy.[16] After R carried out the robbery, it would be possible in addition to the charge of conspiracy to hold D as an accessory to R's crime of robbery. There is no reason why their exposure to punishment for these differential degrees of participation should be the same. But the fact that both are equally liable for conspiracy has suppressed inquiry in common law jurisdictions about whether the two should be liable in different degrees for the homicide. In practical terms, this means that the liability for conspiracy has preempted the more general inquiry into the criteria for complicity.

The criteria of complicity are further suppressed by the doctrine that all conspirators are liable for the substantive offenses committed by their coconspirators in the course of the conspiracy. In a leading case, a coconspirator who had been arrested and was sitting in jail was held liable for the offenses committed by a coconspirator still at large.[17] The doctrine of conspiracy means, in effect, that is impossible under American law to hold individuals liable simply for what they do, each according to his or her own degree of criminal participation.

As if this were not enough, in the law of homicide, as still applied in U.S. jurisdictions, the doctrine of felony murder generates vicarious liability for homicide for any of the participants in a dangerous felony resulting in death. For example, suppose D and R and several others agree to rob a liquor store and they also agree in advance that though they will carry guns there should be no violence. While D is waiting in the car, he sees a pedestrian approach, he gets nervous and fires a warning shot at him, which unexpectedly hits him. Under the doctrine of felony murder, D and R and all the other accomplices are liable for murder in the first degree. Under California Penal Code §189, D is liable for first-degree murder for causing death in the course of a robbery. It does not matter whether in the absence of the doctrine of felony murder, D could be liable for criminal homicide at all. D's liability is imputed to other participants under the accepted criteria of "vicarious liability."[18] The doctrine of felony murder distorts the criteria of liability almost beyond all recognition. England abolished the doctrine in

1957.[19] The Model Penal Code recommended the same reform for the United States,[20] but it has had virtually no effect on state criminal legislation.

The doctrine of felony murder means that if two or more persons engage in a dangerous felony (e.g., robbery, burglary, rape, arson, mayhem) and death results to someone in the course of the felony, there is no point in trying to assess the relative complicity of the participants in the homicide. They are all liable for first-degree murder. Now we must ask the question: Why do Americans tolerate this doctrine? Is it simply an application of private law thinking in criminal cases? I think not. The persistence of the doctrine of felony murder reflects the dominance of utilitarian thinking in American criminal justice. The foundation of utilitarian thinking is cost/benefit analysis. Punishment imposes costs on offenders but generates benefit for the society by deterring future offenders. Therefore, the state justifiably threatens robbers who cause death with an additional punishment in order to make them, as it were, "careful" robbers—they should do everything possible to minimize the risk of death. Imposing this additional burden on them is not considered unjust, for they, as robbers, have embarked on a forbidden course of endangering human life.

The intrusion of these utilitarian criteria make it difficult to explain the American practice simply as a confusion of criminal law and private law thinking. Also, as a general matter, American law pays close heed to the procedural differences between private law and criminal law. Recall the extensive discussion in chapter 2 about the significance in American constitutional law of establishing that a sanction threatened by the state constitutes criminal punishment. If it is punishment, then the panoply of procedural protections, reserved for criminal trials in the Fifth and Sixth Amendments, come into play. These protections include the right to counsel (at the state's expense if necessary), the privilege against self-incrimination, and the right to confront the prosecution's witnesses. A profound shift in procedural protection occurs as soon as the American judge recognizes that the trial is one for crime rather than disciplinary or administrative proceedings. American lawyers are indeed extremely conscious of the difference between a private dispute and a criminal trial, and therefore the thesis of a blurred boundary may explain some slippage at the level of substantive law, but it hardly is as profound as we suggested at the outset of this discussion.

The purpose of this section has been to explore the grounds that might lead Americans or lawyers of other legal systems to accept the principle that, at least formally, all participants in a criminal plan should be punished in the same way. Let us summarize the influence of the various doctrines we have considered in the simple case of D and R who agree to commit a robbery, with D's role limited to driving the car and keeping guard as R executes the robbery. While waiting, D accidentally kills a pedestrian approaching the scene. The following questions may be posed and answered:

1. Is D an accomplice—aider and abettor—in R's robbery? Yes.

2. Will D be punished as severely as R for the robbery? Yes.

3. Are R and D both liable and punishable, in addition, for conspiracy to commit robbery? Yes.

4. Is D liable for accidental homicide independently of the robbery? No.

5. Is D liable for murder under the felony-murder rule? Yes.

6. Is R liable for either accidental homicide or murder? No and Yes, R is liable for the killing precisely as D is liable.

These results bring home a very simple point. American law is in fact indifferent in cases of this sort to assessing liability according to the relative participation of the various parties to the robbery and homicide. At least in this body of cases, the common law categories of principal and accessory carry little weight.

11.2 The Differentiation of Perpetrators from Other Participants

The effort to punish each participant according to his or her own contribution to the crime runs into an immediate problem. Complicity is not a crime in and of itself. No one is charged with complicity in the abstract. An accessory is always complicitous in the acts of another or at least in a crime that a group of people brings about. In this sense, liability for complicity is derivative. You can be liable for an attempt, even if no one else is liable. But complicity presupposes that someone else is engaged in committing the offense.

The derivative feature of complicity raises questions about who is on trial when someone is charged with aiding and abetting the crime of another. Can one escape a charge of complicity in murder, for example, by showing that the alleged principal did not do it? Substantively, the question is whether the alleged principal must actually be guilty in principle, and procedurally, the problem is whether the principal perpetrator must be convicted before the accessory can be indicted. To take the procedural issue first, the common law initially required that the principal actually be convicted before the accessory could be tried. Overcoming this barrier to accessorial liability required a long process of development. By the time of Blackstone, this rule had been relaxed so that the indictment against the accessory was sound if the principal had received a pardon, or had claimed benefit of clergy.[21]

Parliament abolished this procedural impediment altogether in 1826,[22] and soon thereafter in the United States, criminal codes commonly displayed provisions stating that accessories may be prosecuted without regard to the trial and conviction of the perpetrator.[23]

The substantive question with regard to the principal's liability is much more difficult. Suppose that the perpetrator is insane or diplomatically immune to prosecution. Should it follow that the people who aided him in committing robbery will not be liable at all? It would certainly seem odd to let the accessories go just because the state could not secure a conviction against the principal. Yet what does it mean to say that the accessory's responsibility derives from that of the principal. It must derive from *something*. The problem is determining what that "something" is. The two extreme positions are these:

1. The principal must at least be guilty, in principle, of having committed the offense.

2. The principal need not be guilty of anything. Indeed, the intended principal need not have carried out the crime at all.

There is much support, in theory at least, for the first option. And as we shall see, there is growing support around the world for the opposite extreme, which renders liability for complicity independent of the actions of others.

A middle position emerges by asking the questions: What is the minimal condition for liability? What must occur before we can think of holding anyone liable for the offense? The right answer, it seems to me, is that there must arise a criminal state of affairs. This means that some human act must constitute a wrongful violation of the law. Once we know that some individual has acted wrongfully, without justification, in violation of the law, then we can ask the question: To whom is this action attributable? Who should be held responsible, and to what degree, for the unlawful state of affairs. Everyone who contributed causally to the occurrence of the unlawful state of affairs should then answer according to his or her personal culpability.

This abstract way of putting the theory of complicity reduces it to a simple formula. The principal must act wrongfully or unlawfully, as that concept was defined in chapter 5. The principal will be punished for the offense if and only if the principal is also culpable, that is, not excused, for acting wrongfully in violation of the law. An accessory can be punished if and only if the accessory is also culpable, that is, not excused, for having contributed to the occurrence of the wrongful violation of the law.

It turns out that this eminently sensible approach to complicity first received recognition in German private law, long before the idea presented itself to criminal lawyers. Just as American complicity theory draws on private law, Germans could have found guidance by paying closer attention to the 1900 German Civil Code's approach to an employer's liability for the torts of its agents. To hold the German employer liable, the injured party need prove only that the employee wrongfully caused the injury. The employer can then exculpate himself by showing the exercise of due care in the hiring and supervision of the employee who unlawfully caused the harm.[24]

The difference between common-law respondeat superior, based on vicarious liability, and the German Civil Code is illustrated in the following diagram:

	Respondeat Superior	
	Employer	Employee
Wrongful act	0	X
Culpability	0	X

	German Civil Code § 831	
	Employer	Employee
Wrongful act	0	X
Culpability	X	0 or X

This rule illustrates the general principle: the party acting (the employer's agent; the criminal principal) must generate an unlawful state of affairs; the party behind the scenes (the employer; the accessory or instigator) as well as the party acting must be judged on the basis of personal responsibility.

In one of those provocative events that raise more questions than one can readily answer, this idea, already present in the German Civil Code of 1900, made itself felt in German criminal jurisprudence in 1943—at the height of the Nationalist Socialist perversions of law and morality.[25] How this decree came to pass in 1943 is beyond my ken. Yet I believe that it is the correct rule. There is support for it as well in the common law cases.[26] The German code of 1975 confirms its commitment to this way of thinking in several provisions.[27]

One very clear implication of this rule is that if the principal is justified on grounds, say, of self-defense or necessity or consent, the accessory—who may have a criminal purpose—cannot be liable. Suppose that Alex comes on the scene of a fight involving his enemy Victor and a stranger Sam. He assumes that the stranger has started the fight and he joins him in order to do in Victor. It turns out that in fact Victor started the fight and Sam was acting in self-defense. Alex had the worst of motives for joining in the fray. Suppose he even acts with racist motives toward Victor. Should Sam be held criminally liable if with

Alex's aid, he kills Victor? The principle we have derived in this section would lead us to say no. In view of Sam's justification of self-defense, no unlawful state of affairs came into being. There is nothing to attribute to the responsibility of either Sam or Alex. Whether this is the definitive answer to this conundrum concerns us further in the ensuing section.

11.3 Two Problematic Variations

The general theory of complicity as derivative liability confronts two serious challenges. One derives from the situation in which the instigator of the offense totally dominates the behavior of the guileless actor on the scene—say, a child, someone acting under mistake, or someone insane at the time of the act. The common solution to this problem is to treat the instigator as the perpetrator of the offense and the innocent person on the scene merely as a puppet or instrument in the hands of the actual perpetrator. We refer to this doctrine as perpetration-by-means or *mittelbare Taterschaft* in German. It is not actually a theory of complicity at all but a denial of complicity and an allocation of total responsibility to the calculating perpetrator behind the scenes. The perpetrator is treated as if he acted via some other instrument, such as a computer, or robot.

This doctrine denying derivative liability is usually grouped along with teachings and statutory materials on complicity. The Model Penal Code (MPC) provides in its general rule on complicity that an actor is guilty of an offense if, with the requisite state of mind, he "causes an innocent or irresponsible person to engage in the [proscribed] conduct."[28] The German code says simply that the perpetrator is anyone who commits the offense himself or "through another."[29] The new Spanish code provides that the notion of an "autor" of an offense includes someone who realizes the act *"por medio de otro del que se servin como instrumento* [by means of another whom he uses as an instrument]."[30]

It is perfectly understandable that those who manipulate innocent agents should be just as liable as those who manipulate machines in order to achieve their criminal ends. But what should we do in cases in which the actor on the scene is not "innocent." Let us return to the example posed above. Alex, with the worst of motives, assists someone who, contrary to expectations, is acting in self-defense. The pressure to punish Alex is great; principle tells us that there should be no liability.[31]

The doctrine of perpetration-by-means could come to the rescue. Why not treat Alex as the perpetrator acting through the "innocent" Sam. True, Sam is not innocent in the same way that a child or an insane person might be. His innocence derives from a justification rather than an excuse. But why should that matter? The MPC would limit its doctrine of perpetration-by-means to cases in which the perpetrator "*causes* an innocent or irresponsible person to engage in the [proscribed] conduct." But causation is a notoriously elastic concept. If we imagine that Sam could not have killed Victor without Alex's aid, then surely Alex's actions are causally connected to the death. With a little imagination, one could redefine Alex not as an aider-and-abettor but as a perpetrator causing the innocent self-defender Sam to kill.

The conceptual danger should be apparent. Perpetration-by-means, introduced as an exception to cover certain problematic cases, could easily swallow the rule. Anyone who contributes to the criminal outcome could be seen as "causing" the result, and anyone who is exempt from liability might be treated as "innocent." Thus, with a little finesse, the stop-gap rule of indirect authorship could reach all cases in which the theory of vicarious liability fails to generate a desired result of liability.

German courts and theorists sought a decade ago to check this tendency toward expansion of the doctrine of perpetration-by-means by holding that a responsible actor could not be treated as an "instrument" in the hands of another, and therefore, if the primary actor is treated as a responsible party, the person behind the scenes cannot be held as a perpetrator-by-means. The basic idea was that you could not have a perpetrator orchestrating the behavior of another perpetrator.

This position was put to the test in a remarkable case that came to the German Supreme Court in 1988. Two women manipulated a psychologically weak and slightly gullible man into believing in and fearing a symbol or evil incarnate, "King Cat." For personal reasons of jealousy, one of the two women wanted to eliminate a certain N, her former lover's new wife. She induced the man to believe that "King Cat" would claim a million human victims if he, the dependent man, did not kill N. After reflecting on the evil of killing and being convinced that he had to do it to save a million lives, the gullible man actually tried to kill N by stabbing her three times. All three were charged with attempted murder, and all three were convicted as perpetrators.

On appeal to the Supreme Court, the man, who carried out the stabbing on his own, proposed various defenses, such as insanity, necessity as justification (saving all of humanity), and necessity as an excuse. The court rejected all of these arguments, but recognized that he had acted in a good faith but unreasonable (avoidable) mistake of law about the permissibility of killing one person to save many others. Then the question was whether the two women, who had orchestrated the killing behind the scenes, should be punished as instigators or as perpetrators-by-means. At first blush, it is hard to understand why the question is so important, for instigators and perpetrators are punished according to the same rules.[32] But the stigma and psychological signif-

icance of perpetration appears to be greater than that simply of insti-
gating or soliciting the offense.

Taking sides in an ongoing academic dispute, the Supreme Court
decided that it was conceptually possible to have a "perpetrator behind
the perpetrator." And in this situation, where the responsible actor
seemed to be totally dominated and manipulated by people behind the
scenes, it was appropriate to brand all of them principals or "perpetrators."

A few years after this decision, this new doctrine found a pointed
application. With the reunification of Germany on October 3, 1990, the
criminal courts found themselves with the responsibility of gauging the
responsibility of border guards who shot at and sometimes killed East
Germans trying to flee the country. Having decided that the guards
could not justify their conduct, as they claimed, according to prevailing
East German positive law, the courts addressed the question whether
the political leaders who gave the guards their "authorization to shoot"
could be held criminally accountable as well. Several members of the
"Security Council" of the German Democratic Republic were charged
and convicted of instigation to murder. On appeal, the Supreme Court
applied the teachings of the "King Cat" case and reclassified their actions of institutionalizing the use of deadly force at the border as the
"perpetration-by-means" of criminal homicide.[33] The symbolic point
was important: those who direct the killing are still killers, even if the
actions are carried out by responsible agents.

When the agents of the mafia or of a dictatorial state induce the
rank-and-file to commit crimes, then those behind the scenes appear
to warrant the same condemnation. The pressure to make this symbolic
point constitutes one of the factors that have driven the doctrine of
complicity into retreat. A totally independent threat to the role of derivative liability in the criminal law comes from current trends in the
field of attempt liability. If many modern theorists believe that attempters should be punished on the basis solely of what they do, regardless
of fortuitous consequences, then we should expect an analogous doctrine in the field of complicity.[34] In other words, we should expect to
find a tendency to disengage the liability of instigators and aiders-and-
abettors from the conduct of the principals they seek to direct or further. To put it another way, we should expect to find a theory of "attempted complicity" under which the attempter is treated as though
he actually succeeded. For example, suppose the brother of a prison
inmate tries to smuggle weapons into the prison in order to support an
anticipated breakout. The inmates do in fact break out, but before the
weapons could reach the participants. The attempted effort to aid fails
to connect. It has no bearing on the success of the criminal plan. Yet
whether the weapons arrive one hour before or after the breakout

would seem to be an entirely fortuitous event. Why should it matter in assessing the brother's liability? After all, everyone's conduct should be judged on its own merits—on the basis of what he did, not on whether he was successful in aiding a criminal plot.

In light of this argument that persuades many, it is not surprising that the MPC has endorsed the equivalence of attempted complicity and actual complicity. Whether the perpetrator actually receives the aid—or thinks that he has received the aid—turns out in the MPC official draft to be irrelevant.[35] This legislative proposal signals the future of American law.[36] But notice the infelicitous combination of "equivalence" principles. The background assumption of the common law is that accessories should be treated as equivalent to perpetrators, and now comes the modern corollary that attempted accessories are equivalent to actual accessories. This means that anyone who attempts to render aid in a criminal plan is punished as though he actually caused the criminal harm himself. It does seem odd that American lawyers would casually sidestep the principle of punishing individuals according to their respective culpability (e.g., felony murder, vicarious liability, strict liability) but insist on punishing each individual for what he or she has actually done—regardless of the consequences.

By contrast, German law adheres to the principle of individual culpability and, at the same time, recognizes the doctrine of derivative liability in the field of complicity. Aiders-and-abettors are punished only if they *actually* render aid and therefore participate in an actual crime.[37] There is no doctrine of attempted or impossible complicity. There is no inconsistency between focusing on individual culpability but deriving the responsibility of accessories from the wrongful actions of perpetrators.

But German law does slip in the direction of the American trend toward focusing on each accessory as a separate party, punishable according to his or her actions. Section 30 of the 1975 German Criminal Code, drawing on a change introduced in the late nineteenth century, provides that attempted but unsuccessful instigation should be punished as a criminal attempt. This provision also replicates some aspects of the American doctrine of conspiracy by holding liable as an "attempting instigator" anyone "who declares himself ready [to commit the crime], who accepts the [criminal] entreaties of an another, or who agrees with another to commit the felony or to instigate someone else to commit it."[38]

In the end, then, the general theory of complicity based on derivative liability retains its force in very limited areas of the law. It is under threat on the one side from the expansion of the theory of perpetrators behind the perpetrators, and it is under threat as well from those who wish to abandon derivative liability for the sake of judging each actor solely on the basis of his or her own conduct.

11.4 The Expansion of Corporate Criminal Liability

At the beginning of this chapter we noted that there are two distinct ways of assessing crime executed by groups of people. The traditional approach is to isolate some leading figures within the group as perpetrators or principals and then to classify the others as accessories, instigators, aiders-and-abettors, or possibly as "perpetrators behind the perpetrators." The alternative is to focus on the group as such as the agent of the crime—as the "subject" of the offense as we explored that concept in chapter 3. Traditional criminal law has ignored the question of groups as subjects of criminal action, but in fact our experience of this century suggests that groups have become the primary agents of criminal harm. Only groups fight wars, engage in genocide and ethnic cleansing, impose dictatorships, force the "disappearance" of citizens, control the drug trade, develop systems of money laundering, and manufacture defective, dangerous, and polluting products. The "groups" in question range from governments, to ruling cliques, to organized criminal organizations, to respectable corporations. We can refer to all of them simply as "legally created entities."

Criminal actions by "legally created entities" display several peculiarities. Sometimes it is difficult to penetrate the inner workings of the organization to know who did what in bringing about the criminal harm. Or sometimes it might be the case that one person possesses the relevant information, another makes the decision to act, and still another carries out the action. In this situation, the diffusion of function makes it impossible to hold a single individual responsible for the crime. These difficulties, plus the general sense that organized action has an increasing impact on the lives of ordinary individuals, have generated pressure toward the prosecution and appropriate punishment of "legally created entities" that bring about criminally proscribed harms.

The argument against the criminal responsibility of organizations qua organizations is that groups of individuals do not possess the attributes that make criminal action possible. Groups as such cannot act and they cannot act culpably. These objections are most frequently voiced in the German-speaking countries that have taken a conservative stand against the worldwide trend in favor of the criminal liability of legal entities. Germans recognize the liability of legal persons for administrative violations,[39] but they are not prepared for the next step of holding these entities liable for criminal actions. Criminal punishment, they insist as a matter of principle, must be reserved for those who are personally blameworthy for bringing about criminal harm.

Of course, groups cannot be put in prison, but a range of remedies applies nonetheless. These include fines, the forfeiture of profits from illegal activities, prohibitions against the commercial activities that led to criminal harms, and even dissolution of the corporation. Also, as the

Federal Sentencing Guidelines suggest, corporations in violation of the law can be induced to adopt compliance programs that will lead to better guidance of employee behavior.[40]

The argument of principle invites several replies. First, in the popular mind, legal entities do act and do stand responsible for the harm they do.[41] Ford markets the Pinto, a car with a design likely to cause death.[42] Exxon spills oil and endangers the wildlife of the Pacific Ocean. I. G. Farben hires slave labor during the Third Reich. Swiss banks trade in Nazi gold. We have no trouble thinking of these legal entities as responsible for the harms that emerge from their sphere of activities.

It does not follow, of course, that every member of the firm is individually responsible for the harm. The corporation has its own personality and must stand apart from its members. This is the difference between corporate and collective responsibility. Corporate responsibility means that the corporation, an entity greater than the sum of its members, must stand responsible for what it as an entity does in the world. Collective responsibility or guilt would imply that each member of the entity is also guilty and that simply is not true. This is the better way, in my view, to think of the responsibility of nations. The German nation is responsible for the Holocaust, but it surely does not follow that each German living at the time or born thereafter is also responsible.

The notion that legal entities can be responsible for their actions has brought into international favor the American doctrine of vicarious liability, which we subjected to criticism at the outset of this chapter. Using this doctrine, we can see the corporation as having information, making decisions, and acting through its individual members. Thus, the uncoordinated participation of individuals fuses in the corporate personality.

The doctrine *qui facit per alium facit per se* may have no better application than in trying to account for corporate criminal liability. This should not be surprising for "qui facit" is a teaching of private law. Since their inception, corporations have been responsible civilly for their contracts and torts. Under American law, corporations are also "persons" under the Fourteenth Amendment: they are entitled to due process and the equal protection of the laws.[43] The other side of the coin is that they must stand responsible for the harm they cause.

It is not clear, however, that responsibility in the sense of vicarious liability makes corporations actually guilty for the criminal harms they cause. Some lawyers, particularly in English-speaking countries, respond that if the only threat is a monetary sanction, then strict liability poses a lesser injustice than if applied to individual actors. An alternative line of argument, developed recently in Germany, is that a particular form of guilt or culpability attaches to corporate entities. They often cause harm as a result of a flaw in the structure of management—

a fault in the way the entity manages itself *(Betriebsfuehrungsschuld)*. This kind of fault can be understood by analogy, it is argued, with the fault of individuals who commit rape and murder.[44]

But the analogy is strained. The management faults of corporations are generally faults of omission—not of a choice to do evil. It might be appropriate to punish them for these faults for if they choose to do business and receive the protection of the legal order, they must take steps to avoid causing criminal harm. They have a duty to manage themselves in the interests of society, but this duty departs from the moral foundations of the criminal law.

The movement toward corporate criminal liability reflects a tendency to blur the lines between criminal and civil [private] legal liability. Modern societies may be losing their sense for criminal punishment as an imperative of justice. The tendency at the close of the twentieth century is to focus not on the necessity that the guilty atone but on the pragmatic utility of using criminal sanctions to influence social behavior. Therefore, the argument that corporations are not really guilty of crime carries less and less weight. The more convincing consideration is the social utility of disciplining corporate behavior with the tools of the criminal law.

Notes

1. In Hebrew: *ain schlichut bavirah.*
2. See Cramer in Schönke/Schröder, § 25, note 45.
3. Cal. Penal Code § 31.
4. StGB § 27(2). The mitigation is obligatory (Die Strafe . . . ist zu mildern) [the punishment is to be reduced]. In the case of attempts, the mitigation is discretionary. StGB § 23(2) (Der Versuch kann milder bestraft werden)[an attempt can be punished more mildly].
5. Quill v. Vaco, 80 F.3d 716 (2d Cir. 1996); Compassion in Dying v. Washington, 79 F.3d 790 (9th Cir. 1996)(en banc).
6. The statutes in question generally punished both assisting and "driving" others to commit suicide. The constitutional challenge was directed only at the former clause.
7. The Federal Sentencing Guidelines recognize that a convicted defendant's punishment should be reduced for being a "minimal participant in any criminal activity." It is reduced less for being a "minor participant." See Federal Sentencing Guidelines § 3B1.2.
8. Note the switch in terminology. In private law, the "principal" is the person behind the scenes; the agent is the one who actually enters into the contract. In criminal law, the perpetrator, sometimes called the "principal," is the one who executes the deed at the scene.
9. StGB §29 ("Every participant must be punished according to his personal culpability without regard to the culpability of others.").
10. Recall the assessment of punitive damages in tort cases against Bernhard Goetz (43 million dollars), see chap. 4, note 15 supra, and O. J. Simpson

(33.5 million dollars), Simpson Fails in Bid for New Civil Trial, The New York Times, April 19, 1997, 13A, col. 1.

11. On strict liability, the classic case is United States v. Dotterweich, 320 U.S. 277 (1943). Recent decisions seem to disfavor the use of strict liability, particularly if the sanction imposed is more serious than a license revocation or a fine. See United States v. Staples, 114 S.Ct.1793 (1994) (defendant could not be convicted of the felony of possessing a prohibited firearm without proof of knowledge that the "gun would fire automatically"), and State v. Guminga, 395 N.W.2d 344 (Minn. 1986) (defendant as owner of a bar could be liable for criminal penalties for serving liquor to a minor only on proof that he had knowledge of the sale or that "he gave express or implied consent" to the sale).

12. See Ordinance Concerning Conspirators, 33 Edw. (1305). For a general discussion, see Paul Marcus, Prosecution and Defense of Criminal Conspiracy Cases 1–3 to 1–15 (1997).

13. I Hawkins, Pleas of the Crown 348 (6th ed. 1787).

14. See Marcus, supra note 12, at 1–14. Under federal law today, it is a crime for two or more people to conspire to defraud the government. The action of "defrauding the government" need not itself constitute a legislatively defined offense. 18 U.S.C. §371.

15. German law recognizes the analogous crime of forming a criminal organization, namely, an organization with the aim of committing criminal offenses. See StGB § 129.

16. On the overt act requirement, see Rethinking Criminal Law at 223–25.

17. Pinkerton v. United States, 328 U.S. 640 (1946).

18. For a typical case, see Superior Court v. Pizano, 21 Cal. 3d 128, 145 Cal. Rptr. 425 (1978) (After committing a robbery, E took a hostage as a shield and exited the store. A neighbor shot at E and killed the hostage. Even though the neighbor decided on his own to shoot at E, E and two accomplices were liable for the murder of the hostage.)

19. English Homicide Act 1957, c.11, §1.

20. MPC sec. 210.2(1)(b) (accepting compromise that recklessness should be presumed from one of enumerated dangerous felonies).

21. 4 Blackstone 323–24.

22. 7 Geo. IV, c. 64, §9 (1826).

23. E.g., Cal. Penal Code §§31, 971, 972; Mass. Ann. Laws c. 274, §3.

24. BGB §831.

25. Ordinance of May 29, 1943, 1 RGB1. 341.

26. United States v. Azadian, 436 F.2d 81 (9th Cir. 1971) (perpetrator of bribe acquitted on grounds of entrapment; accessory convicted); Regina v. Cogan & Leak, [1975] 3 W.L.R. 316 (Crim. App.) (perpetrator's conviction for rape reversed on grounds of mistake; accessory then held as a perpetrator-by-means); State v. Haines, 51 La. Ann. 731, 25 So. 372 (1899) (dictum to the effect that accessory could be held for rape of his wife if he coerced the perpetrator).

27. StGB §27: An accessory will be punished as an aider-and-abettor if he intentionally aids another in intentionally committing an unlawful act [not necessary that the principal commit a crime]. StGB § 29: Every participant in

a crime will be punished according to his own culpability without regard to the culpability of the other participants.

28. MPC §2.06(2)(a).

29. StGB §25(1).

30. Codigo Penal §28(1).

31. The case would be different if the defendant calculatedly brought about the situation of self-defense so that he could aid the party defending himself. See P. Cramer in Schönke/Schröder, § 25, note 28, at 433.

32. StGB §26.

33. See Judgment of Supreme Court, July 26, 1994, 40 BGHSt. 219.

34. On these developments, see chapter 10 supra.

35. MPC § 2.06(3): "A person is an accomplice of another person in the commission of an offense if (a) with the purpose of promoting or facilitating the commission of the offense, he . . . (ii) aids or *agrees or attempts* to aid such other in planning or committing it." In addition, instigation—called "solicitation" in the MPC—is treated as a separate inchoate offense, punishable as soon as the solicitation is complete. See MPC § 5.02.

36. Many states have followed the MPC proposal. See, e.g., 11 Delaware Criminal Code §271, 533; Illinois Criminal Code §5-2(c).

37. StGB § 27(1).

38. StGB § 30(2). Also see StGB § 129, punishing the act of forming a criminal organization.

39. Ordnungswidrigkeitsgesetz §30.

40. See Federal Sentencing Guidelines § 3572(a)(8).

41. On the general theory of corporations as acting agents, see Meir Dan-Cohen, Right, Persons, and Organizations: A Legal Theory for Bureaucratic Society (1986).

42. See E. R. Shipp, Can a Corporation Commit Murder, The New York Times, May 19, 1985, sec. 4, p. 2.

43. See, e.g., Western and Southern Life Jns. Co. v. State Board of Equalization of California, 451 U.S. 648 (1981).

44. See Günter Heine, Die strafrechtliche Verantwortung von Unternehmen 248–268 (1995).

12

Justice versus Legality

Shortly after the fall of the Berlin wall and the beginning of East German unification with West Germany, a politician from the East was heard to say, "We wanted justice and we got the rule of law." The disappointment was understandable. Justice has the appeal of knowing what is right and securing it immediately. Justice offers instant gratification. The rule of law requires time, patience, and procedures of high ritual. Justice stands to the rule of law as fast food hamburgers compare with an eight-course meal.

The claims of justice come and go. A new party is in power and heads roll. One of Shakespeare's characters even quips, "The first thing we will do is kill all the lawyers." Justice carries all the promise and the risks of a passionate love affair: the rule of law offers the stability of a loyal marriage.

The rule of law evens out the risks of injustice over time. The law accomplishes this goal by insisting on careful procedures, hearing both sides of the argument, suppressing unreliable and inflammatory evidence, and, at least in the common law systems, decentralizing power among judges, lawyers, and juries.

Concentrating power in the hands of the judge makes it easier to convict and therefore increases the risk of a false conviction. The decentralized procedures of the common law are more likely to produce the injustice of false acquittals. Examples of arguably false acquittals have made headlines over the last decade. Just think of the not guilty verdicts in the trial of the four Los Angeles police officers who beat up Rodney King, of the hung jury in the first trial of the Menendez brothers for killing their parents, of the acquittal of O. J. Simpson. These, as well as lesser-known verdicts, have generated widespread skepticism about the ability of criminal juries to distinguish clearheadedly between the guilty and the not guilty.[1]

12.1 The Complexities of Legality

The theory of legality consists in both negative and positive principles. The negative principle holds that the highest concern of a legal system should be to protect the citizenry against an aggressive state that will invariably seek to impose its will on it subjects. The procedures of decentralized power contribute to this security of citizens against the state. The negative principle of legality insists on the principle *nulla poena sine lege*—no punishment without prior legislative warning. The rationale for this principle is twofold. First, in a world of moral disagreement, citizens must be told in advance whether particular forms of conduct will trigger criminal sanctions or not. Of course, they may know this to be the case with regard to the core offenses of violence and aggression, but they cannot be blamed for not being sure about adultery or homosexuality, gambling, offering presents to public officials, or lying to a police officer. In these borderline cases, the principle of legality requires advance warning. Second, the rule of advanced legislative warning serves to bind the judges against zealous decision making for the sake of immediate political objectives. If judges must justify their decisions in the language of enacted rules, shared by the community as a whole, they are less likely to act in idiosyncratic ways.

The principle of negative legality runs into conflict with the values of positive legality, which stands for consistency and completeness in the application of the law. In the field of criminal law, positive legality requires that the law punish the guilty, all the guilty. This value is taken far more seriously in Germany than it is in the United States. It is expressed in the so-called *Legalitätsprinzip* [legality principle], which requires criminal prosecution of all those who are guilty. This may be a difficult goal in practice, but it stands squarely opposed to the principle of prosecutorial discretion, commonly accepted in common law jurisdictions, which permits prosecutors to pick and choose among possible defendants in order to maximize their efficiency. It would not be possible, under the "legality principle" of prosecuting all who are guilty, to grant immunity to some coconspirators in order to convict others.

The principle of positive legality means, in effect, the state is under a duty to enforce the criminal law and even to legislate in order to protect victims protected by the constitution. A failure to prosecute can constitute a constitutional violation, as evidenced by a leading 1975

German decision holding the state bound to legislate and prosecute to protect the constitutional right to life of unborn children. This idea of a "constitutional duty to punish" is unthinkable under American constitutional law. In the United States the state and federal governments are bound to protect the rights of the accused but not to prosecute in order to protect the rights of society and of victims.

The positive sense of legality recoils at the thought that an obviously guilty person would walk the streets and the state would do nothing about it. Suppose that after his acquital in a fair criminal trial, O. J. Simpson confessed that he killed his wife. The American reaction would be, "Well, there is nothing we can do. The prosecution tried to convict and failed. It would be unfair to reopen the criminal proceedings." The German reaction would be, "The confession is new evidence against him. If the statute of limitations has not run, there would be nothing wrong with reopening the case and prosecuting anew. The rule of law demands no less."[2] It is clear that the German notion of the rule of law (the idea of a *Rechtsstaat*) is more aggressive than the American principle of negative legality. It includes positive as well as negative legality. For the German states, the *Rechtsstaat* is a sword; for the American citizen, the rule of law is primarly a shield against governmental power.

These two senses of legality—the negative shield and the positive sword—readily come into conflict. The faith of the negative legalist lies in the constraining effect of the statutory language used in defining liability. If the crime of theft requires the taking of a "thing," then it matters greatly whether the notion of "thingness" is limited to physical objects or whether it lends itself, by analogy, to the acquisition of electricity or electronic signals.[3] If the crime of homicide is limited to the killing of human beings, then it is of critical importance to determine when the quality of being human takes hold of a fetus in gestation and departs a dying body.[4] There is, of course, no easy consensus on these matters, and the language of the law can never eliminate the necessity of good judgment in interpreting the law.

When it comes to the interpretation of criminal statutes, it matters greatly whether the basic rule of interpretation is designed to minimize or to maximize the thrust of legislative efforts to define and punish criminal behavior. The common law courts were always hostile to statutory expansion of the common law, and therefore the basic rule of common law interpretation held that "statutes in derogation of the common law should be strictly construed."[5] This rule of intepretation dovetailed well with the principle of negative legality for it discouraged expansive interpretation of statutes.

In recent decades, under the influence of the Model Penal Code (MPC), the tendency of state legislation has been to take a more generous view of legislative power. The MPC §1.02(3) holds that its provisions should be interpreted according to "the fair import of their terms," and in cases of controversy to further the purposes of the code, which includes subjecting "to public control persons whose conduct indicates that they are disposed to commit crimes."[6] This more expansive approach toward interpretation reflects the influence of positive legality: it is important to interpret statutes broadly with a view to capturing within their scope all those who are guility or who can usefully be regarded as guilty. The boundaries of positive legality readily merge with a utilitarian use of the criminal law as an instrument for controlling "dangerous persons."

The tension between positive and negative legality is only one of the distinctions that we must keep in mind in contemplating the relationship between legality and justice. Additional complications arise from distinguishing among positive law, law as principle, morality, and justice. A few words about the meaning and relevance of each of these concepts would be useful.

1. *Positive law* is law enacted by the legislature. It takes the form of statutes. Virtually all European legal systems employ a special word to designate this form of law—*Gesetz, loi, ley, legge, zakon,* etc.

2. *Law as principle* includes the principles for determining whether a technical violation of the law constitutes wrongdoing, whether these nominal violations can be justified or excused, whether an issue is an element of the offense or a defense—indeed all the major distinctions that define the structure of this book. As European legal cultures have a term for statutory law, they reserve a special term for law as principle—*Recht, droit, derecho, diritta, pravo,* etc.

The idea of "law" in a field called criminal law is always based on this term—law as principle—thus the expressions: *Strafrecht, droit penal,* etc. The point expressed in this usage is that the field of criminal law always includes principles that go beyond the legislated language found in the criminal code.

3. *Morality* enters our thinking about criminal justice in at least two radically different and easily confused ways. We make moral judgments about the interests worth protecting under the criminal law. And in addition, we use moral criteria to determine attribution of wrongdoing. These two uses of morality are confused, but the distinction is clear. There might be considerable debate about whether the criminal law should punish "victimless" sexual offenses. Or whether abortion should be punishable, or whether cruelty to animals should be a crime. These are basically disputes about which interests are morally sufficiently serious to require intervention of the criminal law.

These questions about which interests should be protected distinguish themselves from the inquiry about whether individuals should be held accountable for unjustifiably violating the law under conditions of possible excuse. The question when individuals should be excused under circumstances of duress, personal necessity, mistake of law, or even mental illness requires an assessment of what we expect from people under stress, both physical and psychological stress. The question "what we expect" is not simply an inquiry into conventional mores, but a moral question about what it is proper and fair to expect. For this reason it is appropriate to describe the problem of attribution as an assessment of moral responsibility.

The distinction between morality and "law as principle" is not always subject to easy clarification. For example, there is some dispute about the nature of duties imposed to prevent harm in the case of omissions. (A breached "duty" puts the actor in the same position as if he had caused the harm.) These duties are sometimes imposed on the basis of natural relationships, such as between parents and children. The courts decide these matters on a case by case basis, and therefore it is clear that the duty is not a matter of positive law. Law as principle and morality interweave in this context. Whether a relationship is sufficiently close to warrant a duty to rescue seems to be an irreducibly moral question. Yet the consequence of recognizing the duty is to establish a legal relationship; the duty to intervene is in this sense a legal duty.

4. All these aspects of law and legality confront a challenge from the theory of justice, but note that "criminal justice" must be understood in two distinct senses. In a descriptive sense, the practice of criminal justice refers to the collective experience of the agencies of arrest, prosecution, and judging. What they do constitutes the "criminal justice" of a particular country. In this sense we have American criminal justice and Russian criminal justice. These local practices could in fact be unjust in the ideal sense (and they often are).

The tension between legality and justice requires us to understand justice as an ideal for measuring the performance of a legal system. These two distinct senses of justice are marked in German as *Justiz* (the practice of the courts) and *Gerechtigkeit* (ideal sense). The term "injustice" is used only as the negative of justice in the ideal sense.

The interplay between substantive and procedural justice shapes our assessment of justice in a particular legal system. As we noted in chapter 1, the substantive rules determine guilt in principle; the procedural rules, guilt in fact. Substantive injustice can occur as a result of discrimination or partiality in the definition of what is punished and what is not—for example, punishing the use of crack more severely than the equally noxious use of cocaine.[7] One might hope for perfect substantive justice (avoiding all injustice), but perfect procedural justice is impossible. It would imply the total avoidance of mistakes and that is a dangerous illusion. Courts will always make mistakes, even if the rules of procedure are designed as well as possible to seek the truth as well as to protect the dignity and the rights of the accused. Procedural justice is always imperfect, always subject to improvement.

The nature of legality is not as easily pinned down as one might hope. The conflict between negative and positive legality persists, and the rule of law, properly understood, must account as well as for the influence of law in principle, morality, and justice. Yet because legal cultures are so complicated we naturally gravitate back to the authoritative value of criminal codes. Avoiding a maze of endless argument on value and morality, we invariably find security in the statutory law as written and enacted. Rediscovering the enacted law as written takes us back to the point of departure in this book—the problem of according too much deference to statutory language.

The problem is finding the right balance between the authoritative language of statutes and cases and the abstract philosophical problems that drive systems of criminal law. This tension between authoritative text and abstract ideal is not limited to law. A useful analogy arises in thinking about the way religious cultures accommodate their ultimate concerns with the reliance on holy writ as the common denominator of the culture. Judaism, Christianity, and Islam begin with a written text, indeed the same written text that according to the text itself was revealed to Moses on Mount Sinai. The Bible is, as it were, the basic code of Western religions. Religious life in the West is unthinkable without the Bible, but thoughtful theologians do not stop their reflections about God and the meaning of the universe simply by reading and rereading the text. Theology requires the intervention of speculative reason. Similarly, the legal cultures of the West begin with textual materials, but thoughtful jurists go beyond the text to contemplate the implications of reason for understanding law-as-principle, morality in law, and the possibility of just laws and just procedure.

Religious cultures tend to isolate themselves from the influence of the others. Fundamentalists deny the commonality of their faith with other religions. And the same is true of law when it becomes a national, parochial discipline. When lawyers limit themselves to their own "holy" laws, they fail to recognize the universal impulses that lie behind all legal systems.

Law, like religion, requires an act of faith. Good lawyers must believe that just solutions are possible and that they contribute to the pursuit of justice by beginning with their traditional texts but seeking at the same time to go beyond them. The purpose of this book has been to kindle faith in the possibility of gaining knowledge by going beyond the authoritative texts with which we invariably begin. But then we must ask the question: What kind of knowledge are we trying to acquire?

12.2 The Legal Nature of the Twelve Basic Distinctions

What is the nature of the twelve distinctions developed in the course of this book? They are certainly not a matter of positive law, for the point of the argument is to convince the reader that these distinctions exist implicitly in all legal cultures. They are not a creature of legislative or judicial enactment. They inhere in the very idea of a criminal law that seeks to reflect on the premises of its own operation. Does this mean that these distinctions are a matter of law-in-principle or of morality or of justice? Well, yes and no.

Some of the concepts we have discussed are necessary parts of a functioning system of criminal law. For many purposes, we have to know what a substantive rule is, what causation or self-defense means, or what the boundaries of a criminal attempt are. Other concepts—such as the idea of a subject of a crime or the notion of crime itself—are philosophical concepts that exist outside the criminal law. They may all have moral overtones.

Yet it is not the concepts themselves that are of primary importance in this study. The concepts come in pairs, and as pairs they establish a dialectic tension within each legal culture. The feature common to all legal cultures is this dialectic tension.

The dialectic tension stands for no particular moral value. It is not a matter of law-in-principle, morality, or of justice. The ongoing effort to work these competing conceptual claims defines the universal structure of criminal law. To work in the field of criminal law is to have a view on the contours of substance, on punishment, on the subjects of crime, on human causes, on the nature of crime, on offenses, on defenses, on intentionality, on legitimate force in self-defense, on the range of relevant mistakes, on the scope of attempts, on the distinctiveness of complicity, and on the nature of legality. Each of these terms state one pole in the conflict, and each requires analysis and definition as it stands in relation to the oppositive pole of the dialectic.

Are these the only distinctions that might qualify under the "top twelve." Many people have offered their favorites, but none of the alternatives seems as central and compelling as these twelve. But nothing turns on the exact number, and the reader may wish to propose his or her own additions to the list.

12.3 Implicit Principles

Criminal law, as presented in this book, is an ongoing debate about marking distinctions, finding the point at which each of the twelve concepts finds its boundaries relative to its opposing pole. But this ongoing debate hardly implies that the criminal law as a discipline is a free-for-all of incessant argument. Statutory language and cases restrain our flights of fancy, in the course of the argument, but our reading of authoritative language is limited as well by certain principles of legality, morality, and justice. Here follows a summary of the propositions that were highlighted in the course of the book:

1. Individuals have a right to know what the "law" is at the time that they are said to violate it.

2. Individuals have a right to know that which could make a moral difference in their choosing to engage in the action or not.

3. Causation is a problem only where accidental harm is possible.

4. There can be no criminal liability without wrongdoing attributed to a particular actor.

5. Only crimes of harmful consequences can occur negligently.

Note that the first proposition restates the principle of negative legality. The second interprets this principle as a moral right and gives an account of negative legality as a necessary basis for planning one's life rationally. The third and fifth propositions are conceptual in nature. They both derive from the conceptual argument that some harms are logically independent of actions (e.g., homicide), and other harms are logically implied in the action that produces them (e.g., rape). The properly conceptual conclusion is there should be no crime of negligence rape. Yet today in many legal systems lawyers speak of "negligent rape" in cases in which the defendant is negligently mistaken about whether his partner has consented to intercourse. The current usage of the law does not always fall into line with arguments about how we should develop and maintain our conceptual world.

The fourth proposition illustrates the interplay of logic, law-in-principle, morality, and justice. The "can" in the proposition means: in a proper system of criminal law, there can be no liability without wrongdoing in violation of the law (proposition one), wrongdoing (no justification), and attribution of the wrongdoing to a responsible actor. The principle of attribution requires validation of the actor's moral responsibility. Of course, there can be improper and unjust systems of punishment, systems motivated by political considerations and the utilitarian impulse to confine dangerous people and to punish excessively in order to deter others. These impulses are ever present in the criminal law, in systems of criminal "justice" that become unjust.

Developing an understanding of the distinctions that drive discussions of criminal justice cannot eliminate the political abuse of the system. But if we have a clearer understanding of the issues at stake, we can perceive the difference between merely following the law and seeking justice.

Notes

1. For additional details about these cases, see generally With Justice for Some.
2. See STPO § 362(4) (confession sufficient to reopen case).

3. Theft of electricity is now punishable under special legislation in most common law jurisdictions.

4. See Keeler vs. Superior Court, 2 Cal. 3d 619, 631, 87 Cal. Rptr. 481 (1970).

5. On the common rule of strict construction of statues "in derogation of the common law," see Roscoe Pound, *Common Law and Legislation*, 21 Harv. L. Rev. 383, 404–406 (1908).

6. MPC §1.02(1)(b).

7. See United States v. Armstrong, 116 S.Ct. 1480 (1996) (unsuccessful challenge to the differential prosecution and punishment of African-Americans for using crack).

Index

Acts
  causal theory of, 52–53
  context of, 52
  humanistic view of, 51
  and intentions, 53, 121
  mechanistic view of, 51
  Model Penal Code's definition of, 51
  v. omissions, 45–47
  problem of defining, 51
  requirement of, 44–45
  in sleepwalking, 50
  teleological theory of, 52–53
  under hypnosis, 50
  Welzel's theory of, 52–53
  as willed bodily movements, 44–45, 51
Adversarial system, 54–55, 95
Alfonsin, President, 38
Aristotle, 89
Arson, 61
Assault, 61, 72n.4
Attempts
  abandonment of, 181–184
  conditional intent in, 174–175
  dangerousness of, 177
  as derivative offenses, 172
  impossible, factually, 176–181
  impossible, legally, 180–181
  inapt, 177
  intention in, 174–176
  Model Penal Code's renunciation of, 182
  Model Penal Code's substantial step in, 172
  by omission, 179
  of rape, 175
  voluntariness of, 182
Attempts v. Completed Offenses
  abandonment of, 181–184
  in general, 5, 171–194
  impossibility in, 176–181
  as primary offense, 172–176
  punishment for, 173–174
Attribution
  and blameworthiness, 82, 85
  and culpability, 82
  and excuses, 83–85
  in general, 81–85
  and inculpation, 82

Justification (*continued*)
  putative, 159–162
  self-defense as, 80–81, 132–138
  self-defense, putative, as 88–91

Kafka, Franz, 7
Kahane, Meir, 39
Kant, Immanuel
  blood guilt, view of, 37–38
  ethics v. law, 136
  excuses, theory of, 84
  individual freedom, view of, 144
  means v. ends, view of, 43
  necessity, view of, 131
  punishment, theory of, 31–33, 36–37
  shipwrecked sailors' hypothetical, 132
  victims, view of, 37
Kennedy, President John F., 122–123
Kennedy-Powell, Judge Kathleen, 29
King, Rodney, 39, 90, 207

Larceny, 61, 78
Legality. *See also* Justice v. legality
  duty to punish under, 207–208
  in general 206–211
  negative and positive, 207–211
  as nulla poena sine lege, 48, 107, 207
  in omissions, 48
  as rule of law, 206
  tort law's absence of, 66
Leopold, Richard, 74
Lincoln, President Abraham, 55
Locke, John, 136, 144
Loeb, Nathan, 74

Manslaughter, 76
Mayhem, 76
Menem, President, 38
Menendez brothers, 207
Miranda rights, 55–56
Mistake
  Aristotle's view of, 89
  about bigamy, 156–157
  v. accident, 114

burden of persuasion for claim of, 94
causing harm by, 62
as a defense, 93
about diplomatic immunity, 149
as excuse, 162–163
about factual element of definition, 156
about factual element of excuse, 163–165
about factual element of justification, 158–163
in general, 148–167
irrelevant, 149–155
about jurisdiction, 149–150
about justifications v. elements of the offense, 89
about justification, putative, 159–162
of law, 19, 87
about legal aspect of definition, 156–158
under Model Penal Code, 153–155
about norm of excuse, 165–166
about norm of justification, 163
relevant v. irrelevant, 4, 166–167
in self-defense, 88–91
in self-defense, putative, 137–138
and strict liability, 160–161
Model Penal Code
  action, definition of, in, 51
  attempts in, 172, 177, 179, 186n.39
  attribution, view of, in, 82–83
  complicity in, 197–198, 205n.35
  duress in, 125, 164–166
  excuses, 84–85
  felony murder in, 192–193
  homicide in, 96
  insanity, view of, in, 87
  justification, putative, in, 161–162
  killing v. letting die in, 68
  knowledge in, 122
  legislative power, view of, 208–209
  mistake in, 153–155, 164–166
  mistake of law in, 19, 87
  necessity in, 141–142
  negligence in, 114–116, 118